# The Kashubs:
# Past and Present

# NATIONALISMS ACROSS THE GLOBE
## VOL. 2

SERIES EDITORS:

Dr Tomasz Kamusella
(University of St Andrews, Scotland, UK)

Dr Krzysztof Jaskułowski
(Warsaw School of Social Sciences and Humanities, Poland)

PETER LANG

Oxford · Bern · Berlin · Bruxelles · Frankfurt am Main · New York · Wien

Cezary Obracht-Prondzyński and
Tomasz Wicherkiewicz (eds)

# The Kashubs:
# Past and Present

PETER LANG

Oxford · Bern · Berlin · Bruxelles · Frankfurt am Main · New York · Wien

Bibliographic information published by Die Deutsche Nationalbibliothek.
Die Deutsche Nationalbibliothek lists this publication in the Deutsche National-
bibliografie; detailed bibliographic data is available on the Internet at
http://dnb.d-nb.de.

A catalogue record for this book is available from the British Library.

Library of Congress Cataloging-in-Publication Data:

The Kashubs : past and present / Cezary Obracht-Prondzynski and Tomasz
Wicherkiewicz (eds).
    p. cm. -- (Nationalisms across the globe ; 2)
    Includes bibliographical references and index.
    ISBN 978-3-03911-975-2 (alk. paper)
    1. Kashubes--History. 2. Kashubes--Ethnic identity. 3. Kashubian
language--Social aspects. 4. Kashubian literature--History and
criticism. 5. Kaszuby (Poland)--History. I. Obracht-Prondzynski,
Cezary. II. Wicherkiewicz, Tomasz.
    DK4600.K345K37 2011
    305.891'85--dc23
                        2011026376

Cover image © NASA/Goddard Space Flight Center Scientific Visualization Studio

ISSN 1662-9116
ISBN 978-3-03911-975-2

© Peter Lang AG, International Academic Publishers, Bern 2011
Hochfeldstrasse 32, CH-3012 Bern, Switzerland
info@peterlang.com, www.peterlang.com, www.peterlang.net

Printed in Germany

# Contents

# Acknowledgements

The editors and authors are highly indebted to the University of Gdańsk and the Kashubian Institute in Gdańsk for their financial and organisational support when preparing, translating and editing this volume.

We are also highly grateful to Dr Tomasz Kamusella for encouraging our work, and for providing us with his precious remarks.

We wish to thank wholeheartedly Ewa Michalina Orzechowska (from Baranowo), Justyna Walkowiak and Dr Michael Hornsby, Adam Mickiewicz University in Poznań, for their kind assistance as translators and proof-readers of the original texts.

Last but not least, thanks must go to Maciej Ostoja-Lniski and Jacek Swędrowski for their technical assistance.

CEZARY OBRACHT-PRONDZYŃSKI AND TOMASZ WICHERKIEWICZ

# Introduction

The reason for publishing the present book seems quite obvious: since 1935 (i.e. since the publication of *The Cassubian Civilisation* by Adam Fischer, Professor of Ethnography at Jan Kazimierz University in Lwów/ Lemberg,[1] Tadeusz Lehr-Spławiński, Professor at the Jagiellonian University of Cracow and eminent expert in Slavonic languages, and the German linguist and ethnographer Friedrich Lorentz, with a preface by Bronisław Malinowski) no substantial, compact publication in English has appeared in print presenting the Kashubs as an ethnic community. Clearly, that book was far from complete, as it focused mainly on ethnography and language, in principle passing over social life, political issues and even historical questions, which were discussed only superficially. Since then a few English-language publications have been brought out (mainly articles or papers edited in Poland); most of them, however, have had quite a limited range of publicity and may hardly have reached readers interested in the ethnic scene of East Central Europe, Poland and Pomerania. It even seems that, except for an inner circle of specialists, in particular linguists, the very fact of the existence of the community of several hundred thousand Kashubs is almost unknown.

Meanwhile, interest in ethnic and regional processes is evidently growing, not only in academic circles (among sociologists, linguists, historians and anthropologists), but also among journalists, educationalists and cultural activists. There are various reasons for this, among them the changes which occurred in Poland and East Central Europe after 1989 related to the so-called 'disclosed multiculturalism' i.e. the renaissance of ethnic communities and national minorities, the restoration of local and regional self-government and various integration processes. These changes stirred up frequent

---

1    Nowadays Lviv in Ukraine.

disputes and arguments, from the time of the emergence of Euroregions[2] at the beginning of the 1990s until May 2004, when Poland, together with other countries in that part of Europe, entered the European Union and became subject to the all-European regional policy. The renaissance of interest in regional and ethnic issues can be viewed from a wider perspective – namely, as a sequence of phenomena of global dimension, where on the one hand we have to do with an amalgamation of cultures (the unification of behavioural models and values with a free flow of ideas, finances, and to some extent also people), and on the other hand we deal with the revival of local identity, the verification of 'rootedness' and duration, as well as a growing attachment and devotion to the native land and/or home region.

Understandably, this revival of interest in regional and ethnic issues has not passed by the circles interested in Kashubian matters, hence the unambiguous calls addressed to Kashubian scholarship. There is an unquestionable need for a new English-language publication which presents the current state of the art in Kashubian studies, and discusses the present situation of the Kashubian community, taking into consideration its historical context.

An additional incentive for the authors of this book has been a growing interest in their own roots among Kashubian immigrants in Canada and the USA – in 2008, Canada formally celebrated the 150th anniversary of the arrival of its first Kashubian settlers.

The present book is addressed to several groups of potential readers, one of them being academic circles interested in ethnic, sociolinguistic and ethno-historical processes in Central Europe and the Baltic Sea region, including linguists, ethno-linguists, sociologists, social anthropologists, historians and cultural experts.

The second potential circle of readers includes members of the Kashubian community dispersed around the world, whose greatest concentration is in the USA and Canada, with smaller numbers also in Australia and New Zealand. We would like to present them with a thorough, accessible and above all reliable source of information on the community which their forebears came from.

---

2      Transnational co-operation structures between two or more contiguous regions located in different European countries.

Last but not least, the book is addressed to institutions and organisations dealing with minority issues and ethnic studies in Europe. We are convinced that the Kashubian example can have a universal character – exposing the dangers that small ethnic communities encounter when facing the transformations of contemporary civilisation, but also presenting the challenges which these groups envisage and the modern instruments they are provided with, not only to effectively and successfully protect and maintain their heritage, but also to develop and promote it.

The reason for publishing the book within Peter Lang's series Nationalisms Across the Globe seems more than justified – especially in light of appeals made by the international expert in Slavonic linguistics, Professor Gerald Stone: 'The question has been frequently asked whether Cassubian is not really a separate Slavonic language rather than just a dialect of Polish. If the answer to this is yes, it implies a further question as to existence of a separate Cassubian nationality. There are no known linguistic criteria for the resolution of such questions, but it is, in any case, clear that the question is not purely linguistic' (Stone 1993 and 2002: 759). As the contributors to the present book attempt to demonstrate, the case of the Kashubs and their language is in this respect quite unique – as the question mentioned by Professor Stone has been answered by developments during the last two decades. In that and many other respects, the Kashubs do constitute a distinctive group in the European ethno-linguistic landscape.

The question of the Kashubs' origin, their ethnic identity, the origins and history of the Kashubian movement, its reasonably successful ideology and the practice of regional development, and the Kashubs' successful struggle to upgrade their linguistic status (from the imminent extinction of their dialect, predicted more than a century ago, to its official recognition as Poland's only regional language) – all these, together with the enduring efforts of the Kashubian elites to maintain but also to modernise the basic Kashubian values, make the group an extremely interesting subject of study.

This book should contribute to further debate on the 'Kashubian issue', or rather on the 'Kashubian model', closely observed by other European groups of a similar kind.

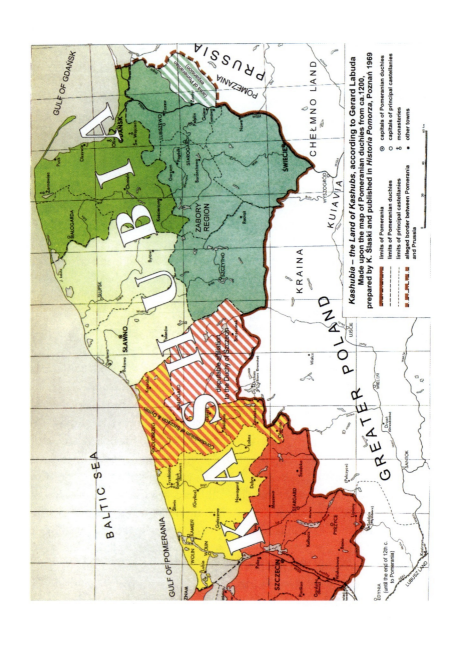

**Kashubia – the Land of Kashubs, according to Gerard Labuda**
Made upon the map of Pomeranian duchies from ca.1200,
prepared by K. Ślaski and published in *Historia Pomorza*, Poznań 1969

JÓZEF BORZYSZKOWSKI

# A History of the Kashubs until the End of Communism

## Sources for research into the Kashubs' history

In order to start writing the Kashubs' history at the beginning of the twenty-first century, one should be aware that it is inseparable from the history of the whole of Pomerania – that is, the territory situated between the Baltic Sea in the north and the Noteć and Warta rivers in the south, and between the lower Oder (Polish: Odra) river in the west and the lower Vistula (Polish: Wisła[1]) river in the east. This ideological, determined shape of the Kashubian native land was attributed to the Kashubs in the second half of the nineteenth century by their foremost representatives, the architects of the Kashubian-Pomeranian movement and ideology.

A particular phenomenon of Pomerania is its role as an area where various worlds, consisting of different geographical, cultural and political realities, came into contact. This is a land where sea and earth abut, a point of meetings (or frictions) and diffusion between two great cultures: the Slavonic and Germanic worlds. Since the end of the first millennium AD, both Pomerania and its inhabitants, the Kashubs, as well as the whole of Slavdom, became the subject of rivalry between the Germanic states in the west and the developing Polish state in the south. Germanic expansion drove towards the east; the Poles strained towards the north, to the sea, being aware of their common Lekhitic[2] heritage with the inhabitants of that coastal land, known as Pomerania.

---

1    Where appropriate, the editors provide respective place names in their Polish, German or Kashubian versions.

2    The Lekhitic languages are a subgroup of the Western branch of Slavonic languages, associated with the territory of Poland and its north-western borderland, including

The proper name of the land and the original name of its dwellers are 'Kashubia' and 'the Kashubs', respectively (in Kashubian *Kaszëbë*, in Polish *Kaszuby*). The Kashub-Pomeranians, the original inhabitants of Pomerania and the native indigenous ethno-cultural community, participated in the Polish-German struggles, often simply as the objects of international politics. They protected and maintained their culture and identity, sometimes against their own dukes and rulers. Since the Middle Ages they have constituted a riddle for their neighbours, who did not understand their linguistic separateness, and determined to absorb both the people and their land. That lack of comprehension resulted in various, often misleading interpretations of the origin of the names *Kashubia, Cassubia* and *Kashubs* by numerous authors.

The question of the etymology of Kashubia and the Kashubs has been discussed both by linguists and historians. Although until now no full synthesis of the Kashubs' history has been compiled, researchers or teachers have at their disposal a few remarkable and comprehensive reference studies. It is worth remembering that they were prepared and published under difficult circumstances, when essential analytical research could hardly be carried out. They had been preceded by numerous noteworthy scholarly articles, mainly by linguists and ethnographers, including such meticulously researched publications as:

1. *Ostatki slavyan na yuzhnom beregu Baltiyskogo morya* [Remnants of the Slavs on the southern coast of the Baltic Sea] by the Russian scholar Aleksandr Hilferding (Sankt Peterburg 1862).

2. *Statystyka ludności kaszubskiej* [Statistics of the Kashubian population] by the linguist and ethnographer Stefan Ramułt (Kraków 1990).

3. *Kaszubi giną* [The Kashubs vanish], on the vanishing Polish land and property in Kashubia, by the Polish activist and journalist Konstanty Kościński (Poznań 1908).

4. *Von einem unbekannten Volk in Deutschland* [About an unknown people in Germany] by a rural teacher and ethnographer from Wdzydze, Izydor Gulgowski (Berlin 1911).

---

Polish, Kashubian (with extinct Slovincian), and the extinct Polabian. The name derives from the name of Lech, legendary ancestor of the Poles.

The climate and context visible in the wording – 'remnants of the Slavs', 'Kashubs vanish', 'unknown people' – is noteworthy. At that time the people, and in particular their history, were unknown – to the Poles as well as to the German-dominated population of Pomerania.

It was Aleksander Majkowski (1876–1938), a renowned activist, physician, writer, politician and poet, who was the first to write a *Historia Kaszubów* [History of the Kashubs]. He started working on the volume before the First World War, and finished it in the interwar period. It was published as a whole only after his death, in 1938 in Gdynia, and republished with a valuable afterword by Professor Gerard Labuda in 1991 in Gdańsk. Majkowski presented a version of the history of the Kashubs as Pomeranians – whom he also called *Veleti* – inhabiting the territory from the river Vistula in the east to the Peene river in the west (in today's Mecklenburg), considering also their ethnic links with the Obodrites, Wagri and Polabians, which makes the work a complete history of the whole of Baltic Slavdom in unity with the Poles, and referring to a *Lekhia* as a supra-community comprised of all the above-mentioned Lekhitic groups.

The second work of Kashubian history was *Geschichte der Kaschuben* [History of the Kashubs], published in German in Berlin in 1926, by the most eminent linguist among researchers of Kashubian, Dr Friedrich Lorentz from Mecklenburg (1870–1937). He presented the history of the Kashubs within the so-called Vistulan Pomerania, taking into account the situation of Kashubian and ethnic relations in nineteenth-century Pomerania. In the opinion of the Kashubs themselves, this is not strictly their history, insomuch as it is the history of their Germanisation.

For more than fifty years, another version of the history of the Kashubs has been in preparation by Professor Gerard Labuda, a Kashub himself and the most eminent mediaevalist among Polish historians. He is the author of the first volume, which encompasses the Middle Ages. His extensive output includes many studies on the Kashubs, published in the volume *Kaszubi i ich dzieje* [The Kashubs and their history] (Gdańsk 1996). When describing the Kashubs, their name and the area where they live, he has addressed the question of where Kashubia – as the homeland of the Kashubs – was located, by quoting the research of Agnieszka Dobrowolska, who stated that 'the appellation of Kashubs/Kashubia was known in the entire coastal area from Holstein and Lüneburg to the Balto-Slavonic lands, being used as the name of a land, a people, as a nickname, as an administrative name, as well as a topographic name, familiar also in Poland' (Dobrowolska 1958: 345). Labuda has also drawn upon the later work of Józef Spors, who after thorough research came to the conclusion that the name Kashub/ia was originally rooted in West Pomerania, from where it spread to Mecklenburg and East Pomerania, to finally become associated with the latter region (Spors 1972). Today the Kashubs (i.e. speakers of Kashubian, conscious of their Kashubianness, and for whom Kashubia-Pomerania is their homeland, with Poland being their encompassing, political homeland) can be found in Vistulan (i.e. Eastern) Pomerania. As such, they develop their native culture, identify themselves with Polishness, and cultivate their Kashubian identity embedded within the Polish one. This is the present situation, and we look to history to find answers to questions about the past: in particular, where did the Kashubs and their name come from?

The assumption that the name of Kashub/ia was formed by the Slavs during the Migration period[3] between the fifth and the seventh centuries and denoted those Slavonic tribes who settled on the southern Baltic littoral is the most convincing. Why the name did not appear in written sources until the thirteenth century is a riddle for historians, since at that time it was known throughout the whole of Pomerania and among the Poles, and even in remote Muscovy/Russia and Rome. This and other questions are discussed by Labuda (2006) in the monograph *Pomorze – mała ojczyzna Kaszubów. Kaschubisch-Pommersche Heimat*, published as a joint project of the Kashubian Institute and the Kashubian-Pomeranian Association in Gdańsk and the Ostsee-Akademie in Lübeck (Borzyszkowski and Albrecht 2000). It is the most comprehensive overview of the complicated history of the Kashubs in the Pomeranian context, based on abundant sources and the authors' own research.

---

3   The Migration period was a period of human migration that occurred roughly between the fourth and seventh centuries in Europe, marking the transition from late antiquity to the early Middle Ages. Migrating peoples during this period included mainly the Germanic and Slavonic tribes.

Among numerous other works, two are particularly worth mentioning: Andrzej Bukowski's monumental monograph on Kashubian regionalism as a scholarly, social and cultural movement (1950), and an essay on the history of the Kashubs by Rev. Franciszek (Franz) Manthey, a professor in the theological seminaries in Pelplin and Hildesheim. This was originally written in German for Germans from Gdańsk and Pomerania, and was republished in Gdańsk in Polish, Kashubian and German (Manthey 1997). These two books offer contrasting interpretations of the complex historical reality of the Kashubs and of the Kashubian revival which commenced in the mid-nineteenth century. Bukowski focuses particularly on the literary culture, enriched by consecutive generations of writers, arguing that teachers of Polish and Kashubian should combine literary analyses with an understanding of the Kashubs' historical legacy.

Looking for the most satisfactory way of presenting the Kashubs' history, Gerard Labuda has stated:

> From a completed outline of the historiography of Kashubia, understood as a political and historical community arisen in the course of history, two possible ways of presenting their history arise, namely, either as the people who inhabit the land called Kashubia, or as the Kashubs who gave their ethnonym to Kashubia – the land of their residence, more or less between the lower Oder and lower Vistula on the one side and between the Noteć and Warta rivers and the Baltic Sea on the other side. According to the second option, the history of Kashubia would be identical with that of Pomerania, which in turn would be the geographical and political counterpart of the Pomeranians. Initially, the Kashubs were, thus, ethnically and culturally identical with the Pomeranians. However, in the course of historical development the latter notion has gained a multinational meaning due to the processes of migration and denationalisation, following the influx of populations of Polish, German(ic), Scandinavian, Scottish, English and Baltic origins. Having lost their own statehood, in the thirteenth century the Kashubs ceased to be the rulers of their lands and became just one of their ethnic components. Originally an active subject of Kashubian history, over time they have became its object. Thus, until the end of the thirteenth century, it was predominantly the 'history of Kashubs and Kashubia', while since then to this day it has been solely the 'history of the Kashubs within the history of Pomerania'. (Labuda 2006: 37)

# Cassubia-Kashubia and the Kashubs in the medieval history of Pomerania

*Kaszuby*/Kashubia is an ethnic, supra-tribal term, which was introduced to the annals of history by the Dominicans and Franciscans. It was recorded for the first time in 1238 in a document by Pope Gregory IX (Wachowiak 2006, vol. I: 225). After that it occurred commonly in the Latin titles of the West Pomeranian dukes, initially in the designation 'dux Slavorum et Cassubia'. Barnim III (1320–68) used the title of 'dux Cassuborum' or 'duke of the Kashubs', while his successors appeared as the dukes of the Slavs, Pomeranians and Kashubs, the titles having been adopted by the Brandenburg-Prussian Hohenzollerns after the extinction of the Gryfit dynasty. The dukes of Gdańsk used the title of 'duces Pomeraniae', while the name of Kashubia was attributed to West Pomerania, denoting the newcomers to Gdańsk and the river Vistula as Kashubian people. At that time there was no awareness of linguistic and cultural bonds, even though they were quite obvious and pivotal. Only once the Germanisation of West Pomerania and the resulting decline of Kashubian had been perceived was the appellation and community of the Kashubs fully revealed in the documents and written sources concerning East Pomerania. Therefore, the Kashubs' history is part of the history of Pomerania, and since the Middle Ages also part of the history of Poland and Germany.

At the end of the first millennium, Pomerania – the native land of the Kashubs, for a short period of time belonging as a whole to Poland – saw the development of three supra-tribal political territories with centres in Gdańsk, Kołobrzeg and Szczecin-Wolin. Gdańsk had already in 997 received the Prague bishop Adalbert (Wojciech), who on his missionary journey to the Prussians, under the auspices of the Polish duke, Bolesław the Brave, spent Eastertide in Gdańsk and baptised scores of the town's inhabitants. In the year 1000 the first Pomeranian episcopate was located in Kołobrzeg-Kamień and included the entire territory of the Kashubs-Pomeranians, from the Vistula to the river Oder. However, Christianity was not easy to introduce along the Oder, as local and tribal communities, who stood out from other Baltic Slavs in the spiritual and material richness of their pre-Christian religion, defended themselves far longer against forced Christianisation, which was brought mostly on the swords of their neighbours – Germans from the west and Poles from the south (Labuda 1993).

The pagan religion on the Baltic Sea was based on belief in the deities of war and peace – Świętowit (Svantovit) and Trzygłów (Triglav) – as well as the worship of nature. An important role was played by priests, who exercised significant influence on daily and political life. With time, the main centre of Kashubian West Pomerania became Szczecin (Stettin). The native Gryfit dynasty, whose name originated from the griffin on their coat of arms and whose primogenitor in the twelfth century was Duke Warcisław, ruled there for several centuries. As a result of devastating military expeditions, Warcisław was forced to recognise the authority of Poland and its duke, Bolesław the Wry-Mouthed, whose patronage, supported by armed troops, enabled the ultimate Christianisation of his state by Bishop Otto of Bamberg. Warcisław, who was not stripped of his authority, enlarged his domains with land belonging to the Alliance of Liutizians, who were close relatives of the Kashubs. His successors also ruled over the isle of Rügen, originally a separate duchy, with a splendid temple in Arkona. This symbol of the pre-Christian era, and of the glory days of Baltic Slavdom in general, was destroyed during the Danish conquest in 1168, under the command of Bishop Absalon. In the tenth and eleventh centuries Pomerania became a bridge in relations between Poland and Scandinavia (Labuda 2006: 75).

In the twelfth century the whole of West Pomerania came under German rule. In 1181, Duke Bogusław I paid homage to the emperor Frederick I Barbarossa, which meant a break in formal relations with Poland for many centuries. Besides Szczecin, the ducal capital was also Wołogoszcz (Wolgast), especially after the division of the duchy into two – the two parts named after the two capitals. At the same time, the Słupsk-Sławno duchy of the Raciborzycs (Ratiborids), prior to 1238, came under the rule of the Gdańsk dynasty of Subisławics (Samborids), who then also became independent from the Polish dukes, although they stayed closely connected with Poland (Śliwiński 1997).

In 1258, Warcisław III, as recorded in the *Kronika Wielkopolska*, '... went to war against Świętopełk, the Duke of Pomerania, with the troops sent from Greater Poland by Duke Bolesław and with the bishop of Kamień. And having come to the vicinity of Słupsk, called also Stolp, he left the bishop and his troops (...) himself bravely harrying Świętopełk's lands with a great army' (*Kronika* 1965: 264). Nonetheless, the victor remained Świętopełk, and until 1307–8 the lands of Słupsk and Sławno belonged to Gdańsk Pomerania, which Labuda calls the 'Kashubian-Kociewian duchy' to distinguish it from the 'Kashubian-Liutizian' duchy in West Pomerania, the latter being under Danish domination until it came under the influence of the Brandenburg Marches.

The above-mentioned Kashubian duchies in Pomerania had never been united into one state. The western duchies surrendered to Germans while the eastern ones fell increasingly within the sphere of Polish influence. Of growing significance in the east was the organisation of the Catholic Church, Christianisation progressing from the west and south. The eastern part of the Kashubian-Pomeranian lands was included in the Kuyavian-Włocławek episcopate established in 1124, and its subunit, the Archdeaconry of Gdańsk and Pomerania. The central part, from the holy Chełm Mountain ('Gollen-Berg' in German) near Koszalin to the eastern confines of the duchy, belonged to the Archiepiscopate of Gniezno and formed the Archdeaconry of Słupsk (Stolp). The territories west of the Chełm Mountain, which in the Middle Ages made up the greatest Marian sanctuary in northern Europe (Szultka 1993), came under the rule of the Episcopate of Wolin (Wollin), founded in 1140, with the seat moved in 1176 to Kamień (Cammin). During the period of Polish-German rivalry in Pomerania, the bishop of Kamień became independent of Gniezno, and from c. 1188 he came under the direct rule of Rome. Next to Kashubian and liturgical Latin in all parts of Pomerania, under the influence of the Church it was Polish in the east and German in the west which became the significant – and later dominant – languages on an everyday basis. The West Pomeranian bishops preferred German, when managing Christianisation and combining it with a settlement action/colonisation based on German town law (the so-called Magdeburg rights). So did the dukes, defending themselves against political dominance by their German neighbours, particularly the

Brandenburg margraves, and considering direct feudal subordination to the Emperor to be more bearable and dignified. With time, the knight and burger classes, as well as the clergy, were represented predominantly by Germans; the native Slavonic Kashubian populace and its upper classes, including the ducal families, were subject to Germanisation too – having preserved, however, their Kashubian names and symbols, and an awareness of their Slavonic pedigree. Therefore, until 1945 (i.e. the end of German rule in West Pomerania, often called German Pomerania) the wealthiest and most influential families were ancient Kashubian houses with Slavonic-sounding names such as Podkomorzy/von Puttkamer, Cycewic/von Zitzewitz, Bork/von Bork, Mach/von Mach, etc.

All of these families cultivated the memory of the Pomeranian Duchy, once under the reign of the Slavonic Gryfits, and above all the eminent Bogusław X Great (1474–1523). In 1478 Bogusław X succeeded in unifying the whole of West Pomerania (Rymar 1995), and when reforming his state and defending it from the possessiveness of Brandenburg, he sought a rapprochement with Poland.

German colonisation and settlement based on German town law also proceeded in East Pomerania during the rule of the native ducal dynasty of Świętopełk the Great and Mściwój/Mestwin II, who for many years defended their independence against Polish dukes and struggled against German domination, represented there mainly by the Order of Teutonic Knights.

In the west, Germans early dominated the local Kashubian population, for whom colonisation and relocation according to the Magdeburg laws brought an improvement in their existence and a civilising influence, accompanied however by discrimination and the decline of Kashubian (for example, in the so-called 'Wendish clause' the Slavs-Kashubs were denied most of the rights of the Germans). As a result of colonisation and Christianisation, Kashubian lost its position as first language, and became the third language after German and Latin. This was reflected also in the social and economic situation of the native Pomeranian populace, who remained faithful to Kashubian. From the thirteenth century, Kashubs became second-class citizens in a state which was still Kashubian-Pomeranian in name, but more and more German in essence.

In East (Gdańsk) Pomerania, following the death of the last duke,
Mściwój/Mestwin II, at Christmas 1294, power was assumed by Przemysł II,
Duke of Greater Poland. This was due to the 1282 Treaty of Kępno, known
as *Zôpis Mestwina* or 'Mestwin's legacy' (Zielińska 1968 and 1990). It was
this unification of Gdańsk Pomerania with Greater Poland that underlay
the renewal of the Kingdom of Poland in 1295.

When Przemysł II lost his life in the same year, his successors did
not manage to ensure the continuity of the Kingdom or the affiliation of
Vistulan Pomerania to Poland. In 1308–9 the territory came under the
control of the Teutonic Knights, who had been settled in Chełmno Land
for a long time. Their rule, which lasted for over one and a half centuries,
contributed to the development of the local economy, and strengthened
Germanisation, mainly through intensified colonisation with the help of
genuine German settlers, both in the towns and the countryside (Biskup
and Labuda 1986, 2000). The position of the local knight and magnate elites
was also reduced, so that the language of Kashubian functioned mainly in
the rural environment, in particular among the yeomanry and peasantry.
It had no opportunities to develop into a public language, with a unified
form, or to be more than a regional dialect within a geographically and
economically diversified country. Therefore the Kashubian community
within Pomerania, dominated by strangers, did not create a supra-tribal
standard, or a basis for Kashubian nationality. The delayed development
of the Kashubian language, and the numerous difficulties faced by those
who used it under Teutonic rule, not only caused a setback in the Polonisation process which had started earlier in Vistulan Pomerania, but allowed
sweeping unification through the Prussification of the Teutonic state. The
name 'Prussia', appropriated by Germans from the extinct Baltic population, survived the Teutonic era.

## The importance of the Reformation and the autonomy of Ducal Prussia for the preservation of Kashubian

The Reformation and consequent Counter-Reformation were turning points of great importance, and had far-reaching consequences in Kashubia and the whole of Pomerania. The Reformation first reached West Pomerania, where it changed the face of the region for many centuries and was extremely important for ethnic, national and cultural processes throughout the whole of Pomerania. The dukes of Szczecin (Stettin) observed the Reformation ideas entering their country from Wittenberg with great tolerance and prudence. The fact that the reforms strengthened the position of the dukes in relation to the Church, and that one of the leading reformers in the north of Germany was Johannes Bugenhagen, himself from Pomerania, was not unimportant. In his 1518 work 'Pomorania' he wrote about the language changes that were occurring in his native land: 'Truly, having adopted the [Christian] faith, the Pomeranian towns soon began neglecting their Slavonic language and becoming Teutonic and Germanic, so those [towns located] beyond Köslin as far as Poland, commenced nursing a grudge towards their brother Pomeranians, who had become German' (Bugenhagen 1900: 38; Szultka 1992: 18). 'Slavonic' here should be read as 'Kashubian'.

The ideas of the Reformation quickly reached all the inhabitants of West Pomerania, including both the German- and Slavonic-language speakers, and were particularly well accepted by the rural and urban middle classes, often heavily indebted to monasteries and other Church institutions, and at the same time quite eager to take over Church properties. Thanks to Bugenhagen, who was supported by the dukes and initially even by the bishop of Kamień, who accepted the need for reform within the Church, Reformation ideas quickly spread to the Oder Pomerania. According to the duke's wish, in 1535 Bugenhagen edited the Church Regulations, a document which was to become the constitution of the Lutheran Church in Pomerania.

The western and central parts of the country were quickly converted
to become uniformly Protestant and German. However, its eastern part –
located east of Jamno Lake (Jamunder See) and the Unieść (Uniesta) river
– and especially the borderland with East Pomerania, which as Royal Prussia
had belonged to Poland since 1466, remained Kashubian and also partly
Catholic. This is where the first religious books complying with Luther's
teachings appeared in print in the Wendish-Slavonic (i.e. Kashubian) language. At the end of the sixteenth century, Simon Krofey, a pastor from
Bytów (Bütow), published Luther's Catechism and Psalm Book (Krofey
1586, 1858). However, they were not written in Kashubian but in Polish with
abundant Kashubianisms. The Kashubs were generally devoid of proper
pastoral care in their native tongue, hence the decline of religious culture,
soon reinforced by the Thirty Years' War, which spread into Pomerania.
At the same time, among some of the local nobility and peasantry, Protestantism triggered new forces in the struggle for the maintenance of Slavonic Kashubian, not only in daily life, but also in the Lutheran Church
(Szultka 1993, 1994).

Simultaneously, although at a slower rate, the Reformation was reaching East Pomerania, becoming popular predominantly in urban centres
populated by Germans, as well as among the nobility, including those of
Kashubian-Polish descent. East Pomerania belonged to the Polish crown
and the Commonwealth of Poland and Lithuania, preserving its political
autonomy as Royal Prussia until 1569. One of its three provinces, known
as Pomerania, included all lands located on the left bank of the Vistula,
including the poorest ones, densely populated by Kashubs, whose distinctiveness made some contemporary chroniclers extend the Kashubian-language area to the entire province, or even to all the Prussian lands – 'since
the Kashubs are here far and wide', as Charles Ogier, a French diplomat,
recorded in his 1635–6 diary of his journey to Poland (Ogier 1953: 137).
In the Kashubian lands there were sparsely distributed small towns, as
the majority of population earned their living from farming, fishing and
forestry, in the shadow of the great town of Gdańsk. All the citizens of
Royal Prussia regarded themselves as Prussians by birth and identified
with Polish nationality, regardless of the culture or daily language of the
extremely diversified local ethnic groups.

Thanks to the progress of the Reformation and influx of various ethnic and religious communities to Vistulan Pomerania, the region kept changing its cultural profile, becoming more and more a mosaic of religions and cultures. The progress of Lutheranism was only limited during the Counter-Reformation, which followed the 1545–63 Council of Trent, and also due to the Jesuits, who took over the education of diocesan clergy. At this time numerous representatives of the nobility and members of rural parish communities returned to the Catholic Church, especially in the Kashub-populated areas. The activity of other monastic orders, such as the Benedictine nuns from Żarnowiec (Zarnowitz) or – to an even greater extent – the Franciscans from the new Calvary sanctuary of Wejherowo (Neustadt), was also of some importance. For a long time religious diversity and the accompanying economic differences influenced the Kashubs' daily life, and they were much tried by wars, in particular between Poland and Sweden, leaving persistent negative traces in the Kashubs' historical memory. This was not the case with the Polish-Turkish wars, especially the 1683 Relief of Vienna, in which Kashubian noblemen and even peasants took part, hence the traditional Kashubian memory of the 'good king', Jan III Sobieski. At that time, numerous members of the Kashubian nobility began to identify themselves with Poland, and some even acquired aristocratic status and were granted such positions as Polish senators or voivodes (governors) in Royal Prussia. The autonomy of that province, and the related right of peerage (in which Polish citizenship was granted to foreign noblemen), as well as separate general provincial assemblies, made the Kashubian nobility in general active in politics. Even the local yeomanry identified themselves with Poland, while still harbouring ambitions to preserve their distinctness within the Commonwealth (Odyniec 1972, 1983). Of equal importance was their experience in representing the Prussian towns in the provincial assembly, where they had greater independence and power than Polish townspeople in general.

The fall of the Republic in the eighteenth century also had an impact on the situation of the Kashubs in Royal Prussia. Already, during the first partition of Poland, Royal Prussia had been seized by its rapacious neighbour the King of Prussia, who had wielded power in West Pomerania since 1637 when the Gryfit dynasty died out. In 1648, after the Thirty Years' War,

the West Pomeranian Duchy was divided between Sweden and Brandenburg, which joined together later as the protestant Kingdom of Prussia, a
state which included all Pomeranian lands between the lower Oder and
Vistula rivers.

## The Kashubs in the Protestant state of Prussia

In the Prussian state Protestantism became the official religion, and as
such it served the policy of Germanisation, directed essentially against
the native Kashubian or Polish population. One of the representatives and
implementers of that policy, Christian W. Haken, a superintendent from
Stolp (Słupsk), wrote at the end of the eighteenth century:

> The Kashubs' great national pride is the main reason for their longstanding resistance
> against the complete extinction of the Sarmatian[4] tribe. It is that pride that does not
> allow them to mix with German blood in any way, all the more so as they treat the
> Germans as plunderers of their hitherto fatherland. This pride also contributes to
> the shame felt when using the German language (...). There exists a prescript order-
> ing preachers to get rid of the Kashubian language as far as possible, and to impose
> solely German teachers, and not to confirm children who cannot read German. This,
> however, requires certain wisdom, caution and attention, to not make them aware
> that their language is to be eradicated, since the Kashubs would certainly rebel against
> and resist such a plan. One should also make Kashubs, who communicate in German
> with difficulty on an everyday basis, able to understand religious instruction in the
> German language (...). Both reasons together have been an obstacle for eliminating
> Kashubian in my synod. After ten years of my stay here, with my pastors' assistance,
> I have caused the parishes with vacancies to appoint preachers without knowledge
> of Kashubian, provided the local patrons are not too stubborn, as within the next
> five to six years the elderly people, who are illiterate in German, will die out. Some
> parishes will need some fifty years for that.

---

4    A reference to the legendary relationship of the Polish gentry to the Iranian tribe of
     Sarmatians.

The parishes where sermons are delivered in Kashubian can be divided into two groups:

1) where the pastor has to preach in Kashubian, as a half or even two-thirds of the listeners do not understand German sufficiently; these are the parishes of Gardna Wielka [Groß Garde], Rowy [Rowe] Smołdzino [Schmolsin], Główczyce [Glowitz], Cecenowo [Zezenow], Skórowo [Schurow];

2) where Kashubian will disappear soon; these are the parishes of Damno [Dammen], Łupawa [Lupow], Mikorowo [Mickrow], Nożyno [Groß Nossin], Budowo [Budow]. (*Gryf* 1908/9: 204–5).

These were prophetic utterances, although the process of the extinction of Kashubian in this area lasted half a century longer, as a result of the attitude among the Lutheran Kashubs themselves and those few pastors who understood the need to preserve Kashubian, pastors who were recruited from among the local communities or who came from Sorbian Lusatia. In general, however, pastors went to any lengths in order to eliminate Kashubian from local churches. These actions were also described by the Swiss scholar Johan Bernoulli, who in 1777 visited the Prussian Minister for Foreign Affairs, Count Otto Christoph von Podewils, a landlord in Zipkow (Szczypkowice) near Stolp (Słupsk):

> The Kashubs understand Poles quite well, but the latter have problems with understanding the former. The count's cook, who had served in Lusatia, where Slavonic is much spoken, can understand Kashubian quite well. Moreover, the great difference between that language and German is unpleasant to the nobility, who possess landed property in Kashubia. Therefore, the landowners do everything, although so far with no remarkable success, in order to spread the German language and to eliminate Kashubian. They ordered sermons to be delivered in German immediately after Kashubian, and the congregation had to listen to them; German-only sermons, however, would be premature, as it is not yet commonly understood. Gradually, the expected changes will probably come, partly because the Kashubs increasingly blend with the Pomeranians, partly because of many German colonists settling in the country as a result of the reclamation of swamps and thickets. (Bernoulli 1779: 139–40)

That document, a foreigner's account, shows the common identification of Pomeranian with German in West Pomerania, and describes Protestant Kashubs as persistently maintaining their native language, customs and traditions.

That Kashubian persistence worried even Frederick II, who otherwise esteemed the somewhat disdained Kashubs – and all the Pomeranians – as a recruiting base for his army. With that aim he established cadet corps in Stolp (Słupsk) and Culm (Chełmno), where Kashubian youth, especially from the local yeomanry, were trained in strict obedience and commitment to the king. The Stolp school gave the Prussian army many officers, even generals from Kashubian families, known in Poland to this day, and who originated predominantly from the lands of Bütow (Bytów) and Lauenburg (Lębork) (Szultka 1992). That Kashubian part of West Pomerania bore the name of the Azure Country, referring to the natural cheerfulness and cultured aspect of its populace – the image, however, was far too heavily idealised. The living standards among its inhabitants actually differed significantly from the all-Prussian standards. Of crucial significance in improving the conditions of Kashubs' existence in Pomerania were the Prussian enfranchisement reforms, which regulated the ownership situation in the countryside and granted freedom to peasants, and hereditary tenure of land to some of them, often in the form of quite large farmsteads. This was a consequence of the French Revolution and the victorious Napoleonic War against Prussia, where the wiser representatives of the Junker ruling class, who wanted to save the state, showed concern for granting freedom and property to peasants, and reforming the government system in towns, in public education and in military service.

The Napoleonic Wars marked the start of the nineteenth century, in the history of the Kashubs and Pomerania (as well as the whole of Europe) a period of transition from feudalism to capitalism, from class society to civic society, and from monarchies to democracies, even if – as was the case in Prussia – a monarchy was preserved. It was a period of ethnic and national awakening, with the formation of numerous societies in East Central Europe whose activities aimed at regaining independence or creating their own state. The changes in culture and consciousness were conditioned by social and economic changes, the participation of the hitherto 'oppressed masses' in the progress of civilisation, and decision-making when introducing representative institutions into self-government and entire states.

The formation of a modern society was determined mainly by changes occurring in the first half of the nineteenth century within property relations in the countryside and also methods of farming. The enfranchised peasants, like the noblemen-landowners, had become a part of the huge organism of the Prussian and later all-German state, where the development of a free market required more and more education and economic administration. Every landowner of a larger farm, like each craftsman, merchant and manufacturer, became an entrepreneur, who managed the work of the people they employed: family members and workers. Their prosperity was dependent to a large extent upon the development of the entire national economy, where Pomerania, together with Greater Poland and Mecklenburg, provided a food base for Germany's growing industrial regions.

In the lives and mentality of the Kashubs, huge changes took place. From being inhabitants of villages, parishes and neighbourhoods, tied to their land and dwelling place, more and more of them were becoming citizens of towns and countries, citizens of quite an alien state, however – sometimes almost citizens of the world, when wandering far from their homeland as free persons in search of work and livelihood, and a better future. The starting point for these huge changes was the previously mentioned enfranchisement of the peasants.

Only through enfranchisement did the Kashubian peasant become the legal owner of his farmed land, and his properties were entered into the real-estate register under his name. The real-estate register had been introduced in 1776 by Frederick the Great, at first in relation to noblemen's properties. The nobility of Royal Prussia had to document their rights of usufruct in front of civil servants of the king – their new lord. Some of them were evicted from their properties during that regulation process, in cases where they did not own the required documents or could not provide a neighbour's testimony. To this day, some families and estates in Kashubia own such documents and mortgage registers from the end of the eighteenth century.

Farmsteads were not given their entry in the mortgage registers until the enfranchisement process. These registers contain interesting materials concerning everyday life, and besides the registration acts of new owners also contain sale and purchase contracts, documents of lease and rent, liabilities and mortgage debts, wedding contracts, property inventories, last wills, and sometimes even records of court proceedings. (A folk proverb says: 'if you want to know the character of the Kashubs – have a look at the records of court proceedings'.) Without an analysis of these mortgage and legal documents, the image of the history and everyday life of the Kashubs and of Pomerania would not be complete.

The enfranchisement included firstly the regulation of property relations. In royal and state demesnes this followed the 1808 edict, and in private properties the 1811 law, complemented by the 1816 government declaration. In noblemen's properties, the proprietary rights were originally given only to the richest peasants, who owned their own draught teams. Others were granted their right after the Springtime of Nations, while most of the smallholders were ousted by noblemen and became ordinary workers, who were not covered by the enfranchisement. The regulation of property relations was followed by the abolition of peasants' obligations towards the manor (*corvée*, rent, tribute in kind) and noblemen's obligations towards the village (construction and repairs of peasants' buildings, emergency assistance in case of crop failure). As the value of the peasants' obligations was higher, they had to buy themselves out, most often through repayments spread over many years or with part of their farm land. The latter form of repayment was prevalent in noblemen's properties throughout the whole of Pomerania, and resulted in the increase of noblemen's acreages.

Separate laws and agreements at the end of the nineteenth century regulated the buying out of peasants' and estates' obligations towards the Church – the so-called tithes or 'mass-donations'. According to the law, the tithes were to be submitted on St Martin's day,[5] but actually they were collected during the priests' Christmas visit. Whereas the inhabitants of larger villages used to submit a definite amount of rye or oat grain, sometimes also eggs, those who lived in isolated settlements or single farmsteads far away from the church had more diversified tithes. For instance, in the parish of Brusy (Bruss), the villagers of Giełdon, besides rye and eggs for the priest and rye for the organist, submitted sixty silver groschen a year in cash, dinner during the Christmas visit, eight units of oats for the priest's horse, and four units of oats for the organist's horse. The agent during the

5    On 11 November.

buying out of these obligations was the *Rentenbank* of Königsberg, which provided parishes with securities, from which the priest and organist collected annual interests. Despite that, the remnants of tithes still functioned for a long time, even into the second half of the twentieth century in some parishes in Kashubia and Pomerania.

The third important issue which formed part of the enfranchisement process was the elimination of servitudes (i.e. the peasants' rights to use the estates' properties of nobility and royalty – mainly pastures, woods and lakes – and the rights of nobility to hunt on the peasants' land), as well as the partition of communal properties. The most important servitude in Kashubia and Pomerania was the right to fish for one's own needs in the royal lakes and rivers, or sometimes in private ones. Fish, mushrooms and other products of nature's bounty constituted a very important component of their everyday diet for the inhabitants of Pomerania. For a long time, the Kashubs defended themselves against the liquidation of these privileges, but it finally happened in the second half of the nineteenth century. To this day, they have still not accepted this, and see it as a wrong inflicted by the Prussians, and maintained by the Polish state. Therefore, according to numerous observers, poaching became a common phenomenon, often not regarded as theft by the local community.

A commune at that time was composed of a manor with grange and village, most often with common ownership of pastures, sometimes woods, ponds and small lakes. The first to be liquidated were the common pastures (whereas ponds are often to this day the communal property of a village); these were divided according to the law exclusively among the landowners, in proportion to the areas of their farmsteads. Therefore, the richest – the manor and the rich peasants – were given the most, the smallholders less, and the landless nothing, although it was the landless to whom these communal properties had been of most importance.

The course of reforms varied in individual villages. The entire process in Vistulan Pomerania was directed by the General Commission in Bydgoszcz (Bromberg; where interesting documents concerning the process have been preserved in the local State Archives). The General Commission took all final decisions, based both on examination of the situation and also on agreements between the interested parties, prepared by county and special commissions. There were often arguments and court trials, which resulted in decades-long regulation of individual cases, some of them even lasting as late as the beginning of the twentieth century. For the parties involved, the most significant issue was the 'in-perpetuity' separation and allocation of land belonging to individual owners, both noblemen and peasants. The separation of the estates' land from that of the peasants' was called the general separation, and that of individual peasants' farmsteads the special separation. The latter was more important, as the former had often taken place earlier. At this time the role of land surveyors and geodesists increased significantly. The work of marking out the peasants' and noblemen's fields was difficult, and it was often hard to agree on any final conclusion. A lot of conflicts and long-term disputes accumulated as a result of the individual separation; therefore it became a symbol for the entire process of enfranchisement.

Teodor Kossak-Główczewski, in his history of a village and family from the vicinity of Brusy, has written about the grandfather Michał, who owned the property of Milachowo and pieces of land in Rolbik:

> In 1856, after the separation of 1850, he built a beautiful building by the lake, a farmyard and a large house for workers and bequeathed all this to his son Mateusz in 1859. (...) Mateusz was born on 16 September 1832 in Wentfie near Kościerzyna. He attended schools first in Kościerzyna and later from Wentfie to Leśno. For several years also he went to the secondary school in Chojnice. Returning home from school, he had to plough with oxen; often he said that when they were driving out the oxen, the sun was rising over the fields. He was drafted into the army, served three years in Greifswald, Stralsund and Amsterdam. Not a single leave. In Greifswald at that time there was no Catholic Church and in the town there was just one Catholic priest, who celebrated mass in a rented room, so he regularly participated in the services. (Główczewski 1982)

This quotation contains a reference to one of the most serious results of the enfranchisement, the separation – the special and architectonic development of the village and region. It was mainly peasants who built new dwellings, and they sometimes located these in the middle of their land, outside villages. Hence the multiplication of single settlements (which had characterised Kashubia and Pomerania even earlier); isolated buildings and plots surrounded the centre, the old village. The role of innkeepers and craftsmen, merchants and workers, villeins and tenants increased. They lived next to wealthy peasants and smallholders and often worked additionally for the landowner or looked for a better life, at least for their children, in the nearby town or in faraway lands.

At the same time the central and local administration and municipalities were re-organised. The army was reformed in 1815 through the introduction of compulsory military service and new criteria for officers' commission, which were based on education, merit and seniority. This reform, however, was not a success, since – as with the bureaucracy – the deciding factors in the army were the Junkers' power and traditions. The Junkers, particularly from Pomerania, were mainly opposed to the broader reforms and to democratisation. The Junker nobility, by preserving significant privileges within the bureaucracy and the army, identified themselves particularly strongly with the King and later with the Emperor. The nobility's Kashubian component was limited through Germanisation. Only a few families, besides the descendants of the former minor knights, had preserved their Kashubian identity, and most often they had already developed a German or Polish identity. Many Poles were deprived of their property as a result of competition with the Germans, as they could not stand the conditions imposed by the government, which was not supportive towards Kashubian or Polish separateness. The process of the Germanisation of the nobility was accelerated through privileges within military or administrative careers, and even within the educational curriculum. The strong Germanising influence of the army and of garrisons located in Kashubia and Pomerania is an acknowledged fact.

In the highly militarised Prussian state, the army and its garrisons were also important factors in the economic development of towns and regions. Beside the capital Gdańsk, other Kashubian towns which hosted garrisons in the second half of the nineteenth century were Chojnice (Konitz) and Wejherowo (Neustadt), as well as the by then German-dominated Lębork (Lauenburg) and Słupsk (Stolp). Compulsory military service, also open to many Kashubs in privileged royal or imperial units, created an opportunity for visiting distant and foreign towns and lands. Participation in splendid military manoeuvres, or even victorious wars, strengthened devotion to the court and state. The feeling of otherness was lessened through attendance at school, where loyalty and love to the King and the state were taught, as well as the dominant German language. It was the Kashubian and Polish languages, as well as the Catholic religion, that marked out the feeling of separateness among the Kashubs of West Prussia, whereas in the province of Pomerania the only factor was the Kashubian language and the native Slavonic tradition. Therefore a great role was played by churches and Prussian schools, which, together with the army, were able to reach the general public, and particularly the children and youth (even if only the male half). Souvenirs and skills were brought back from service in the army, as well as knowledge of military songs and traditions, which were also taught in schools and aimed at the strengthening of the German spirit among their Slavonic subjects.

## The role of the education system and the development of a local intelligentsia

The development of a common education system in Pomerania took place only after the Napoleonic wars, on the initiative of the authorities and – to a large extent – thanks to the endeavours of local elites, particularly priests, who performed the duties of school inspectors. For a long time the function of teacher was combined with that of organist, and the residence of the organist also housed the school. As early as 1825, a common and compulsory schooling system for children from the age of six to fourteen was introduced in the Prussian state. However, in the eastern provinces, the conditions for the fulfilment of this order were insufficient for a long time. Parents were punished by fines if their children were absent from school without an excuse, and in cases where they could not pay the fine, they might be imprisoned. The children of parents who did not appreciate education were often kept at home in order to help with urgent work, or sometimes because of a lack of shoes in the winter. In the normal course of events, the resulting fines were usually settled with teachers. Elderly

Kashubs still remember with a smile how much a goose, chicken or pound of butter offered to the teacher could help on such an occasion. The teachers, who came from local communities, tried to avoid such conflicts; therefore they were not too zealous in fulfilling the state directives. The educational authorities had problems finding appropriate candidates for teachers, and the townships had problems with maintenance of schools. In the first half of the nineteenth century the vast majority of schools consisted of one grade, with one teacher employed. At that time education was still provided simultaneously in Polish and German; there was no mention of Kashubian.

The class schedules and school inventories from the time reveal a lot about the level of education, equipment and furnishing in schools. Education was limited to reading and writing in Polish and German, arithmetic and Biblical history, as well as practical knowledge of nature and farming, with time allowed for singing. In 1845, the school in Czyczkowy was attended by 157 children (eighty-nine boys and eighty-eight girls). The school inventory for that year mentions, beside single copies of handbooks for basic subjects which were probably used only by the teacher, twenty-six copies of *Lesebuch für Denkschüler* [Reader for Thinking Pupils], seventeen copies of *Lesebuch für Volksschulen in Preußen* [Reader for Elementary Schools in Prussia], twenty copies of *Kinderfreund* [Children's Friend] by A.E. Preuss, twelve Polish-German primer-books, fifteen tables (including one desk), twenty-six writing slates, two blackboards and two bookcases. Other school inventories mention a school-bell. The handbook *Kinderfreund* was also published in a Polish version as *Przyjaciel dzieci czyli książka do czytania* [Children's Friend, or a Reading Book], for Catholic elementary schools, re-written by the teacher of Polish K.F.A.E. Łukaszewski and published in Berlin in 1864.

Schools were mostly denominational. In Pomerania, except for the regions of Lębork and Bytów, they were almost exclusively Lutheran, while in West Prussia most were Catholic; there were also 'simultaneous' (bi-denominational) schools. The Lutheran schools in West Prussia were attended mostly by the children of immigrant civil servants (forest and post administration workers, etc.), who had come from the interior of Germany. These schools enjoyed preferential treatment from the authorities. They were identified with the Prussian state and with Germanness. An 1872 law abolished the inspection of Catholic schools by priests, a practice which was supposed to hamper the pupils' civic education.

The parish archives of Brusy have preserved the text of an oath taken in Polish by Aleksander Goebl in 1848:

> I, Aleksander Goebl, swear to the Omniscient and Holy God, that as a teacher called and installed at the school of Zalesie and at all other offices I might hold in the future, I shall be obedient and faithful to His Majesty, the Prussian Monarch, Frederick Wilhelm IV, my Benefactor, King and Lord and to his Royal House; I shall conscientiously obey the Constitution, multiply the welfare of my Fatherland as far as possible, according to my vocation, perform conscientiously my official duties according to state laws made and to be made by authorities, train the youth given to my custody as pious, good and wise people, attempt to be tender and zealous, lead a Christian and constructive life of a reliable teacher; so help me God and his Gospel!

This oath shows how much the school was harnessed into the state political system, which aimed more and more at the acceleration of Germanisation in Polish children and the community. Their instruments were teachers, whether Kashubs, Poles, or people like Aleksander Goebl, who originated from a German family. Goebl worked in Zalesie for sixty years, followed by his son Konstanty, who worked as teacher for another half a century. Their family were completely Polonised and Kashubised in Brusy and its vicinity, and became famous in the memory of their compatriots from the southern reaches of Kashubia. As a rule, however, it was the other way round and most Kashubian or Polish teachers and their families became Germanised; the decisive factor was economic.

The Prussian authorities, in realising the programme of Germanisation, limited use of Polish to the lowest grades at school in the former Polish territories, Kashubia included. From 1873, Polish could only be used during religious instruction and church singing classes. In 1887 it was abolished from the school curriculum. Petitions, manifestations, press campaigns and the intervention of parents, Polish deputies and Catholic bishops did not help. Eventually, even religion was taught in German from the first grade. In 1906, this policy caused a school strike, which spread through Greater Poland and West Prussia, where the Kashubian population was the most engaged. The aim of the strike was to restore the teaching of religion in Polish. The participants in the strike action, both parents and schoolchildren, received numerous penalties, including corporal punishment, fines and other forms of persecution. Teachers, sometimes contrary to their own personal convictions, participated in the suppression of the protest. One of them was still mentioned in the 1980 reminiscences of Franciszka Knitter of Klonia (one of the strike participants): 'He was a Pole, he spoke Polish, but he had to beat us otherwise he would be dismissed. When Poland became independent, he moved away towards the Russian border. Feeling pricks of conscience he left Kashubia, but stayed in Poland'.

During Prussian rule, especially after the war with France, Kashubia and Pomerania witnessed significant development of the schooling system, mainly at the primary level. Numerous school buildings were constructed, typically made of red brick and covered with steep roofs. The number of teachers increased; they were educated in well-organised teacher training colleges, for example the colleges in Kościerzyna (Berent) and Grudziądz (Graudenz). Many were also imported from the interior of the Reich and paid special allowances or granted college scholarships. Some of them turned into ruthless promoters of Germanisation; others mingled with local communities and became more multicultural, like the society surrounding them. However, the local Germans rarely mastered Polish or Kashubian, whereas the Kashubs often knew three languages. Apart from their native Kashubian, the Kashubs spoke German (often in two varieties, High and Low German, the latter called Plattdeutsch) and Polish, studied in catechism classes, in churches and through reading at home, especially newspapers.

An important factor in the modern development of Pomeranian and Kashubian society was middle-level education, from vocational winter farming schools to classical secondary schools and university studies. For a long time, there were just two Catholic secondary schools in West Prussia, most willingly attended by Polish youth, including the Young-Kashubs. These were in Chojnice (Konitz) and Chełmno (Kulm). As a result of grassroots activity among the citizens and the endeavours of the bishops of the Chełmno Diocese, new secondary schools were gradually established in almost all district capital towns. The best and most famous remained the schools at Chojnice and Chełmno, where secret groups of Polish youth had been active almost uninterruptedly since the 1830s. Their actions in Pomerania were facilitated by the relatively long survival of Polish classes within school curricula. The high level of education and the calibre of the teachers in these schools (who often successfully avoided direct engagement in the struggle against Polishness) was conducive to the development of a Polish intelligentsia. Of great significance was the scholarly activity of secondary school teachers, who later co-founded regional learned societies and, above all, participated in the achievements of Polish and German scholarship, including studies in Kashubian history.

An institution of immense importance and merit for Kashubia and for the Polish character of Vistulan Pomerania was the 'Society of Academic Assistance for the Youth of West Prussia', founded in 1848 in Chełmno. Thanks to this society, the Polish intelligentsia were supplied with numerous clergymen, journalists, physicians and lawyers, who had mostly originated from the peasantry and the middle classes. Among them were the future 'awakeners' of the Kashubian people and founders of Kashubian regionalism, as well as representatives of the Pelplin- and Toruń-based schools of history and other disciplines cultivated within the frames of the Learned Society in Toruń (Thorn), established in 1875. German learned societies, mostly from Toruń and Szczecin, also played a considerable role in shaping historical and national identity.

The alumni of Pomeranian secondary schools received their higher education at universities located outside their Vistulan homeland, predominantly in Prussia and other German areas. Before 1904, when the Institute of Technology in Gdańsk was founded, the only institution of higher education had been the seminary in Pelplin. Kashubs, Pomeranians and Poles from West Prussia most often studied in Berlin, Breslau (Wrocław), Königsberg (Królewiec), Greifswald (Gryfia), Münster, Würzburg or Munich – all university centres in Germany – and less frequently in Cracow, Warsaw or Zurich. When visiting other German lands, provinces and towns of the Prussian state, they frequently discovered their own Slavonic past, as well as the richness of the native Kashubian-Pomeranian traditions on the Baltic Sea. Of great importance in that respect was the University of Wrocław, where Kashubs met Polish students from all three parts of the partitioned country, mainly from Greater Poland and Silesia. They also met brother-Slavs, Czechs, Slovaks and Lusatian Sorbians, among whom forces were developing that were to contribute to their national awakening.

## The Springtime of Nations in Pomerania, and Florian Ceynowa, father of Kashubian regionalism

In European historiography, the term 'Springtime of Nations' usually refers to the events of 1848–50. This was also an interesting time in Pomerania, between the Vistula and the Oder, with a significant role played by Königsberg. It was preceded by a 'pre-spring', which was the Polish democratic revolution in Galicia and the Greater Duchy of Poznań (the Austrian and Prussian parts of partitioned Poland), which had been inspired by the Polish Democratic Society, active mainly in exile. One of the participants in those events was Florian Ceynowa. Ceynowa was the son of a Kashubian peasant from Sławoszyno (Slawoschin) near Puck (Putzig), a member of the Slavonic Literary Society in Breslau, and at that time a student of medicine at the University of Königsberg, In February 1846 he unexpectedly became the commander of the insurgent units that were to seize Starogard Gdański (Preußisch Stargard). The operation ended in failure, and Ceynowa was sentenced to death in the Berlin prison of Moabit. It was in that prison, after his death penalty was commuted to life imprisonment, that he summed up his life's achievements and wrote about the history and future of the Kashubs. When he looked for partners to continue his work, he could not find any among his compatriots. Finally, he found one in the Society for Pomeranian and Ancient Studies in Stettin, but the general attitude towards Kashubian studies was not friendly there either.

In the spring of 1848, thanks to the revolution in Berlin, Ceynowa was released. A breath of liberty and democracy, as well as announcements concerning the introduction of a parliament, brought about activity among Polish and German patriots in West Prussia. However, it soon became apparent that their goals were contradictory. The Germans wanted to change the political system of the Prussian state, whereas the Poles wanted to recover their statehood. Each of the groups and their elites worked towards separate and even opposite goals. On the initiative of Polish deputies to the Prussian Diet, on 25 June 1848, the all-Prussian Polish National League was established. Its goal was the legal protection of Polishness, mainly through the development of the education system and the improvement of living conditions, as the most important means of strengthening national identity. The Polish League, with the assistance of numerous clergymen, spread its dense network of local organisations throughout almost the whole of West Prussia, Kashubia included. Its leaders, often representing a plebeian point of view, conceptualised a programme of 'organic work' which included activities in the fields of education, politics, culture and economy, and which they hoped would be realised by future generations. The League contributed also to the development of a Polish press. The first serious articles on the Kashubs were printed in its organ *National School*. It was also in this newspaper that Ceynowa – who in the meantime had graduated in Berlin and, after getting his M.D. in 1851, had settled as a physician in Bukowiec near Świecie (Schwetz) – published two manifestos addressed to his Polish brothers and fellow Kashubs. There he developed his outlook on the future of the Kashubs, who he saw as living between Polishness and Germanness, endangered by Germanisation (which was made possible by the weakness of Polish activity in Kashubia), unaided and doomed to solitude and self-reliance.

In Ceynowa's 1850 publication in *National School* entitled 'From the Kashubs to the Poles', he outlined his vision of an independent path for the Kashubs' ethnic revival, in a spirit of community with their brother-Poles and their Slavonic kin. This publication sums up the Kashubian programme:

> You, our Polish brothers, are not satisfied with the development of the Polish education system in Kashubia; this is because we Kashubs have a poor understanding of Polish, as nobody has taught us the Polish tongue: our priests are Germans, the teachers are afraid of their superiors, and the noblemen do not care about education. It was different when Poland ruled here, but nowadays we are left to our own resources; we believe, however, that through maintenance and development of the language of our fathers and forefathers, the language we are not ashamed of, we will manage to save our Slavonic speech forever; let us pray to God for our children – according to the natural law – to speak always the same way as their parents; any debate with Germans concerning national rights is therefore absolutely pointless, as the more you stroke a cat, the higher it raises its tail and the louder its purrs. (Bukowski 1950: 25)

This moderate manifesto, written in a Polish spirit, led to accusations of Kashubian political separatism and to attacks against clergy and nobility, fomenting unrest and indignation among Polish elites, which had not been Ceynowa's intention. Offence was taken more at the form rather than the content. This could have been because a Kashub in a political journal had addressed the Poles (i.e. the nobility and elite) in Kashubian – that is, in a peasants' tongue, something which had no precedent. Ceynowa's main focus – protection against Germanisation, which had proceeded particularly quickly in his homeland – was disregarded. This manifesto initiated a peculiar conflict between Ceynowa and the Polish elites – although the very fact of its publication in *National School* proves that the editor-in-chief Reverend Dionizy Knast, a real democrat and an advocate for the large number of Polish rural communities inhabiting the Vistulan Pomerania, held a different attitude.

In the meantime, Ceynowa developed his literary activities, established new contacts with circles of Slavonic and German scholars and cooperated with the Society for Pomeranian and Ancient Studies in Szczecin and the Academy of Sciences in St Petersburg. His writings were addressed to Kashubs and other Pomeranians and to the Slavonic world. They displayed a knowledge of the historical literature on Pomerania as the Kashubs' homeland; they contained, for example, a description of Pomerania's borders: 'Already in ancient times the Kashubian lands spread from the waters of the Baltic Sea, or – as we call it nowadays – the Great Sea, up to the rivers of Noteć and Warta, between the Oder and Vistula. The local people were given different names by chroniclers: Venets or Vendians, Slavs, Pomeranians, Kashubs' (Ceynowa 1850b: 5–6).

One of the most valuable works by Ceynowa is the *Skorb Kaszëbskosłovjnskje mowë* ['Treasure of the Kashubian-Slavonic language'] – the first ever journal in Kashubian, published between 1866 and 1868 in Świecie. On its title page it contained a characteristic motto, three Kashubian proverbs that constituted a socio-political, if not civic, message which is still valid:

Our troubles/poverty shall last longer than their masters.
The most reliable poison for lords is flattery and idleness.
Nobility shall add no fat to a cabbage.

Ceynowa's writings and their significance are addressed in another chapter. Undoubtedly, the primary result of his rather solitary work and his public activity was the introduction of the Kashubs to European scholarship. Within the nineteenth century, he gained wider recognition among his compatriots, and soon, in the twentieth century, he was to acquire the name of father of the Kashubian movement. During his lifetime, he experienced much unpleasantness from the elites, but also received much esteem and respect from common people, especially in the Kociewie region where he practised, and with which area he identified himself – becoming a link between the wider Pomeranian community and the Kociewie community. In spite of everything, he was also respected by his opponents, even those among the Kashubs who intended to follow a different, less Kashubian and more Polish path. His first biographer and critic, Reverend Gustaw Pobłocki, pointed out rightly that in everyday life '[he was] a zealous Pole, who loved his nationality, and an enemy of Poles, namely the Polish nobility, in his writings' (Pobłocki 1887: X).

Indeed, Ceynowa was a real democrat, with a personality which was not aristocratic but civic and all-Slavonic. The most famous nineteenth-century Kashubian poet, Hieronim Derdowski (1852–1902), in a poem produced immediately after Ceynowa's death, wrote the following lines about his love of the Kashubian people:

> People, as people usually do, were shaking their heads a bit
> And you wandered and looked for a heart among the Slavs
> One shrugged his shoulders; another scolded: fool!
> The third smelled betrayal:
> You were sustained by your faith!
> When the son of fame kneels on your grave, shed tears;
> Your faith and hope will lighten his heart,
> And the Aeolian harp will sound in your soul:
> There is no Kashubia without Poland, and no Poland without Kashubia!

Florian Ceynowa passed away on 26 March 1881. He was buried in a parochial cemetery in Przysiersk near Świecie, where his grave still remains a meeting place for different people in the spirit of Derdowski's words.

## National and religious relationships in Pomerania: the problem of Kashubian identity and national choices

In spite of the fact that in the nineteenth century the whole of Pomerania and all the Kashubs were located within the Prussian-German state, the differences and barriers between Catholic Kashubs in West Prussia and Lutheran Kashubs in West Pomerania had not been obliterated. Each of the provinces represented a different world of national and religious relationships. In West Pomerania, except for the region of Lębork and Bytów, it was the German element and the United Protestant Church that dominated. A sparse Kashubian community of a few thousand Lutherans on the Łebsko Lake (Leba-See) was losing its Kashubian-Slavonic identity and language, partly as a result of the Kashubian language having been driven out of the churches. The Lutheran Church and its ministers, who in the sixteenth century had introduced the Slavonic Polish-Kashubian language into their churches, now hardly used it, preferring German as the official language of state and church. Their attitude towards the Kashubs and their language was at most passive and was only rarely empathetic, or engaged in favour of Kashubian identity in the Pomeranian provinces and the Prussian state. The pastors, usually inspired by scholars or by the authorities, produced documents reporting on the vanishing Slavonic world, but without any activities aiming at its maintenance, not to speak of its development. The overwhelming majority fought against the maintenance of the Kashubian identity through a variety of means.

The vitality of the Kashubian and Slavonic spirit evoked surprise among many inhabitants of West Pomerania, who felt themselves German and could not understand this obstinacy and the stubbornness of resistance against the loss of the Kashubian identity. Their most prominent spokespeople were pastors employed among the Kashubs. One of the most interesting examples is the 1835 report of G.L. Lorek, pastor in Cecenowo (Zezenow), who wrote the following earnest and tragic words: 'Utmost thanks be to the highest royal authorities for the blessed development of schools and for the abolition of the teaching of Kashubian in schools!

May it also be soon removed from churches for the happiness of these people!' Such sources were among those used by Zygmunt Szultka, the most prominent researcher of this issue, who has written about the figure of Johann G.L. Kosegarten (1792–1860). Kosegarten was a historian of West Pomerania, a theologian and a linguist. He was born on the island of Rügen, and became a professor in the University of Greifswald. His output included abundant lesser-known Kashubian materials from the 1830s, which still await research by linguists fluent in the Slavonic and German languages of Pomerania. Zygmunt Szultka wrote the following on Kosegarten's assertions concerning West Pomeranian Slavdom:

> J.G.L. Kosegarten was of the opinion that until the mid-thirteenth century, the only language [used there] was Slavonic, described in documents as lingua slavica. Only the influx of the German population brought about the spread of the Low Saxon language and German place names. As far as he was concerned, the name of Pomerania was given in the thirteenth century to the state of Duke Świętopełk I, located westward of the Vistula and including the Baltic lands from Łeba as far as the Peene. He claimed that in ancient times the name of Kashubia was understood in two ways; in a narrow meaning it denoted the 'land of Białogard on the Parsęta, including Szczecinek', in a broader one, 'all the Baltic Slavs (Vendians), who called themselves Slavs'. In the second quarter of the nineteenth century, the Slavonic language and customs were preserved only among the Kashubs of the eastern part of West Pomerania. (Szultka 1992: 60)

Such a view has been shared by most Polish researchers, particularly Kashubs. Because of religious differences in the nineteenth century, the Catholic Kashubs from Vistulan Pomerania, except for a few representatives of the intelligentsia, generally viewed the fate of their Lutheran compatriots from the vicinity of Łeba quite indifferently. Their tragedy was seen as a peculiar divine retribution for their apostasy from the original Catholic faith and the 'real Church', which directly led to the loss of their ethnicity, their language, and eventually their land.

In the face of increasing Germanisation and pressure on the part of the Lutheran Church, the role of the Catholic Church and its priests in the life of the Kashubs grew systematically. In the nineteenth century, national and religious relations in West Prussia, where the Kashubs lived in compact communities, were very much differentiated spatially and temporally. The crucial factor was that two communities – Polish and German – lived next to each other, at times together, but often as strangers. The local Germans did not constitute an exclusively immigrant population, although that factor had a strong influence on relations between Poles and Germans. The majority of Kashubs identified themselves with Polishness, the crucial factors being religion and a church community, since it was in the 1850s that the final transformation of the Kashub-Catholic into the Kashub-Pole took place. The two nationalities made three religious communities – Catholic, Protestant and Jewish. The Jews identified themselves with the Germans, in the same way as the Kashubs identified themselves with the Poles. Prussian official statistics always aimed to register a higher number of citizens declaring themselves as German. According to the official data from 1855, West Prussia was inhabited by 511,335 Catholics and 582,997 Protestants, Jews and representatives of other religions. According to Polish estimations, 457,000 of the Catholics were Poles. With time, the number of Poles was increasing, but their share in the total population of West Prussia decreased – in 1861 it amounted to 34 per cent. A few years later, it was noted: 'In East and West Prussia the situation is the most convenient, as our population forms an arc with ends based on the Baltic Sea in Kashubia and on the borders with the Kingdom of Poland. (...) Between West Prussia and the Grand Duchy of Poznań there is a wedge that encroaches and divides those ancient Polish settlements; its end falls in Bydgoszcz' (Szymański 1874: 10–11). In 1900, among 1,563,523 inhabitants of the province, some 50 per cent were Catholic, 48 per cent Protestant, and 1 per cent Jewish. 35 per cent were Poles and 65 per cent Germans; the Germans formed an evident majority. At the same time, while the statement 'Lutheran means German' corresponded with the facts, the catchphrase 'Catholic means Polish' should be regarded only as a political slogan, used in national conflict and strengthened during the *Kulturkampf* period. At the end of the nineteenth century, the ratio of Poles to Germans among Catholics amounted to two to one, while the Kashubs were crucial for the Polish advantage in most counties of West Prussia on the left bank of the Vistula. It is important to note that the central counties of Vistulan Pomerania that were economically less dynamic were the most Polish-Catholic in character. The social structure of the Polish population was also less advanced: no bourgeoisie, no large lower-middle class, sparse landed gentry and intelligentsia. Polish society, and Kashubian society in particular, was predominantly but not exclusively agrarian, and the most numerous group were farm labourers. The Germans were in the majority, especially in the towns, and the policy of forced Germanisation applied by the authorities and state institutions (which significantly influenced the attitudes of the local population, Kashubs in particular) affected not only families and local communities, but on a larger scale the entire Church Diocese of Culm (Chełmno), whose borders largely corresponded with those of the state province.

The diocesan capital of Pelplin, an ancient seat of the Cistercians who had arrived there in the thirteenth century from Bad Doberan, constituted a particular religious centre for the Poles and even more so for the Kashubs. The crucial factor was the status of the bishop and the seminary, where generations of Polish and German clergy had been educated, and where everybody had to know Polish (which facilitated the understanding of Kashubian). Their role had been increasing in importance since 1836, when the bishop's 'pro-gymnasium' was founded as the Collegium Marianum, which became known as a centre of Polish nationalism. It increased further in 1869, when the journal and publishing house *Pielgrzym* were established. The elevated position and financial status of a clergyman constituted for many Kashubian-Pomeranian families, especially rural ones, a professional climax to their sons' careers. A Kashubian proverb said: 'Who's got a son in Pelplin, who's got a daughter in a convent or who's got a priest in the family, won't be touched by poverty'.

Although the bishops of Chełmno (Culm) Diocese in the nineteenth century were exclusively Germans, they were predominantly local men and partially of Polish origin. Even if they were dependent on the king and government and receptive to the Germanisation policy, they took into consideration the linguistic and cultural distinctiveness of their Polish diocese and tried to appease nationality conflicts in compliance with Church teaching and Church interests. The situation among the clergy as a whole was different; numerous clergymen engaged overtly in national matters, whether Polish or German. Northern Kashubia, more Germanised, had fewer Polish spiritual leaders among their priests, but in the central and southern parts the clergy had more effect. Generally, the role of the Catholic clergy in the life of Polish and Kashubian communities, as well as German ones, was extremely important, increasing in particular from the period of the Springtime of Nations. There were also many priests who felt close to the Kashubian tradition and language.

Of particular importance was the scholarly and educational activity of the Church. At the turn of the 1860s, the 'Pelplin School of History' was established, based on earlier research in Church history which had been carried out mainly in German. The School was soon to accelerate the national awakening of the Kashubs. Its founder, Augustyn Hildebrandt, who originated from the Kashubian village of Wielki Kack (Groß Katz; nowadays a district of Gdynia), wrote:

> Some news of the former Pomeranian archdeaconry published in Polish and German in 1865 in Pelplin: At present, the number of Kashubs amounts to more than 120,000 souls. In modern times, among all Polish tribes, those people have been exposed to the highest danger of losing their tongue and native customs because of the German element. Indeed, in spite of numerous unfavourable circumstances, the Kashubs have faithfully preserved their holy Catholic religion as well as both their tongue and the customs of their forefathers. One should expect that they shall still preserve their mother tongue and transmit it to their children, together with the native customs and virtues which have guided their forefathers. Although the language of the Kashubs differs in some words and ways of pronunciation from the pure Polish language, it does not mean that they form a nation separate from Poles; as various German tribes who speak different vernaculars do not constitute separate nations. The Kashubs always speak purely Polish, if one speaks to them in a clear and slow way. They use prayer books in correct Polish and the priests also reach out to them in correct Polish. And nobody who thinks fairly would refuse respect to clergymen who truly care about the safeguarding and maintenance of the mother tongue among their parishioners. (Hildebrand 1862).

But such a respectful attitude towards the Kashubs and their language was quite exceptional for a long time. No doubt the Catholic Church and its priests occasionally tolerated Kashubian, but they often preferred Polish or German. It was their attitude, teaching and example – together with the later Germanisation policy of the Prussian government – that influenced the identification of Polishness with Catholicism among the Kashubs, and encouraged their sense of a Polish identity from the mid-nineteenth century onwards.

In West Pomerania the role played by the Lutheran Church was totally different from that in West Prussia, where it was identified, not without reason, with the Prussian state, Germanness and Germanisation. An illustrious exception in West Prussia was Krzysztof Mrąga-Mrongovius, a preacher from Gdańsk (originally from Mazuria), who is known in historiography for his defence of his mother tongues, Polish and Lithuanian, within the Lutheran Church and the Prussian school. In the mid-nineteenth century the Lutheran Church and its newly established parishes formed governmental and church agencies, made up mainly of immigrant Germans. After large financial expenditure, new churches and schools were founded which represented a purely Prussian-German character, in contrast to Catholic institutions. This phenomenon intensified particularly after the 1870s and the Prussian-French war, in the period of *Kulturkampf*.

This was a period of crucial importance for the development of national relations in Pomerania and for the formation of Kashubian identity. Ceynowa remarked that the so-called Polish agitation, carried on by the clergy and gentry, only yielded modest results, as it promoted the model of an aristocratic culture, quite alien to the rural and small-town Kashubian populace. Instead, he intended to awaken the spirit of Kashubianness among his compatriots through the appreciation of the Kashubian language and through the presentation of the Kashubs' history within Pomerania. The language was for him as valuable as any Slavonic language, whereas the Kashubs in general treated their tongue as inferior to Polish or German. More importantly, though, many Kashubs were impressed by the efficiency and power of the Prussian state, which assured conditions of increasing prosperity for all its citizens. Symbolic of that development in Prussia was the figure of Bismarck.

Prince Otto von Bismarck, known as the 'Iron Chancellor', creator of the united state of the German Reich, had a personal connection to the Kashubs. His fiancée, Johanna von Puttkammer, was from Barnow in the parish of Alt Kolziglow (Kołczygłowy), located outside West Prussia in the Bytów land of West Pomerania. In a letter of 1866, bored with the silence and remoteness of a Junker manor and longing for her absent fiancé, Johanna complained: 'in the middle of nowhere only the howls of wolves and Kashubs could be heard'. This attitude was repeated in Bismarck's memoirs, without him realising how important his conclusions would become for historians. The Polish-language liturgy for Kashubs in the parish of Kolczygłowy had been abandoned as long ago as 1740; yet, even after 125 years, the Kashubs disturbed Miss Puttkammer in her thoughts of Bismarck.

Part of the Prussian and Bismarckian myth in Pomerania (and also part of the historic reality, although these things seldom go hand in hand) was the impressive economic development of Prussia after the Prussian-French war, made possible thanks to the gold of the defeated side. This economic development concerned mainly the Eastern 'Junker' parts of Prussia, including West Pomerania, and to a lesser extent also West Prussia. The development of the building trade and of road and railway construction was now gathering strength and enabled connections between remote regions of Pomerania, as well as connections with other German lands and with the capital, Berlin. The construction of the railways was of immense strategic and social importance, and accompanied the development of agriculture and industry and the growth of the cities. The railways contributed to an increase in employment, and enabled people who had previously been attached to their land to see the interior of Germany and beyond. Their construction was followed by both seasonal and permanent migrations of tens and hundreds of thousands of people, particularly to Rhineland-Westphalia and Berlin, less frequently (and mainly seasonally) to agricultural Mecklenburg and West Pomerania. All details, including the duration of the stay, were controlled by Prussian law. From this point onwards, the Polish community in Berlin began to expand, and many Kashubian Pomeranian families now had relatives there. In Rhineland, and in Lower Saxony and Hanover, there were now streets not only inhabited but also owned by Kashubs (Borzyszkowski 1993–4).

From the 1870s onwards, the Polish church ministry network began to develop in Rhineland-Westphalia, organised by priests from Chełmno Diocese. Also emerging were the Polish national movement, various associations, press organs, workers' unions and above all the Polish Labour Union, which was soon to spread into the entire Prussian sector of partitioned Poland. The leaders were Pomeranians – Rev. Franciszek Liss from Lubawa, Jan Brejski, a journalist from Kociewie, and Rev. Józef Szotowski, who originated from Ermland (Warmia) and graduated from Pelplin. Workers returning to their rural homes now not only brought money, presents and manufactured novelties, the products of German industry; they returned as enlightened Poles. Szotowski, after he was forced to leave Rhineland, became the parish priest of Chmielno in Kashubia, where from the end of nineteenth century onwards he stimulated national, economic and cultural activities, and was finally granted the nickname of 'Kashubian Polish king'.

Bismarck encouraged the development and unity of the Reich by promoting laws directed against the Catholic Church. According to his intentions, the Catholic Church was to be subordinated to the state, following the example of the United Protestant Church. His legislation separated civic matters from the influence of the Church, introduced public registrars' offices and secular school inspectors, and initiated internal reforms within the Church; it often had adverse effects. The anti-Polish dimension of the *Kulturkampf* policy, directed against the Catholic Church, solidified the stereotypes of Catholic Pole and Lutheran German. An 'index of forbidden books' was introduced, a register of court orders which forbade the distribution of publications hostile to the government. These were mainly Polish but included the few existing Kashubian books. Jan Karnowski, a student of theology and law, wrote the following in his dissertation, published both in the journal *Gryf* and separately as *Ludność kaszubska w ubiegłym stuleciu* [Kashubian People in the Previous Century]:

> The Kashubian population is characterised mainly by two attributes: religious fervour and a sense of justice. Religious feelings are the fundamental breath of the Kashubian soul, not guided by reasoning, but deeply felt emotionally; it is customs, tradition and above all the personality of priest that stand in for reasoning. The justice of a Kashub is firm and unbending, making no allowances. This may be the reason for the famous suing mania, the relentless stubbornness and persistence in defending their own rights. A Kashub is ready to forgive all faults and grudges, but he will never forgive an injustice. It is enough to hurt those two aspects of a Kashubian soul and hostility shall last forever! Such was the effect of the Prussian government's anti-Polish policy. As already explained, the Prussian government enjoyed a significant confidence within the Kashubian population more or less until the period of Kulturkampf. The cultural struggle, however, opened their eyes. 'When a policeman turned up in front of a rectory, the people already saw their sacred possessions in danger and immediately took

a critical stand against the government (...)' The cultural struggle was not conducted everywhere with equal severity and ruthlessness; it depended on the energy of individual administrative officers, but it was severe enough that everywhere the naive threads of trust were at once broken between people and government. Even though the influence of the cultural struggle was similar in other regions, nowhere was it as significant as in Kashubia; where trust in the government was not so considerable, the disappointment was not so painful. (Karnowski 1911: 26–7)

The reason for that damage to the myth of a good Prussian king and state was Otto von Bismarck. His repressive policies created national solidarity among the Kashubs, and stimulated programmes of social, cultural and economic development among the Kashubs and among Poles in general. On the other hand, they accelerated migration, mainly overseas to the USA and Canada, but also to South America and New Zealand. This was facilitated through frequent recruitment campaigns by agents, and by the policies of the states hoping to attract migrants. Economic factors were decisive in stimulating migration, because of the desire to improve living conditions, but both in personal accounts and in the press we can also see evidence of a wish to live in freedom from Prussian oppression. According to Ramułt (1899: 243), the number of Kashubs in Europe in 1899 exceeded 200,000; together with the Kashubian population in America it even approached 300,000.

With time, the role of the Kashubs in the Polish national movement in Pomerania started to increase, and they began to perceive themselves as the defenders and true owners of the Polish coast and of Pomerania. More attention was paid to their presence and role in the town of Gdańsk (Danzig). The Kashubian issue (the question of who the Kashubs were: Poles, Germans or a separate nation?) was creating interest and dispute among academics and politicians. For a long time, the Kashubs themselves were the objects of manipulation in the struggle between the Poles and the Germans, something which was particularly striking during electoral campaigns for the Prussian or German Parliament (a Polish candidate had always been victorious in the Kashubian districts).

From 1903, electoral campaigns were unified across the entire Reich and corresponded with parliamentary representation in Berlin. In the north of Kashubia, the *Gazeta Gdańska* was extremely influential – this was a newspaper mostly identified with the Kashubs. Among the deputies who represented the Polish population of West Prussia in Berlin, there were a dozen or so intellectuals and landowners from old Kashubian families, although they sometimes distanced themselves from the Kashubian peasants' language and traditions. Members of the Janta-Połczyński and Sikorski families were exceptions to this rule. All the Polish deputies aimed to secure the free development of the Polish press, and fought for even a nominal presence of Polish in schools, as well as seeking freedom of activity for the Catholic Church and various other aims, among which the condition of landowners' farms was of some importance. A minimum of liberty for the development of Polishness was guaranteed by the fact that, in spite of anti-Polish legislation, Prussia stood out from other European states as far as law and order was concerned, and also had a relatively stable economic basis. This also held true for 'Prussianised' Germany, where some lands and their inhabitants were characterised by a specific distance from Prussian bureaucratic and military traditions, and particularly from the nationalism practised by the Union of the Eastern Marches. Such a situation created a somewhat more favourable atmosphere for the development of the Kashubian-Polish intelligentsia and for scholarly research, which contributed to the process of the Kashubian revival.

The scholarly, cultural and political activity of the Poles, the Polish press, and the efforts and achievements of the Kashubs themselves (for example, the Wdzydze teacher Izydor Gulgowski and the Mecklenburg linguist Friedrich Lorentz) began to popularise Ceynowa's ideas and Derdowski's literary work among members of the young intelligentsia. The first initiative was taken in 1905 by Aleksander Majkowski, editor of *Drużba – Pismo do polscich Kaszubów* [Friendship – A Letter to Polish Kashubs], a supplement to *Gazeta Gdańska*. In 1907, the *Verein für kaschubische Volkskunde* (Kashubian Ethnographic Society) was founded in Kartuzy. This was an academic society, German in spirit but devoid of German nationalism; it published its own scholarly journal. In the same year, within the student union 'Polonia', the Circle of Kashubologists was established by Jan Karnowski. From 1908, in Kościerzyna, Majkowski started editing *Gryf* [Griffin], the first Polish and Kashubian social, cultural and literary journal in West Prussia. All these developments led to the establishment of a movement of the young intelligentsia, called the Young-Kashubs. Under the motto 'everything Kashubian is Polish', the Young-Kashubs pursued the revival of Kashubian, predominantly as a native culture within the Polish nation, and also sought the economic, cultural and political development of the Kashubs. They saw Gdańsk as the Kashubs' spiritual and economic capital, so it was in Gdańsk, in 1912, that the first cultural and political organisation was formed during the Young-Kashubian congress. It was called Towarzystwo Młodokaszubów (The Society of Young-Kashubs), and its main founder and intellectual leader was Aleksander Majkowski, who acted as the Society's secretary. The president was Rev. Ignacy Cyra, a parish priest in Drzycim (Dritschmin) in the Kociewie region (Borzysz-kowski 2004: 195–395).

As the continuers of both Ceynowa's and Derdowski's ideas, the Young-Kashubs created a movement which could be called Kashubian-Pomera-nian. They stressed the regional community of Kashubia-Pomerania, and alongside the Kashubian identity also emphasised a national Polish iden-tity. They made themselves and the world realise that the Kashubs were a community of various cultures – Kashubian, Polish and also German. The crowning achievements of the Young-Kashubs, besides the *Gryf* journal and numerous literary works, were the Kashubian-Pomeranian Library and Museum in Sopot (Zoppot), as well as the development of Kashubian spelling and the dissemination of Kashubian culture on a European scale, in particular to the Polish and German publics.

Their programme was most fully expressed in *Gryf*, where Majkowski wrote in an article entitled 'The Young-Kashubian Movement':

> This is the programme of objectives specified by a handful of younger native Kashu-bian intelligentsia, who set themselves the task of introducing Kashubian tribal ele-ments into the all-Polish culture under the motto: 'everything Kashubian is Polish', and decided to base their social and political activity on realistic conditions, which required consideration of the different conditions prevailing in other regions of Poland. The primary goals of the Young-Kashubian movement are nowadays of a cultural nature, as it is the field, where most of the sins against Kashubs have been committed. Since they found themselves under the rule of the Teutonic Knights, until the partition of Poland, they played the role of Cinderella in relations with both their fellow countrymen and with foreigners. Nobody took pains to learn the folk

base of the Kashubs, according to the spirit of the times, when the only representatives of nations and tribes were supposed to be scholars and noblemen. The latter,
however, even if inclined toward Poland and accepting the Polish culture, hardly
admitted their Kashubianness. It is from them that contempt for native features
filtered down to the common people, fuelled by the open hatred of Germans, who,
since the times of the Teutonic Knights, have always played an important role in
Kashubia. (...) Therefore, our aspirations – as Young-Kashubs – should flow in the
common river bed of Polish aspirations. (...) Working in such a spirit, we shall ensure
the Kashubs their due role in the history of the Fatherland and provide them with
a team of defenders, aware of their tasks and being the real executors of Mestwin/
Mściwój's legacy. (Majkowski 1909: 7)

In spite of those very patriotic and pro-Polish declarations, the activities of
the Young-Kashubs met with opposition not only from the Germanisers,
but also from some of the former elites of the Polish nationalist movement
in West Prussia – especially from the circles of the clerical *Pielgrzym* journal and the middle-class *Gazeta Grudziądzka*. Attacks, libels and accompanying lawsuits (later won by the Young-Kashubs) caused the decline
of that group. Nonetheless, the very movement disclosed the force of the
Pomeranian spirit among the Kashubs, their will to maintain and develop
their language and culture, and their desire to obtain and strengthen their
own political identity.

The collapse of the Young-Kashubian movement, whose campaigners
were vigorously involved in other aspects of Polish national activity in West
Prussia, was mainly caused by external factors, in particular the outbreak
of the First World War.

## The Kashubs and industry, trade, seafaring and fishing: the influence of Gdańsk

The second half of the nineteenth century was marked not only by the
development of formerly industrialised Prussia and Silesia, but also by
significant progress in this respect within West Prussia. The growth of the
shipyard and machine industry in Elbląg and Gdańsk, represented by firms

such as Schichau's Company which produced agricultural machinery for domestic and foreign customers, as well as warships for the Russian and German navies, was also of some importance. In consequence, among the workers in the Gdańsk factories there were always quite a number of Kashubs, who kept arriving there looking for work. The price they had to pay for obtaining a job was the loss (or at least the superficial loss) of their identity, their Kashubianness becoming weaker and weaker in successive generations. A similar process, although less marked, occurred in other towns where the German population dominated, such as Chojnice or Wejherowo.

A particular phenomenon in West Prussia was the development of the timber industry at the end of the nineteenth century, especially in Czersk. Czersk was a village located on the border between Kashubia and Tuchola (Tuchel) Forest, which mainly attracted workers from the surrounding areas. Just like the Schichau Company in Elbląg and Gdańsk, it was the name of H. Schütt that symbolised industrial progress in Czersk. After a time, Schütt's factory (which produced mainly for the Berlin market, using raw materials from Russia) evolved into a company; one of the shareholders was Stanisław Sikorski, Kashubian landowner and Polish MP. Importantly, Sikorski was to co-operate with Ignacy Kliński, a landowner from Kłodnia, who was also a merchant but who identified himself with the Kashubs and supported the development of the Polish language and culture. In the tiny village of Kłodnia and in industrial Czersk, a famous group of actors from the Polish Theatre in Poznań (Posen) appeared for many years in a row, as guests of the Klińskis.

One of the results of changes in the industrial and economic landscape was the formation of a significant Kashubian middle class – owners of handicraft workshops, timber mills, water- and windmills, inns, restaurants and shops. Some combined these activities with farming and helped their children to launch small businesses in bigger towns, even in Gdańsk. Among this middle class, the strength of their Kashubian identity was heavily influenced by economic interests and by the policy of Prussian authorities. Unlike the workers and peasants, they seldom became involved in the activities of Polish organisations, even in singing circles. Wincenty Rogala, singer, conductor and organiser of Kashubian theatre and choirs, wrote in *Gazeta Gdańska*:

Wiele, Chojnice county, February 23rd, 1911.

There was a German theatre here on the 21st of the current month. Nobody envies the good fun the Germans had, but it is those who call themselves Poles who should be blamed for their participation in the German Vergnügen [entertainment] and their singing over and over of 'Heil dir' ['long live!'].

The young, the elderly are singing – so are the village idiot and the clown,
A nationalist merchant and a banker from Wiele are singing,
And another one, who's got a vote in the bank council, is singing loudly.
A peasant from Osowo is singing, so is his neighbour – a righteous lad.
Stall-keepers have gathered to sing for their business.
A neighbour near the shrine is singing, not shirking to raise his hand,
He wants to drink a 'Bier' with the gentry and to sing 'Hoch, heil dir!'
Oh, all the 'gentry' shall tread a lovely measure, worthy of each other!
Those from squadrons and the land inspectors ... (Ostrowski 1977: 29)

The Kashubs have been no strangers to opportunism. However, it is important to remember that all the bigger villages and towns witnessed harsh economic and cultural competition between Germans and Poles.

A typically Kashubian domain of activity in the early twentieth century was seafaring, particularly service on merchant ships and warships, and above all sea fishing, in partnership with Germans from Puck (Putzig) or Hel (Hela) and from Gdańsk and the western part of Pomerania. Generations of involvement in maritime trades was the norm among coastal Kashubs, especially in Hel. The sons of Kashubian fishermen sailed under various flags and visited the entire world. Having earned some money, they returned to their homeland and became members of the existing fishing companies, built or bought their own boats, barges or cutters, and engaged in fishery or coastal transport of goods and passengers. A well-known chronicler of Kashubian fishermen and seafarers from the Baltic coast was Augustyn Necel (1902–79). Necel was born in Chałupy, himself a fisherman, and at the end of his life became a writer living in Hel and Władysławowo. His novels recorded the realities of Kashubian life, mainly covering the nineteenth century and the first half of the twentieth century, and set in the German coastal lands as well as in America. Fishing was dominant in the life of the Baltic Kashubs, as well as among the German Pomeranians west of Żarnowiec Lake (Zarnowitzer See). The most interesting record of this area of Kashubian life and history was written by Rev. Hieronim Gołębiewski (1845–1918), a parish priest from Jastarnia (Putziger Heisternest). It is worth reading as a whole, but here we quote a fragment:

In order to fish salmon and eels, the entire peninsula is divided into fishing unions, so-called 'maszoperias'. (...) Such a union is lead by a skipper. Earlier, when the waters (so-called 'depths') were more or less hereditary, he was an important figure, nowadays, when they yearly change waters ('depths') by government's order, he is of minor importance. Members of 'maszoperias', usually twelve to fifteen, are called 'maszops'. They usually gather on the third Christmas day at the skippers in order to confer, which of the younger men or those from other unions should be admitted. The meeting turns into a joyful conversation over copious jugs of beer and a few half-quarts of wine. In February, the 'maszops' gather again in order to set and sew together dragnets, and when winds are suitable at the beginning or end of March, they carry the dragnet out to the beach ('make a fill'), where again they cannot dispense with several jugs. And the jugs are a treat of God's Providence, as they are to be paid for from the future earnings. (...) Each 'maszoperia' has a certain place on the beaches of the Baltic Sea and the Gulf [of Puck], where only its dragnets can be cast and eel nets can be set, and such a place is called a 'depth'. These limitations are absolutely necessary in order to avoid arguments. A salmon dragnet consists of a middle main part, a 'mother', two wings and two ropes, sometimes as long as 100–200 cubits. With such a dragnet they put to sea in a flatboat, obviously having left an end of one of the ropes on the edge, they gradually leave the rope at a suitable distance out to sea, then one wing, the 'mother' and the second wing, and afterwards they return to the shore, with another end of the rope. Now they begin to pull out the dragnet by means of both the ropes, and not only the 'maszops', but also their wives and children, boys and girls from ten years of age, are engaged in this. – During the salmon fishing season, the local schools have a holiday. They pull the nets out by means of a so-called harness, going backward one after another. Sometimes an hour passes, before such a dragnet is pulled out. The caught salmon are thrown onto the beach sand, where they are beaten with knobbly sticks; otherwise they would toss around and loosing scales they would become smaller and therefore less marketable. Sometimes it happens that one, two three score salmon are pulled out at once; this is a unique sight, when fifteen- and twenty-pound fish in such a quantity toss around like porkers. Having cast such a dragnet up to 6 times a day, still in the evening or the morning, they go to Gdańsk – the most profitable place to sell the fish. Puck is almost out of the question. (Gołębiewski 1975: 34–5).

Kashubian fishermen of the Baltic coast went almost daily to Gdańsk for work, trade and shopping; they spent far more time there than farmers from the interior of Kashubia, from the regions of Kociewie or Żuławy. Some farmers came to the city with their products once or twice a week; but most of them sold their products to retail traders and travelling merchants who specialised in the Gdańsk market. In Gdańsk, fishermen from Hel (both Kashubs and Germans) were an important part of daily life, and not only in the Fish Market. It was no coincidence that the old names of Gdańsk streets and squares, preserved until 1945, included Kashubian Market and Kashubian Road, located within the northern confines of the city.

Herman Wünsche, in his 1904 PhD thesis prepared at the University of Leipzig, researched the question of the Kashubs' national identity:

> The largest part, i.e. almost three fourths of the peninsula population is of Polish nationality. Researchers of languages maintain that the local vernacular is more closely related to the Kashubian branch of Polish kin – such as that spoken in the vicinity of Łeba in Pomerania, than with Poland itself. The native Poles, e.g., from the vicinities of Toruń are said not to be able to communicate or can hardly communicate with the inhabitants of Hel, whereas the population of the peninsula do not admit their close relation to the Kashubs. They claim to be native Poles and every doubt they consider an insult.

> If somebody in a Gdańsk market intends to call me a Kashub, I will hit him or insult him back. This utterance illustrates the local conviction concerning ancestral affinity. The locals do not joke in this matter, as the following event shows: during the 1900 population census the inhabitants of Chałupy categorically requested to be registered as Poles in the census questionnaires – not as Kashubs, God forbid! In Władysławowo it came to scandalous events, even riots, during which a revolver was brandished at a teacher and commune authorities who had required the inhabitants to declare such an allegedly insulting status. (Wünsche 1904: 45–6)

This researcher interviewed subjects with a very strong idea of their national identity. Admittedly, Kashubs in Pomerania and in North America (especially in Canada) also identified Kashubianness with Polishness, although during the above-mentioned census many declared themselves simply as Kashubs.

Józef Łęgowski, Polish researcher of everyday life in Vistulan Pomerania and a teacher in Prussian secondary schools, wrote in his work published in Poznań in 1892 under the pen-name *Dr Nadmorski* ('Dr Coastal') that out of all the Poles, only the Kashubs were really connected with the sea.

Kashubia, as part of the Baltic region, participated in the cultural transformations that occurred throughout the whole of Pomerania and across other Northern German lands, as well as on the Baltic. In this way, the internal diversity of the region grew, something which was particularly evident in its rural architecture. Of great importance was the activity of office-building, usually carried out by Prussian architects and insurance companies, which paid noteworthy fire compensations and thereby helped in converting many Kashubian villages from wood to brick.

In 1912, Antoni Chołoniewski wrote:

> The Polish shore extends from Gdańsk north-west to the point where the river Piaśnica disgorges itself into the sea, both today and in the past dividing Pomerania from Royal Prussia. (...) In some villages on the sea the population lives from fishing, but purely fishing settlements can be found only in Hel, and on the mainland in Rewa. The entire small coastal region is predominantly Polish. (...) The national movement awakened in recent years has even affected the towns, which had become German centuries ago, and where during the last elections to the Prussian Parliament, Polish constituents came out of ballot boxes for the first time (...) The Kashubian shore is perfectly cut off from Poland. That unwitting handful of guardians of the Polish sea has been left stranded. The open hands of mightier compatriots, so generous on the Silesian banks of the Olza, do not reach here in a material or moral respect. Even Poznań does not seem to impinge here, not to mention more distant regions. The great centres of the Polish movement abroad – Warsaw, Cracow, Lwów [Lemberg] – are as far away as the thoughts of their inhabitants concerning that sad remainder of our political insolvency on the Baltic coast. Nobody cares about them at all; it is good if they are known to exist at all. (...) Gdańsk somehow fills that void. From the Old Town Hall on the Motława river, from the Green Gate and Long Market comes everything that rises above the everyday drabness of the Kashubian shore. It has been the same for centuries, and it is the long-lasting influence of the German culture that constitutes the factor mostly hindering any revival. (Chołoniewski 1912: 8–9)

Chołoniewski evidently felt that there was significant separation between the Kashubs and the Polish centres, and a lack of interest in the northern borderland on behalf of the Poles. Numerous contemporary accounts show an interest in the 'Polishness' of Kashubia, and in Kashubianness itself. One belongs to Stanisław Thugutt, who became a socialist politician after 1920. In his *Autobiography* (1984) he wrote:

> I have travelled several times to Kashubia, which I have walked all over many times; I have met many outstanding local activists: the late Dr Majkowski of Kościerzyna and Judge Chmielewski of Sopot; I have also read a lot about Pomerania. Later we have brought Kashubian sightseeing groups to Warsaw. I have always been interested, how they find Warsaw – poor and pre-war, as they are quite worldly and know

Gdańsk, often Berlin, occasionally also Westphalia. One such group was simply daz-zled by two objects: first of all the bookshop of Gebethner & Wollf – as they had not assumed that there could be so many Polish books in the world, and the palace of the Zamoyski family, which they could visit inside – as they had not supposed that such great lords could not only be Poles, but that they could be unashamed of their Polishness. (Thugutt 1894: 73–4).

Too little attention has been paid to the great diversity of everyday interac-tions between the German and Polish cultures in pre-1914 Kashubia.

Maria Wicherkiewiczowa, a writer from Poznań and a famous physi-cian's wife, who lived in Gdańsk in the 1890s, left a vivid picture of everyday life in the city in her *Story of My Gdańsk*:

> There is a lot of traffic on Długa Street, lit brightly by gas lamps. Ladies in round hats and cloaks lift their long dresses. (...) The German language is heard almost exclu-sively. Only occasionally a passing- worker or craftsman utters a greeting in Polish. Sometimes a peddler with basket of fruits calls in Kashubian – loud and resolutely. When I ask her: Where are you from? – she answers: I'm from Kashubia, Madam! Boys are speaking with hushed voiced, so as not to hear a contemptuous: Wasserpo-lacke, 'Grobkaschube' [derogatory: 'watery Pole, crude Kashub']. And I keep listen-ing with pleasure to those unknown sounds, as I am under the strong impression of Derdowski's poetry 'On Mr Czorliński, who went to Puck for net'. And I take delight in the soft local Kashubian dialect. Even earlier I was enchanted by Klonowicz's 'Flis' ['Rafter']. How different was the then Polish Gdańsk from the present one, under the hydra-headed HaKaTa of Hanemann, Kennemann and Tiedemann, powerful heir of Bismarck's policy, suppressing the Polish spirit.
>
> The humour of Gdańsk, the Kashubian dialect, the pomposity of 'Protz' rich men, 'flowers from barrack yards', political allusions, have found their author, who has gathered half-truths, polite and gutter jokes. He has gathered those spicy seeds of humour, listening in the streets and on the Motława. The young editor Jaenicke used to write columns in the German newspaper in Gdańsk, signing them 'Pogodke' ['Cheerful']. His motto was 'I drink, smoke, and write – with humour!'. Those articles were willingly read. They reflected private life, with a touch of crudeness given by Plattdeutsch [Low German language] and seamen's anecdotes. Comical situations resulted from a certain narrow-mindedness among the bourgeoisie who, however, tried to keep up worldly appearances and English manners. That contributed to the specific character of the 'great world' of Gdańsk. (Borzyszkowski 1982b: 150–1).

That great world of Gdańsk with its Polish and German cultural elites was also vividly present in the life of the Kashubs. Germans were also fascinated at that time by the Slavonic past of Vineta or the isle of Rügen being uncovered by archaeologists and historians (sometimes they were more interested in these places than in the closer Kashubian neighbour-hood). This Slavonic past was also embedded in the Kashubian traditions and legends, and in the consciousness of the historically small elites.

## The Kashubs and the First World War, the interwar period and Nazism

When fighting in battles on various fronts of the First World War, the Young-Kashubs in enemy German uniforms continued to think about the Kashubian question and about the possibility of Poland gaining independence, together with the Kashubian lands. Many of them suffered numerous painful experiences during the war; Jan Karnowski, known as the conscience of Kashubian regionalism and the brains of the Young-Kashubian movement, protested in his poems against the atrocities of war and the degradation of the soldiers (Karnowski 1981 and Obracht-Prondzyński 1999).

During the war, there was a general increase of common piety, and this affected the Kashubs as well. It found its expression in the construction of a Calvary in Wiele in southern Kashubia, mainly funded from donations made by Kashubs and other inhabitants of Chełmno diocese, as well as by emigrants. Faith in the revival of the Polish state was also increasing – and it finally happened in 1918. The German Revolution and the restoration of Polish statehood in the former Austrian and Russian territories stimulated and mobilised both Kashubs and Pomeranian Poles to intensive struggle, even armed combat. Their aim was to attach Pomerania and other lands under Prussian partition to Poland, and many took part in the Greater Poland Uprising in the winter of 1918–19. On 12 April 1919, the County People's Council in Kościerzyna (Berendt), during a rally devoted to the unification of Kashubia with Poland, resolved:

We, the Kashubs of the Kashubian town of Kościerzyna and vicinity, numbering one thousand at this meeting of the People's Council, solemnly announce to the entire civilised world that our forefathers, grandfathers and fathers and ourselves are Poles to the core with all our hearts and souls.

Our Kashubian land is Polish, unless Brandenburg is not German! Our Kashubian language is the Polish language, unless the speakers of Low German are not Germans. We are and will remain Poles, like our brothers in Greater Poland, the Kingdom, Galicia, Silesia, and Mazuria. No German historian or politician, no socialist or HaKaTa activist shall pull out our Kashubian – Polish heart. Germans! Don't you dare classify us, our mothers, wives and children as a different, foreign tribe! Hands off! We, the Kashubs, are and will remain Poles in our land! We shall not perish! The Kashubs shall never be destroyed! (Wojciechowski 1981: 123).

The First World War and the Peace Conference in Versailles created a new Europe. The Kashubs, who for generations had dreamt of release from Prussian oppression, saw a better future for themselves in a reunited Poland. But not all of the area inhabited by the Kashubs was incorporated into Poland, and Pomerania (together with its population) was divided into three parts, which the Kashub leaders saw as a defeat. The Kashubian part of the Pomeranian voivodeship formed a wedge between lands that still remained within the German Reich. In the west was the former province of Pommern, with remnants of Lutheran Kashubs on the Łeba Lake and quite a numerous Catholic community in the counties of Lębork and Bytów. To the east, the Free City of Danzig was established, dominated by the German population, but inhabited also by considerable groups of Poles and Kashubs, who now felt more alienated than they had done before the war. A similar situation existed in the regions of Bytów and Lębork and in other regions of Germany, where German society seemed to believe the new situation was temporary, and was only a result of the military defeat of the Reich. The Kashubs and Poles in Gdańsk and in the Pomeranian province found that they were still – and even more obviously – a minority. For those who stayed in Germany, this was a consequence of their national attitude before the war; to a greater extent than in Gdańsk, which remained tied to Poland. In many cases, economic factors and an attachment to the native land were decisive.

Moreover, the Polish army and the new government administration (only partially recruited from among local people) were not able to avoid mistakes and failures, which destroyed the Kashubs' joy in their return to Poland. This was what lay behind an article written in 1925 in *Gryf* by Majkowski. In spite of their enthusiasm for their regained independence, some Kashubs almost immediately began to express their pain at seeing another partition of the Kashubian-Pomeranian lands between various states. Majkowski wrote:

> It is quite painful that the vivisection of the ethnic Kashubian body has taken place without any protest or lively reaction from the Kashubian intelligentsia which had been called upon to do this. We realise that Gdańsk, the natural capital of Kashubia has been cut off. (...) A simple consequence of such conduct has been the separation of Kashubs from the source of their traditions, from the place consecrated by the graves of Kashubian dukes, magnificent Oliwa, incorporated into the territory of the Free City of Danzig. Maybe today, those who, before the war, had been so afraid of the Young-Kashubian movement as a mouthpiece of the tribal identity of Kashubs, will think it over, when the diplomats speak now not about 'Kashubia' but rather of the 'Korridor'.[6] (*Gryf* 1925: 1)

Majkowski shows his disappointment with the attitude of his own circle, as well as sorrow that in the past the activity of Young-Kashubs had not been appreciated by some Polish circles (particularly in Gdańsk), and that, therefore, the chance of acquiring Gdańsk and a greater part of the Kashubs' Pomeranian homeland for Poland had not been seized. Majkowski saw the division of Kashubia into three parts, and the fact that Gdańsk remained outside Poland, as defeats both for his movement and for Poland.

As a result of the new borders, old economic ties were broken and job opportunities within the previously large and prosperous German state were lost. The Kashubs' recovered freedom was not always used in a proper way in the political arena. Admittedly, the Kashubs were often thanked, even

---

6    The Polish Corridor (also known as Danzig Corridor or Gdańsk Corridor) was a territory located in the region of eastern Pomerania provided the interwar Poland with access to the Baltic Sea, thus dividing the bulk of Germany from the province of East Prussia.

publicly, for the return of Pomerania to Poland; however, the economic problems were noticeable on an everyday basis, as was the arrogance of bureaucracy and the dislike felt by some newcomers from inland Poland for the incomprehensible Kashubian populace. Kashubs were frequently excluded from participation in the ongoing land reforms, or from better jobs in the newly built town and harbour of Gdynia. Only Kashubian landowners sometimes had the chance to become wealthy. Importantly, the National Democracy Party – which thanks to the Church was the strongest political party in Pomerania since the partitions, and was quite popular among the Kashubs – never came to power. It was therefore a dominant opposition force, often using the moods of the Kashubian-Pomeranian populace as an instrument in its political struggles, particularly against Józef Piłsudski's *Sanacja* camp after 1926 (Kutta 2003).

After the May 1926 coup d'état, the local Church tried to stimulate integration. Bishop Okoniewski, associated with the independence political camp and with the followers of Marshall Piłsudski, who ruled the country from 1926, did his best to revive Polishness in Pomerania. He identified himself with Pomeranian traditions, awakened the national and regional spirit among members of the Church and stimulated them to social activity. He was able to use the intellectual resources of the diocese's clergy, and to promote genuine and reliable academic research and social work among the seminary professors. His co-workers were also priests known for their Kashubian self-identity, including the precursor of liturgical reform Rev. Dr Kazimierz Bieszk, and also Rev. Konstantyn Dominik, rector of the seminary in Pelplin and famous for his piety (Borzyszkowski 2000, 2002).

At a national level, Pomerania was distinguished by an abundance of civic organisations as well as by high cultural standards, in spite of significant unemployment and other problems. A youthful intelligentsia grew rapidly, educated at Polish universities and assembled into organisations of Polish students, associations and corporations, such as 'Pomerania' in Poznań and 'Cassubia' in Warsaw. As far as scholarship was concerned, Kashubian and Pomeranian issues were researched mainly at the university centre of Poznań, but also by the meritorious Learned Society in Toruń, the capital of the new Province of Pomerania, and the new Society of Friends of the Arts and Sciences in Gdańsk. The most interesting achievements of Polish scholarship in that period concerning the Kashubs and Pomerania were made under the auspices of the Baltic Institute in Toruń, which later moved to Gdynia. The Baltic Institute gathered co-workers from all university centres in Poland and from abroad, published its own journal and other publications (including publications in foreign languages), and presented the Pomeranian issues researched by Polish scholars to a European audience. The showpiece of the Baltic Institute was the monograph *The Kashubs – Culture and Language*, edited by Józef Borowik (Boduszyńska-Borowikowa 1972). Local initiatives in Gdańsk included the reissued Young-Kashubian journal *Gryf*, with a supplement called *Gryf Kaszubski*, whose editors later established the Regional Kashubian Association in Kartuzy and published the journal *Zrzesz Kaszëbskô* (Borzyszkowski 2004: 621).

Also of substantial importance was the activity of the Pomeranian Broadcasting Station of Polish Radio in Toruń, which broadcast special Kashubian radio programmes.

These efforts were supported by the press, which created an atmosphere favourable to various artistic and cultural activities. The banners of most Pomeranian organisations contained the image of the Kashubian griffin, or traditional Kashubian embroidery patterns. These symbolic Kashubian motifs were also visible in the school system, and even in visual arts and music. Kashubian painting was represented mainly by Marian Mokwa and Kazimierz Jasnoch, while Feliks Nowowiejski composed music based on maritime motifs; he later also composed the Kashubian anthem and the opera *The Legend of the Baltic*, which described the prehistory of the whole of Pomerania, including the myth of the ancient town of Vineta.

From its beginning, the Kashubian movement had been interested in the past and in the culture of the Germanised Slavonic tribes of the island of Rügen and the German provinces of Pommern and Mecklenburg. This interest boomed during the interwar period. Various centres, from Toruń to Gdańsk and Gdynia, witnessed the blossoming of diverse Kashubian circles and organisations, which published their own journals and represented various ideas and political options, continuing the activities of Ceynowa, Derdowski and the Young-Kashubs. In spite of numerous efforts, though, no single organisation was established to represent Kashubian interests on the provincial scale, even if Kashubian matters were a subject of interest

among the authorities and among various social milieux in Poland and
Germany. The Kashubian movement was also observed by both the Polish
and German intelligence services, the latter trying – in vain – to weaken the
Kashubs' identification with Poland. In turn, the Polish *Sanacja* authorities
often succumbed to the fear of Kashubian separatism, encouraged by the
Kashubs' political sympathies with the opposition National Democracy
Party (Kutta 1989).

Many Kashubs had close relatives in the Free City of Danzig and in
Germany, and this bolstered the strength of the Polish minority within
Germany. Their organisations included the Union of Poles in Germany
(its Fifth District was called 'Borderland and Kashubia'). Many Kashubs
also held leading roles within the Polish community in Gdańsk.

Just before the Second World War, Józef Kisielewski travelled from
Hamburg via Stettin (Szczecin) to Danzig (Gdańsk). He discovered traces
of Kashubian culture and met living Kashubs in the vicinity of Gdańsk.
In his brilliant 1939 reportage *Ziemia gromadzi prochy* [The Land Accu-
mulates Ashes], he called them the last redoubt of the Lekhitic tribe of
Pomeranians, with Gdańsk (a town of two faces: merchant and Kashubian) as their capital. He claimed the Kashubs on the German side were
perishing in great distress. By this time Hitlerism was spreading in the Free
City and in Germany, in preparation for the war, which was to start with
the attack on Poland.

In order to fully understand Kashubian attitudes in the interwar
period, attention should be paid to the economic situation in the region
and to the policy of the Polish authorities. When the first euphoria over
unification with Poland was gone and the negative consequences of the
new social and economic reality came to light in Pomerania, dissatisfaction
arose with the many injustices resulting from the authorities' weakness. In
place of the Germans who left Pomerania, a wave of settlers and civil servants arrived, including many looters from the Polish interior, who treated
the region as an area of new colonisation and its inhabitants as people of
inferior class, Germanised and alien to Polishness. The authorities maintained martial law or a state of emergency here for a long time, especially
as at the same time the Polish-Soviet war broke out and the Red Army
entered the region of Chełmno. Bitterness overflowed when parity was

created between the hitherto strong Deutschmark and the weak Polish mark, which meant financial losses for the Kashubs-Pomeranians and great profits for their compatriots from the interior.

In such conditions, in the mid-1920s, on the initiative of a group of Pomeranian deputies, the Polish Parliament sent a special commission to Pomerania to investigate on the spot the authenticity of the complaints against the authorities and to undertake possible remedies. That Pomeranian Commission was headed by Rev. Feliks Bolt, who knew his native Pomerania, Kashubia and Kociewie well. In the report, in the chapter on the general overview of the administration and conditions in Pomerania, we read:

> The general impression of the Commission was not comforting, often in fact depressing. A blind eye has often been turned to shortcomings prevailing in the whole country, caused either by the war or by post war conditions. (...) The mood of the population is the best barometer of a normally functioning administrative system. That mood is generally better and favourable towards the state on the right bank of the Vistula, where the patriotic feelings and consciousness are deeper. Therefore, various troubles and shortcomings are endured with patient tolerance and a strong belief in a better future. On the left bank of the Vistula, especially in the northern counties, bitterness, dislike and even hostility towards the state are reaching a climax. (...) Kashubia needs the bravest civil servants. The latter are of various origin, and it is understandable that their tasks are often beyond their capabilities. To Pomerania and particularly to Kashubia and the sea-coast, one should send the bravest and most exemplary people, good Catholics who are well acquainted with local conditions.
>
> (...) Therefore, one should take into consideration, as far as possible, the candidates from Pomerania who more easily understand the spiritual fabric of the Pomeranian population. (...) The county governors and other officials are too permissive towards Germans. They should be convinced to treat Germans fairly but firmly. We have had the impression that the Germans still do not feel themselves to be Polish citizens, expect political turmoil, and – as a certain German expressed it – they 'still glance with one eye toward Berlin'.[7]

The Commission also took note of the complaints of local Germans, many of whom had opted for Germany in the past and left Pomerania in the 1920s. No wonder that those who stayed 'glanced towards Berlin', and continued

---

7   *Sejm Rzeczypospolitej Polskiej o Pomorzu w 1920 roku* (1985), 30–2.

to do so until 1939 and during the Second World War. The German minority in the Polish part of Pomerania, thanks to their previous privileges and wealth, constituted a well-organised economic and political power, and they were also supported financially by Berlin after 1920. Only a minority identified themselves with Poland and most considered the post-Versailles state of affairs temporary.

The Kashubs, hardened by the reality of the Prussian state, expected the Polish state to approximate to their ideal. Majkowski, in a 1921 article, wrote under the pseudonym of Jan Starza:

> The Prussian system created and justified a type of uniform citizen, created according to the same model, with the state as a dominating juggernaut. According to that system, the state was the goal and the citizen a medium – an individual deprived of inherent rights. Not only individuals and opposition associations within the German nationality suffered under such uniformity. Citizens of a foreign type and nationality, as e.g. Poles, whose existence as such, not to speak of their natural tendencies to unify with their brothers in other parts of the partitioned country, constituted an everlasting insult to the principle of the homogeneity of citizens (…)
>
> Following the model of victorious Western democracies, the state for us is a medium, while the goals are the citizens and nation. The state is a house we built for ourselves and for that reason it is beloved and should be fought for till the bitter end. Its defender and builder is the citizen – free, enlightened, noble, and aware that a part of personal freedom must be sacrificed for full civic freedom. The stronger, more enlightened and nobler the citizen, the more powerful the nation – a collective guardian of the state. In a state understood as such, it is various tribes and individuals that on the one hand find opportunities for their full development, and on the other hand, represent not weakness, but richness and support for the state. The Pomeranians with their highly developed state-building sense shall be an important acquisition for Poland. (Majkowski 1921)

Such an ideal of the civic society, and of a democratic state rich in diversity, had no chance of realisation at that time. Polish Pomerania, until 1926, was a furnace of emerging democracy, and after 1926 of a 'moral cleansing policy' inclining towards a totalitarian system. The internal temperature was increasing as a result of the Polish-German conflict. The situation of the Kashubs was especially difficult – they were poorly organised but were on course for further development of their own culture and identity within the Polish nation and state.

The policy of Polonisation or re-Polonisation in Pomerania, led from above in accordance with the aspirations of the majority of Poles, often backfired. The maritime policy, which brought positive effects as far as the economy and general identity of the Poles was concerned, had a negative impact upon the Kashubs, who themselves constituted a vital part of that general myth of 'the sea and Pomerania'. The presentation of the Polish coastland and all things maritime (for example through guidebooks, and through the activities of various organisations) popularised the Kashubian issue in Poland and rewarded the Kashubs for their allegiance to Polish ideas. Apart from the Kashubs, it was Catholic clergy who were praised as local community leaders in their fight against Germanisation. An example is the text published by Piotr Paliński, former editor of *Gazeta Gdańska*, in his 1934 guidebook to the Polish Baltic coast and Kashubia: 'Poland has been resurrected indeed! (...) And here, on the Baltic, it is the hardened and brave fellow Kashubs who have faced the sea and defended it against the perennial enemy of the Kashubian land and sea. (...) The fact that the Baltic is ours today is thanks to our faithful and fearless fellow Kashubs and the most respectable clergy of that land! Their memory shall be blessed for centuries!' (Paliński 1934: 46).

The grandiloquence of those words is typical of the period. Such sentiments provided the Kashubs with a momentary satisfaction, and were doled out generously during numerous anniversaries and national ceremonies, where the Church and Catholic clergy played an important role and eagerly accepted and popularised similar opinions.

However, everyday life both in Prussia before the war and in Poland after 1920 was far from the picture presented in ceremonial speeches. Socially and economically, the people most affected were Poles living in the western districts, especially the Kashubs, who mainly inhabited the infertile regions of Pomerania. On the one hand, those regions had been cut off and isolated from the richer and better developed German state, where many Kashubs could easily find jobs. On the other hand, as a result of unification with the former Russian and Austrian parts of Poland, Pomerania had to pay the costs of amalgamation and fund the construction of a new economic system. An additional problem, perceived by the Kashubs as discrimination against the native population of Pomerania by the central authorities, was the limitation of Kashubian participation in the landowner reforms of the 1920s and in the developing labour market in Gdynia. Both land and labour were in short supply in Pomerania, and were retained for newcomers from the overpopulated and economically weaker regions of southern Poland. Groups of highlanders from Podhale and the Tatra mountains could be found in communities created on the estates of former landowners such as von Krockow; they gradually became Kashubianised.

Alongside the development of Gdynia as the most modern Baltic harbour (which had positive results for the Kashubs, both those from Gdynia itself and those from villages absorbed by the town, where Kashubs often owned building land), another project of great importance was the main coal line constructed in the 1920s to connect Silesia with Gdynia through Kashubia. The construction alleviated the negative effects of the broken economic links of Kashubia with Gdańsk, and West Pomerania and Słupsk with Berlin. Unfortunately, the road and railway connections between Berlin and Königsberg ran through the so-called 'Corridor'. It is worth mentioning here the economic initiatives of the administration of the province of Pomerania and local communal self-governments, such as the development of power plants in Gródek on the river Brda in Rutki and on the Radunia near Kartuzy. These investments alleviated the effects of the great economic crisis at the end of the 1920s.

The inland and Baltic fishery was also developing relatively well. Hel – both the peninsula and the town – acquired a railway connection with the interior of the country and developed into a tourist centre, where health resort visitors came in droves. New boarding houses appeared to host legions of tourists as well as the political and artistic elite from Warsaw. In this way, knowledge of Kashubian issues increased throughout the country. Despite considerable development of the region, substantial spheres of poverty remained, and the economic differences between the native and immigrant populations increased. The immigrants, especially after 1920, were called 'barefoot Tonys' [*bose Antki*]. This was an insulting allusion to the frequent use of the Christian name Anthony (*Antoni*) and to the shortage of footwear and other worldly goods among those who looked for a better standard of living among the Kashubs in Pomerania. They didn't always put down spiritual roots there, often looking down on the native Kashubs and seeing them as culturally alien, German, or at least close to Germanness. The Germans who stayed in Kashubia did not help to relieve the conflicts between their culturally and ethnically differentiated neighbours.

Undoubtedly, the administrative and territorial self-government which accompanied economic self-government stimulated economic development and constituted a new phenomenon in the political culture of the region. In spite of slumps during crisis periods, the administrative system remained stable, thanks to the strong and developed structure of co-operative institutions. This was a soothing factor during changes in the international and internal policy of central governments. The Kashubs functioned quite well within this administrative and economic system, rarely advertising their ethnic identity. They frequently held prominent posts at the local and provincial level, perhaps even more frequently than their fellow-citizens.

## The Kashubs and the Second World War

The 'friendly' visit of the training battleship Schleswig-Holstein to Gdańsk in the summer of 1939 initiated, on 1 September, the biggest war in the history of the world. The names of the Polish soldiers who shielded Westerplatte[8] (among whom there was one Kashub, the military chaplain Rev. Jan Bemka) went down in history, as did the names of the defenders of the Polish Post Office in Gdańsk, where more Kashubs fought. The ashes of the murdered postal workers were still being found in Gdańsk as late as 1992. In September 1939, Gdańsk triumphantly returned to the Reich. Crowded streets and ringing bells welcomed Adolf Hitler into the city.

The execution of people hostile towards the Nazi Reich now began. The first to die were the Jews, followed almost immediately by the Poles. The *Sonderbuch* – an address list of those previously designated for extermination

8    Westerplatte is a military stronghold near the naval harbour of Gdańsk/Danzig.

– was a great help to the murderers, who were often neighbours of the victims dressed in the uniforms of *Selbstschutz* ('Self-defence'). The most potent remaining symbol of those days in Gdańsk is the *Victoria-Schule*, where Polish activists were imprisoned before being loaded onto transports and taken to the Stutthof Concentration Camp, which had been under construction since September 1939. The name of that village (now Sztutowo), located on a Baltic sand bar, became synonymous with the fate of many Kashubian families and many other peoples of Baltic Europe. The camp – with dozens of branches and labour sub-camps, including separate ones for the Jews – operated till the last days of the war, even after the prisoners had been evacuated (ahead of the approaching Red Army) in the famous 'Death March'. Besides Stutthof, hundreds of places in Kashubia and Pomerania (many of them since named 'Death Valley') are still marked with the symbols of martyrdom. These included Szpęgawsk in the Kociewie region (where Rev. Leon Heyka, the Kashubian educator and poet, perished) and – above all – Piaśnica Forest between Wejherowo and Krokowa. Tens of thousands of Kashubs and Poles from Northern Kashubia were buried at Piaśnica Forest, as well as many citizens of the Reich, from Brandenburg and Mecklenburg, whose poor health or Slavonic origin did not correspond with the ideals of the 'pure German race'. The autumn of 1939 came to be known as 'the bloody autumn' and affected the entire local elite including the clergy, most tragically in Pelplin, the diocesan capital. Rev. Franz Manthey, Professor at the Seminary in Pelplin until 1958 and later a German citizen and an activist in the West Prussian Compatriots' Society, wrote the following in his work *A History of the Kashubs*, published in the 1997 series *Truth and Testimony*:

> Decisive for the ultimate attitude of the Kashubs in national matters was the autumn of 1939 with all its atrocities, which afflicted the local population of many places in Kashubia. The cemetery of Piaśnica then became a symbolic monument to rejecting all things German, and it is commonly known that the dead constitute a greater force than the living. Certainly, some Kashubs fought during the war in the Wehrmacht, here and there, there were some people with a positive attitude towards German rule. Many more simply rejected Bolshevism and Russianness. But the events of the autumn of 1939 in that ill-fated land can be forgotten only in the future – and who knows if they can ever be forgotten – or if it the will to forget even exists – there, in the Kashubian cottages, forests and fishing boats. (Manthey 1997: 86–7).

These words from a German clergyman, whose homeland was West Prussia, the land on the Vistula, correspond with the saying: 'To forgive is a Christian duty; to forget is a sign of weak will'.

The wartime fates of the Kashubs and other Pomeranian-Poles, and the various attitudes of the local Germans, are preserved in individual and collective memory and also in literature. Most of these accounts depict experiences on the front line, as well as stories of various escapes, concentration camps and POW camps, and forced labour within Germany and other countries occupied by the Nazi invaders. There were also of course Germans who helped others to survive, both in Kashubia and beyond the river Oder.

From the autumn of 1939, the extermination policy in Pomerania was accompanied by mass displacements into the territory of the Generalgouvernement. Bronisław Brandt of Kościerzyna, recollecting this period in the journal *Pomerania*, remembered the amazement of the inhabitants of Podlasie, far away on the river Bug, when the deported Kashubs arrived:

> After another 2–3 hours, a cavalcade of wagons reached the big village of Kornica – the seat of a township and parish. The local authorities, perhaps warned earlier of our arrival, started to allocate us to individual families. This must have been an unpleasant duty for them. Our family was put up in a farmstead located almost at the end of the 6-km long village. That part was called Sołtysy; our host, probably quite poor, which could be seen from the buildings, was called Chromiec.
>
> One could imagine the amazement and terror of people awoken from sleep and forced to take in under their roof a sizeable group of strangers. We stared at them, and they at us.
>
> We explained, who we were, from where we had been deported. They could hardly understand. (Brandt 1996: 38–41).

These people suffered a lot of hardships, but some escaped from Kashubia and Pomerania to the Generalgouvernement of their own free will. It was easier to hide there from the Gestapo and the SS, as it also was in the interior of Germany. They could feel more secure than if they stayed in their native neighbourhood. Stefan Fikus of Luzino near Wejherowo spent most of the war as a forced worker near Schlepkow. Later he recollected:

Still worse news was coming from Luzino. The local 'Volksdeutsche' [ethnic Germans] allowed themselves to behave so nastily and stupidly, that the villagers were petrified. Nobody knew when their time would come. Before the war they had been beggars, rascals and the worst frauds, but at that time they sported the black and yellow attire and they did what they wanted. They could point their finger at somebody, and he was sent to Stutthof, to labour or was imprisoned. Stefan's neighbours, of whom nobody would have thought they were Germans, at that time sported their brown or black uniforms stuck out their chests and wore high boots. His colleagues and good friends could not speak Polish. Most of his friends were dispersed throughout the world and other were as quiet as mice so as not to be pointed out. Terrible times came to Poland! At moments Stefan thanked God that he was in Schlepkow, not free, as he did not have to see and experience all that at home. (Fikus 1981: 178)

Not all Kashubs behaved with dignity. Their homeland was incorporated directly into the Reich as District Danzig – West Prussia, where Hitler's representative was Albert Forster, who intended to Germanise Pomerania swiftly and entirely. Those Kashubs who stayed and tried to maintain their dignity found themselves on the compulsory DVL or *Deutsche Volksliste* ('German ethnic list'), which for men meant military service in the Wehrmacht. In 1942, the so-called 'Germanisation' (*Eindeutschung*) of the 3rd group of the DVL actually included all the Kashubs. The aim was the total elimination of Polishness, at least formally, with the intention of striking terror into the resistance and – above all – gaining Kashubian conscripts. Those who left for service in the Wehrmacht were reported to have sung Polish songs on their trains, and even to have shouted 'we are the Polish army!'. Those sent to the front remained under the vigilant surveillance of their superiors and colleagues. But even so, many went over to the other side, to the Polish Army in the West and East, or even to the French Resistance.

It is difficult to comprehensively depict the complicated history of Pomerania and the Kashubs in the Second World War. One has to remember that alongside the extreme events – the murders, the national and individual dramas – normal life continued. Both Germans and Poles had their joys and their worries. The intensity of these changed with the course of war, and the war began to afflict the Germans, the nation of winners, with horrifying results. Only a few Germans, in Pomerania as elsewhere, dared to publicly express their disapproval of or objection to the Nazi totalitarian system and its ideal of German domination throughout Europe. A noteworthy example, though, is Dietrich Bonhoefer from Breslau (Wrocław). Bonhoefer was a Lutheran pastor in Pomerania who condemned Nazism, was arrested in 1943 and was executed just before the end of the war, on 9 April 1945, in the concentration camp of Flossenburg.

The Nazi occupation of Pomerania also had tragic consequences for the Catholic Church, as more than half of the clergy in the Chełmno Diocese were murdered. It is worth mentioning the role of the Gdańsk bishop Carl Maria Splett, who issued a number of unprecedented orders, including a ban on hearing confessions in Polish. It could be argued that he felt more attachment to the Nazi ideology than to the Polish souls for whom he was supposedly responsible. Fortunately, not all the priests subordinate to him rigorously observed the ban; among the dissenters was Franz Manthey, as well as some priests who had been imported from the interior of the Reich.

From the first days of the war, the struggle took place on various different fronts, not only in the military arena. There was an organisation of underground state structures in Pomerania, as in many other areas. The most extensive was the secret military organisation *Gryf Kaszubski*, founded in 1940 and soon renamed *Gryf Pomorski*, which co-operated with the all-Polish Home Army, but shrank from total subordination to the headquarters in Warsaw. Its statute outlined as its basic tasks:

3. Armed combat with the enemy in order to liberate the homeland (Pomerania) and attach Gdańsk, East Prussia and Baltic coast together with Szczecin and the isle of Rügen to Poland. (...)
4. Restitution of all churches previously belonging to the Catholic Church (both before and after the partitions of Poland) and taken away by the enemies of the holy faith, and where possible – the erection of holy crosses and re-erection in traditional places of monuments to Christ the Lord, the Blessed Virgin Mary and all the Saints.
5. Underground struggle against the enemy through spreading defeatism within German society, desertion within the German Army, imperceptible sabotage, delaying the course of labour in all domains of life controlled by Germans.
6. Keeping up the national spirit among compatriots, spreading trust in regaining the country's liberty; dissuading Poles from accepting German nationality and joining the German army.

7. Supporting Poles persecuted by the German authorities as well as POW's from allied states. Providing help to Poles a) kept in POW camps, b) displaced, c) in penal camps, d) in extreme poverty; hurrying to the medical and religious aid of all compatriots in hiding.

This kind of activity penetrated all levels of the Kashubian-Pomeranian community, especially in the rural areas. *Gryf Pomorski* was connected politically with the pre-war National Democrats, and points 3 and 4 in its programme are worthy of notice. They reveal the Kashubs' persistence in perceiving the whole of Pomerania as their homeland, as well as the identification of their own fate with the interests of Poland and the Catholic Church.

Among the leaders of *Gryf* there were representatives of the Young-Kashubs, including the commander of their headquarters, Rev. Józef Wrycza. There were many representatives of the young generation of intelligentsia and folk activists who had been educated in the interwar period.

From 1942, the Kashubs were forcibly added to the *Volksliste* and conscripted into the Wehrmacht. Those who deserted or were taken captive joined – whenever possible – the Polish underground army, the Polish Armed Forces in Western Europe or the Polish Army in the East. There were also Kashubs and Pomeranians in the United Kingdom, whose aim was to see the whole of Pomerania, included Rügen, incorporated into Poland. They formed the 'Pomeranian Union' of soldiers, established in 1944 by Lech Bądkowski, and their vision was for Pomerania to stay within the borders of Poland as a land of multiple cultures and languages. At that time it was impossible to imagine the mass displacements which were to afflict both Poles and Germans in the eastern territories of their states, and were to change entirely the ethnic structure of Pomerania and the situation of the Kashubs.

In the final stages of the war, the Kashubs also had to contend with the mixed benefits of liberation by the Soviet Army. There were deportations into deepest Russia, often beyond the Urals and into Siberia, and many never returned. This particularly affected younger people, including members of the resistance (Jastrzębski 1990).

Simultaneously, the mass migration of Kashubs into West Pomerania started – a peculiar and symbolic return of Kashubian to its roots. Migration particularly affected the areas bordering on the former Province of Pomerania, but also reached to the very limits of the new state territory, as far as Szczecin. Many Kashubs and Pomeranians settled in Gdańsk, together with their compatriots and migrants from the south. The fate of the Kashubs, Poles and Germans under Nazism was depicted by the German writer Günter Grass in his novel *Tin Drum* (Grass was proud of his Kashubian roots). The character of Anna Koljaczkowa, grandmother of Oskar, the German hero of the novel, represents the fate of the Kashubs, caught between Poland and Germany at the end of the war. When bidding farewell to Oskar before his departure from Gdańsk, Anna tells him about the recent experiences of her close Kashubian family, as tragic as the experiences of the Germans:

> I've had my trouble too; pains all over, in the heart and in the head where some numbskull hit me 'cause he thought it was the right thing to do … Yes Oskar that's how it is with the Kashubs. They always get hit on the head. You'll be going away where things are better, only Grandma will be left. The Kashubs are no good at moving. Their business is to stay where they are and hold out their heads for everybody else to hit, because we're not real Poles and we're not real Germans, and if you're a Kashub, you're not good enough for the Germans or the Polacks. They want everything full measure. (Grass 1961)

## The Kashubian movement after 1945: persistence and development

Initially, after the creation of the People's Republic of Poland, the Kashubs were very eager to participate in developing its civic structures and building the new democratic Poland. In 1946, the first Kashubian Congress was convened in Wejherowo. It was made up of activists who had survived the war and who were associated with the *Zrzesz Kaszëbskô* journal, edited in Wejherowo at that time, and supported by the local and provincial authorities. They asserted their right to administrative posts in the new regime, and appealed for help for the Germanised Slovincians⁹ from the Łebsko (Leba) Lake. They also wanted to create favourable conditions for the development of the Kashubian language. Later, in September 1946, Szczecin hosted the Congress of Kashubs-Poles-Autochthons, who aimed to convey in a modern form the eternal right of Poland to the Kashubian lands (Borzyszkowski 1997, 1998).

Soon, however, both Poland and Pomerania became dominated by the communists, and the state itself by the Soviet Union, which meant the erasure of any dreams of democracy and free civic activity, including the development of the Kashubian community and other regional communities. Ukrainians who had been expelled from their homeland in southeastern Poland in 1947 were settled in Pomerania; properties formerly owned by Germans, as well as major Polish estates, were nationalised; peasants were forced into collectives. Collectivisation, however, proved unsuccessful, thanks to the Kashubs' resistance. Similarly, the authorities did not manage to weaken the position of the Church.

The accompanying development of the education system and of industry, however, contributed to the survival of the regional movement, even under conditions of socialism – although initially it had to be limited to folklore and folk traditions. The Kashubian Museum in Kartuzy was founded by local activists, as were various folk ensembles; and the production of folk art was established.

The survival of that folkloristic trend meant that after the political thaw in October 1956 a revival of Kashubian organisation was possible. In December, the Kashubian Association was founded with the aim of gathering together all active members of the Kashubian movement, even if they had represented different political options during the interwar period (Bolduan 1996; Obracht–Prondzyński 2002, 2006). The president of the founding committee was Lech Bądkowski, former leader of the Pomeranian Union in the United Kingdom, while the first president was Aleksander

---

9    Lutheran speakers of Kashubian, who lived on the Gardna and Łeba lakes.

Arendt, a civil servant and the last chief commandant of the *Gryf Pomorski*. The main goal of the Association was the cultural, economic and political development of Kashubia. The programme and activities of the Association, especially under the presidency of Bernard Szczęsny, resulted in such important regional investments as the 'Kashubian Road' and the Factory of Kashubian Chinaware in Łubiana. The energetic development of the organisation and the proliferation of its branches in Kashubian towns and villages, even in Szczecin, testify to the immense vitality within the Kashubian community at the time. An event of historical significance was the Kashubian demonstration in June 1957, which accompanied the unveiling of a reconstructed monument to Derdowski in Wiele. In the years to come, an important role was played by the official journal *Kaszëbë* (1957–61), edited by Tadeusz Bolduan, which promoted knowledge of Kashubian history and modern regionalism. Soon, however, the Association – named officially a 'bastard of October [the 1956 thaw] – began to feel that the communist authorities were moving away from the post-thaw ideals. Some activists were subject to prosecution, including imprisonment and confiscation of their manuscript records. Nonetheless, the Association continued its work. Its activity was particularly strong among a young group who formed the Club 'Pomorania', founded by Bądkowski in 1962, and who aimed to support the civic and public development of Kashubian-Pomeranian activists.

In 1964, the Kashubian Association incorporated a group of activists from the failing Kociewie Association and changed its name into the Kashubian-Pomeranian Association (ZK-P). In spite of obstacles placed in its way by the state administration, it now included the whole of Pomerania in its activities.

Despite some crises and failures, the activities of ZK-P stood out from other organisations in the country, and even attracted members of the Communist Party (PZPR) and its satellite Peasants' Party (ZSL). Importantly, they had a policy of accepting members from various regions of Poland, particularly representatives of the intelligentsia and of literary and scholarly circles. They especially attracted members from the lost areas in the East, who were putting down roots in the Kashubian traditions of Gdańsk and Pomerania. Kashubia was becoming more strongly identified with the whole of Pomerania, something which actually accorded with the traditions and ideology of the Kashubian movement. A new formula for the regional movement was developed, predominantly by Bądkowski, stressing the principles of democracy and ideas of self-government on a regional and national level. This new ideology became popular within the Kashubian-Pomeranian community through publication of literary and scholarly works – 350 titles altogether. It was also supported by co-operation with the Learned Society of Gdańsk, and by numerous initiatives at the grassroots level and in local institutions. These included the foundation of the Kashubian Ethnographic Park in Wdzydze, the Museum of Kashubian-Pomeranian Literature and Music in Wejherowo and the Museum of the National Anthem in Będomin. There was also a growing body of work published in the association's journal *Pomerania*, edited by Wojciech Kiedrowski and Stanisław Pestka.

Another success of the Kashubian community and the ZK-P, which gained attention both nationwide and abroad, was the development of its own circle of writers and scholars. These came not only from Gdańsk and Vistulan Pomerania, but also included representatives among the national elites. Professor Gerard Labuda was the most eminent ambassador of Kashubian scholarship, and at the end of the 1980s Labuda became president of the Polish Academy of Sciences.

An expression of the independence of the ZK-P during communism was its close co-operation with the Catholic Church, especially with the two Kashubian-Pomeranian dioceses, Pelplin and Gdańsk-Oliwa. One example of this co-operation was the autumn Pelplin Meetings, which between 1980 and 1999 gathered together a large circle of regional activists, scholars and clergy to discuss the most important questions concerning the past, present and future of the Kashubs and Pomeranians, focusing particularly on moral principles and civic duties.

An important test of the power of the Kashubian-Pomeranian regional community and the ZK-P came with the events of August 1980 and then with the 1981 imposition of martial law in Poland. The ZK-P was one of the earliest organisations to support workers' protests and the formation of the *Solidarność* trade union movement, and later defended the movement's ideals, which for generations had constituted the core of Kashubian-Pomeranian principles. Lech Bądkowski was advisor to the Strike Committee in the Gdańsk Shipyard, the first spokesman of the *Solidarność* Trade Union and the chief editor of the *Samorządność* ('Home Rule') journal. Under martial law, the ZK-P, in spite of attempts by the communist authorities to create a new regional organisation, preserved its former structure and profile. It gave shelter to the persecuted, supported the formation of new organisations, both legal and illegal, and co-operated with regional activists, in 1987 founding a Club for Workers' Self-Government. Moreover, the ZK-P contributed to the normalisation of Polish-German relations, a significant role being played by writers, historians and sociologists from Gdańsk. It is worth mentioning the impressive monograph on the Kashubs prepared by Gdańsk sociologists (Latoszek 1990).

One of the most momentous occasions in modern Kashubian history was the 1987 pilgrimage of Pope John Paul II to Poland. During meetings in Gdynia and Oliwa he addressed the crowds of Pomeranians: 'My dear Kashubian brothers and sisters! Protect your values and your heritage that prove your identity!'. These words strengthened the Kashubian spirit, and had a particular effect on the local clergy, facilitating their acceptance of the presence of the Kashubian language within the Church. Thanks to the resulting increase in sympathy, Eugeniusz Gołąbek's translation of the New Testament into Kashubian was published by ZK-P in Gdańsk-Peplin in 1993 and was approved by the Polish Episcopate.

The achievements of the Kashubs and the ZK-P in various domains of social and public life, especially in the 1980s, undoubtedly set the scene for the developments to follow in and after 1989.

The everyday life of the Kashubs and the activities of the ZK-P have not been free from dangers, fears, weaknesses, defeats, conflicts and the unskilful exercise of liberties. Nevertheless, from the perspective of past generations and future challenges, the phenomenon of Kashubian endurance during communist times is noteworthy. Their achievements include the development of the Kashubian-Pomeranian movement, the formation of a new Kashubian-Pomeranian community, the induction of new generations into ancient Pomeranian traditions, and a new vision of Pomerania as a region of multicultural encounters and traditions, with continuity and progress made secure by its Kashubian core principles.

The history of the Kashubs has confirmed the conviction shared by
their leaders that the decisive factors in securing a prosperous present and
future for a community are inner strength, creativity, fundamental hard
work and education, both in the social and individual dimensions. The
traditions of self-government, freedom, responsibility and everyday work
– according to the Cistercian motto *ora et labora* – give spiritual power to
the Kashubs, and to their work and accomplishments.

JERZY TREDER

# The Kashubian Language and its Dialects: The Range of Use

## Kashubian as a Slavonic language

If the notion of language is attributed to an ethno-cultural group (and not to a nation-state), its distinct identity depends primarily on such factors as:

a) sufficient distinctness of the linguistic sphere;
b) its own literary tradition;
c) deliberate development of the language, literature and culture;
d) considerable specificity of the socio-cultural sphere;
e) a feeling of separateness shared by the intellectual elite as well as the community at large.

If this is the case, then Kashubian (in particular in its written literary form) should be treated as a language (Treder 1990: 80–1).

Kashubian is one of the Slavonic languages. It has emerged gradually from the Proto-Slavonic as one of the Pomeranian dialects within the Lekhitic languages (see below). Almost from the outset it has been subject to influence from Polish dialects, and later also from literary Polish, as well as interferences from German. The most important ancient distinctive features of Kashubian are: the evolution of Proto-Slavonic $*e \ge i$, later also $\ddot{e}$ (*jastrzib, jastrzëba* 'hawk'); so-called 'Kashubation' (*sedzec*, Polish *siedzieć* 'sit'); vowel *shwa* (*ë – Kaszëbë*, Polish *Kaszuby* 'Kashubia'); affricatisation of consonants *k', g' ≥ cz, dż* (*tacé nodżi*, Polish *takie nogi* 'such legs').

The status and position of Kashubian, as the only survivor of the historical dialects of Pomerania on the southern coast of the Baltic Sea, has been subject to heated discussion in the past. Its affiliation with the West-Slavonic languages has remained undisputed, while disagreements have arisen regarding their subdivision, namely the so-called Lekhitic group, which also comprises Polish and Polabian languages (Ramułt 1983). The common features shared by the Lekhitic languages are:

– preserved nasal vowels (as in *miãso* 'meat', *ząb* 'tooth');
– lack of a shift *g* > *h* (in comparison with other Slavonic languages e.g. *droga* 'road', *tego* 'this' (Genitive/Accusative));
– preserved *dz* < Proto-Slavonic *\*dj* and *\*g* (*ksãdza* 'priest' (Genitive/Accusative), *nodze* 'leg' (Dative));
– umlaut of Proto-Slavonic *\*ě* > *a* (*wierzëc* 'believe': *wiara* 'belief') and Proto-Slavonic *\*ę* > *ã* (*klic* or *kląc* 'curse': *wëklãti* 'cursed').

Within the geographical area of the Lekhitic languages, the western extreme was formed by Polabian, which became extinct in the eighteenth century. Polish has constituted the eastern boundary of the Lekhitic language region, with Kashubian acting as a transitional continuum.

For centuries, Kashubian has existed in numerous dialectal varieties as *kaszëbskô mòwa* or *rodnô mòwa* ('Kashubian/native tongue'). The formation of a common language, with partial standardisation, started in the mid-sixteenth century in West Pomerania (Krofej 1586). It redoubled in intensity from the mid-nineteenth century onwards in East (Gdańsk) Pomerania, as the result of a deliberate decision, and through the fruitful activity of Florian Ceynowa (1817–81). Ceynowa, born in Sławoszyno near Puck, created the Kashubian alphabet and orthography, establishing a language standard (with grammar) and providing samples of various texts based on his native (northern) vernacular. Since then, Kashubian has been deliberately cultivated as a means of communication, but it is still merely *in statu nascendi*, with a slender degree of polyvalence (Rogowska-Cybulska 2006) and a continually insufficient range of standardisation. This standardisation is highest in orthography, and there is also partial standardisation of inflection. As a standard language, it functions mainly in written literature, although it is used, to a much lesser degree, as a spoken language, and various Kashubian dialects are used as local varieties.

Stefan Ramułt, when compiling his dictionary, *Słownik języka pomorskiego*, used the term 'Pomeranian language', in order to 'express [his] viewpoint concerning the position of Kashubian among the Slavonic languages, as well as to remind the descendants of Pomeranians of their ancient and proud name' (Ramułt 1893: X). Friedrich Lorentz may have been referring to this in his *Gramatyka pomorska*, when he used the term 'Pomeranian' to describe the 'language of indigenous Slavs, situated in the northern part of so-called West Prussia and in the eastern part of German Pomerania' (Lorentz 1927: 7).

The literature created by Ceynowa came into being during the Springtime of Nations, alongside the national, cultural and linguistic demands of Czechs, Slovaks, Lusatian Sorbs and other peoples influenced by Slavophile ideas, according to which all Slavonic idioms are dialects of a single Slavonic language. The Kashubs were all the more interested in the right to their own language because at that time Poland was partitioned, and Kashubian was acknowledged as a barrier against Germanisation. The development of literature was intended in the first instance to stimulate tribal pride, and to strengthen the progress of civilisation among the Kashubs, and later to reveal more of their cultural identity.

## The range and differentiation of Kashubian: local groups

Nowadays, the Kashubs as an ethnic group inhabit a small part of Gdańsk Pomerania i.e. the eastern fringe of the vast territory of Pomerania. Kashubian has always shown a considerable internal diversification, and the first descriptions of the language originate only from the mid-nineteenth century, from Ceynowa's period. In 1856, the Russian researcher Hilferding divided Kashubian into: 1) the Slovincians' dialect (e.g. Wielka Gardna, Kluki, Smołdzino) and the Kabatks' dialect (e.g. Główczyce, Rowy), which are now extinct; 2a) dialects from the Łebsko Lake (e.g. Izbica, Łeba) 2b) dialects from east of the Łebsko Lake (e.g. Charbrowo, Sarbsk, Osieki); 2c) the dialect from the Bytów region (e.g. Bytów, Grzmiąca), now preserved only in the latter area, for example in Rekowo; 3) the dialect spoken in the former West Prussia, e.g. in Żarnowiec, Swarzewo, Chałupy, Wejherowo, Kartuzy, Stężyca, Kościerzyna, Leśno, Skarszewo. This final area has generally stayed Kashubian.

At the beginning of the twentieth century this division was updated by Lorentz, who delineated two primary areas (north and south, differentiated by duration), twenty-one groups and seventy local dialects, all richly illustrated with texts. The situation from the mid-twentieth century onwards has been described in the 1964 *Atlas językowy kaszubszczyzny* [Kashubian linguistic atlas], where the following areas were assigned: 1) the more archaic north e.g. the Puck and Wejherowo regions; 2) the more innovative centre, mainly focussed on the west; 3) the Polonised south, especially the eastern part. Here the Kashubs adjoin the neighbouring Kociewians and Borowiaks,[1] who speak sub-dialects of Wielkopolska (Greater Poland), sharing some linguistic features with Kashubian. These features include: a) diphthongal pronunciation of vowels i.e. former: $\bar{a}$ ≥ ôə (e.g. *ptôəch* 'bird'), $\bar{o}$ ≥ óə ‖ *uó* (e.g. *sóəl* ‖ *suól* 'salt'), ŏ ≥ *uo, ue* (e.g. *muewa*, 'gull'); b) lack of *mazurzenie*[2] i.e. pronunciation: *cas* ('time'), *sari* ('grey'), *zaba* ('frog') – comp. Polish *czas, szary, żaba*; c) diminutive suffix *-iszk* (*-yszek*) e.g. *grzebiszk, kamiszk* ('little comb', 'little stone'). Some other features connect Kashubian with the Mazovian dialect, for example: a) voiceless inter-word phonetics e.g. *ôjców nënka, brat ôjca* ('father's mother', 'brother of father'); b) consonant levelling: *y = i*, e.g. *dim* ('smoke'), *bùdink* ('buildings'); c) the productive suffix *-iwac* ‖ *-ëwac* in iterative verbs such as *pisëwac, wëmachiwac* ('[now and then] write, wave'), in place of the earlier *-owac* e.g. *pisowac* (comp. Polish *skupować* ‖ *skupywać* 'buy up').

The Kashubs themselves perceive their own internal linguistic and cultural differentiation, and it is reflected in the names of their ethnic subgroups. The names originate from: a) topography e.g. *Kaszëb*s, *Lesók*s < *las* ('woods'), *Zôbòrë* (< *bór* 'forest'); b) linguistic properties e.g. *Bëlók*s,

---

1   Inhabitants of the regions of Kociewie and Bory.

2   *Mazurzenie* or mazuration is the replacement of consonants 'cz', 'sz', 'ż', 'dż' with 'c', 's', 'z', 'dz'.

*Gôchs, Krëbans, Slovincians*; c) occupations e.g. *Rëbôks* who live by the sea (*rëbôk* 'fisherman') in comparison with *Kònicë* (< *kóń* 'horse') or *Gbùrs* (*gbùr* 'farmer'); d) clothes e.g. *Kabatks* (*kabat* 'sleeved vest'); e) social status e.g. *Parcanô Szlachta* ('sackcloth gentry'). Further, the *Bëlôks* in the north-east pronounce general *ł* as *l*, e.g. *bél, bëla*, while in Polish: *był, była* ('he was', 'she was') – what is known as *bëlaczenie*. The *Półbëlôks* ('half-*Bëlôks*') in the north-west, who speak the dialect of Żarnowiec, manifest this phenomenon only partially (it is also called *Leżcë* – after *leżka*, Polish *łyżka* 'spoon'). The *Lesôks* in the middle-east use their own dialect, so do the *Gôchs* in the south-west, and the *Zôbòraks, Zôbòrôks* and *Krëbans* in the south-east. Distinct dialects were spoken by the extinct Slovincians in the area of lakes Gardno and Łebsko and by the *Kabatks* in the parishes of Cecenowo and Główczyce.

## Stages in the development of literary Kashubian

Kashubian elites have been developing the common Kashubian language for over 150 years, while forced to accept the dominant position of Polish as the official language. The evolution of literary Kashubian can be divided chronologically into five periods, related to literary groups and attitudes to the linguistic questions under discussion, such as language enrichment and writing systems. These periods can be described as:

1) Florian Ceynowa
2) Hieronim Jarosz Derdowski
3) The Young Kashubs and Bernard Sychta
4) The *Zrzesz* circle
5) Post-war writers (after 1945).

1) Florian Ceynowa recognised Kashubian as a separate language to be used as a universal means of communication, and not just for literary purposes. The language of Ceynowa's writings was linked to the vernacular of his native village of Sławoszyno (Puck county), and it generally represented

the idiolect of a person educated in Polish language patterns, switching from literary Polish to his mother vernacular. Retained, but not stressed, were some local northern attributes in his language, particularly in vocabulary. His spelling, firmly based on etymological criteria, displayed uniform Kashubian features, although revealing – as any orthography will – numerous phonetic features.

Ceynowa used the Polish language as a general reference pattern, and did not dissociate himself from Polish either in theory or in practice. This can be seen clearly in the lexicon (e.g. *czatë, konwulzyje, materia, indukcje, wnioski* – comp. Polish *czaty, konwulsje, materia, indukcje, wnioski* – 'ambush, convulsions, matter, inductions, conclusions'), in the syntax (e.g. participial verb-less sentences such as *czëtającë, zrobiwszë* – comp. Polish *czytający, zrobiwszy* – 'reading, having done'), and in junction markers (e.g. *abë, chtëren* – comp. Polish *aby, który* – 'in order to, which/who'). This meant Ceynowa's texts were incomprehensible to those Kashubs who had a poor knowledge of Polish, despite his argument that the ability to communicate was the main reason for the standardisation of written Kashubian. He occasionally used German forms (e.g. *dëcht*) and neologisms. Some of the neologisms were part of his grammatical terminology (*doraznjk* 'stress', *jistnjk* 'noun', *położnjk* 'case'), but he also used *szkòlôk* 'school kid', *zdobëtk* 'trophy' (similar to *dobëtk* 'belongings') and *zemstwò* 'vengeance'. Examples of semantic neologisms are *mapa* (that is, *krajobraz/zemiobrôz* – German *Landkarte*) and *towarzëstwo* 'society'.

Since Ceynowa's time Kashubian has functioned in two varieties: the well-rooted old local dialects and a new written literary variant that has required constant maintenance. As far as language standardisation is concerned, he displayed considerable radicalism in eliminating dialectal diversity in phonetics and, even more notably, in inflection (see Treder 2005: 71–114). His norms were adopted by Ramułt in his 1893 dictionary, and were referred to later by the *Zrzesz* members.

2) Hieronim Jarosz Derdowski – according to whom Kashubian was 'a dialect of Polish' or 'a weak shade of the Mazovian dialect' (Treder 2005: 125, 134) – saw Kashubian solely as the language of belles-lettres, alongside the official Polish language. He felt that knowledge of Polish among the Kashubs should be deepened, as it could act as their weapon of defence

against Germanisation. He did not believe that 'dialectal grammar' could be 'taught in elementary schools' (Derdowski 1885: 6), or accept the written version of Kashubian elaborated by Ceynowa, which he saw as 'expressly northern and at the same time too Polonised', and thereby 'alien' to the Kashubs. Derdowski's Kashubian was based on the local dialect of the village of Wiele in the south (e.g. *nodzie* – Polish *nogi* 'legs' or *babusia* 'granny, old woman'). It included some properties of other local varieties of Kashubian; Derdowski wrote that in order to make 'my *opuscules* accessible to compatriots from the [banks of] the Warta, Vistula, San and Niemen rivers, I use in writing a south Kashubian sub-dialect, which is closest to the bookish Polish language, however with many similarities to the northern dialects' (Derdowski 1885: 7). There were also references to Ceynowa's work (e.g. *knega* – Polish *księga* 'book'), as well as links to Slovincian (e.g. *ga* – Polish *gdy* 'when, if'). The nature of the Polonised southern dialect was a guarantee that this version of written Kashubian would be comprehensible e.g. *przeciwny* (Kashubian/Polish) 'opposite'; *swietnie* – Polish *świetnie* 'splendidly'; *ukosnie* – Polish *ukośnie* 'obliquely'; *wząc kogos w obrotë* – Polish *wziąć kogoś w obroty* 'to handle somebody'. Derdowski did not avoid Polish and German forms used in spoken Kashubian e.g. *amtman* – Polish *urzędnik* 'clerk', *beniel* Polish *chłopiec* 'boy'. He created no neologisms and used semantic neologisms only rarely, for example *nórcyk* – Polish *skarbczyk* 'strong-room'.

About himself he wrote: 'Using [...] the sub-dialect from the Chmielno region, the author reconciled the northern and southern varieties of Kashubian; moreover, in his work, he equally matched the words and forms from the coast with those from the dialects of Kościerzyna, Człuchów and Chojnice counties. Obviously, in this way, he wanted to create a unity within the Kashubian dialect, and to give it such a form, that each Kashub could identify it with their own vernacular and understand such a book' (Treder 2005: 144). Furthermore he adopted a phonetic spelling, confining himself to the Polish alphabet, which was familiar to at least some of the Kashubs.

3) Derdowski's version of Kashubian, together with his aim of using it solely for Kashubian literature, was adopted at first by Aleksander Majkowski. However, he later abandoned it in his 1938 novel *Żëcé i przigòdë*

*Remùsa* [The life and adventures of Remus], creating a new type of language. The Young-Kashubs made use of Ceynowa's and Derdowski's experiences in creating their own 'universal' variety of Kashubian. This can be seen in the spelling system, which remained halfway between the peculiarly Kashubian spelling of Ceynowa and Derdowski's spelling which conformed to the Polish system. They used the distinct letters <ô é ë> only for avoiding ambiguity e.g. *kôta* 'hut': *kota* (nowadays *kòta*, < *kòt* 'cat' (Genitive)): *kóta* 'hoof' (< *kót* 'hoof' (Genitive)); *jem* 'I am': *jém* 'I eat': *jim* (Dative) 'them'. They also used *przë-* as opposed to *prze-* (prefixes in e.g. *przëńc* 'to come' and *przeńc* 'to pass/cross') and *wë-* as opposed *we-* (prefixes in e.g. *wëszedł* 'he came out' and *weszedł* 'he came in'). Their literary language norm showed features of local vernaculars, e.g. in limiting the range of the Kashubian *ë*: *Kaszuba, Lipusz* (cf. contemporary *Kaszëba, Lëpusz*). Worth mentioning are the forms of the Genitive Singular *bez pozwoleniu*, verbal forms (type *znajesz* 'you know') and auxiliary forms (e.g. *jesta* 'he/she/it is' and *sąsma* 'we are') as well as the past forms *obuwołes, zapalołes* ('you put on shoes, you lit up') next to the occasional *jo noseł* ('I carried'). The vocabulary in their works is of a genuinely southern origin.

It was only later that Majkowski created a language independent of the various regional vernaculars, and intentionally enriched with features from other parts of Kashubia (Treder 2005: 169–201). In his novel *Remùs* Majkowski assigned to Kashubian literature significant cultural and social tasks, which resulted in questions relating to the status of Kashubian. According to him: 'our idiom should be always perceived as spoken vernacular in relation to the literary language [...] while our beautiful vernacular can come into use in belles lettres, in fairy stories and songs, in amateur theatre' (Majkowski 1909: 198). The Kashubian language was therefore assigned broader functions than ever before. In this way, Majkowski polemised with Derdowski, being already by this time unquestionably under the influence of the radical *Zrzesz* circle.

4) The *Zrzesz* circle (*Zrzeszeńcy*, after the journal title *Zrzesz Kaszëbskô* or 'Kashubian Association') included such figures as Stefan Bieszk, Aleksander Labuda, Jan Trepczyk, Jan Rompski and Rev. Franciszek Grucza. They considered Kashubian to be an autonomous language and a universal medium, hence their plan to introduce it into the education system and

their reference to the work of Ceynowa. In the literary realm, on the other hand, they followed the Young-Kashubs. Their observations of the work done by their predecessors, however, did not result in any profound conclusions, hence the low degree of standardisation of their literary variety of Kashubian, except for spelling and writing. It was excessively dependent on various local features, in particular their own native variety of the language from the borders of Kartuzy and Wejherowo counties. They did extend the language to some extent by using phonetic archaic neologisms such as *starna* 'side' or *lékarztwo* 'medicine, remedy', and introducing pronunciation *rz* < *rs* (after Ramułt).

They pointed out rightly that previous attempts to create a general standard of Kashubian had grown out of the substrate of southern dialects and therefore were too much dependent on Polish, as was also the case with their precursor Ceynowa and with the contemporary *Klëka* circle. They themselves, born in the border area between the centre and the north, knew the northern dialects comprehensively, and made them a foundation for the Kashubian literary standard, assuming correctly that this was a better preservation of an archaic form of Kashubian. This assumption was confirmed by the research results of the dialectologist Friedrich Lorentz.

All the members of the *Zrzesz* circle, as well as the Young-Kashub Heyke, took advantage of *licentia poetica* in their poetry and made use of phonetic differences and morphological variations which were used actively in vernaculars. They tried to widen the usage of some features, such as the central type *sjat*, *sjāti* ('world', 'saint'), or the pronunciation of *krjewa* 'cow' from Luzino. They preferred Lekhitic properties from the north-west, avoiding features from southern Kashubia if they conformed to Polish. For the *Zrzesz* circle the literary Polish standard was nothing more than a general model; where possible they clearly avoided it, some of them even finding it easier to accept German elements. Above all, they programmatically applied neologisms, in effect making their language difficult, often quite 'mysterious'.

They partially achieved their aim of setting out a path for the normalisation of literary language, with the central dialect as the basis, enriched by the northern properties and their compatible neologisms, which on the whole also determined a certain tightness of their language. They also managed partially to 'fix' these elements, thanks to their considerable and manifold creative activities, their long literary careers and their numerous achievements. In the sphere of language, the dictionaries by Labuda and Trepczyk are most notable; in the sphere of literature, the quality of their poetry and prose deserves mention (Treder 2005: 202–65). They were truly appreciated within the community. Jan Trepczyk wrote: 'Kashubian is not a corrupted Polish dialect or a speckled variety of German, but an original Slavonic tongue, the last non-Germanised dialect of Pomeranian. To this tongue – its maintenance, care and development – I have dedicated my writing. With each word I try to stress its specific properties (...) I select exclusively Kashubian vocabulary, in order to save it from oblivion' (Trepczyk 1986: 236).

In opposition to the *Zrzesz* circle was the *Klëka* group (after the journal *Klëka*, 1937–9). This included Józef Ceynowa, Paweł Szefka, Leon Roppel and Franciszek Sędzicki (who was also active long after 1945). Generally, the *Klëka* group carried on the ideas and practices of Derdowski and the Young-Kashubs in their belief in a subordinate role for Kashubian, functioning only in the artistic sphere. They ignored Kashubian distinctness, brought the spelling close to Polish (see Roppel's norm of 1939) and cultivated an entirely comprehensible language with clear Polish influence. Their model of Kashubian reflected the idiolect of an average Kashub, educated in Polish, and preserving some properties of the native tongue, for example through the work of Roppel who came from the vicinity of Wejherowo (Treder 2008c: 55–72).

5) In the first years after 1945 the situation remained much the same as in the 1930s. Officially, political conditions were more favourable towards the *Klëka* group, but it was the *Zrzesz* circle who were more widely appreciated and later also more active. The question of the autarky of Kashubian was not openly raised, even after the foundation of the *Zrzeszenie Kaszubskie* [Kashubian Association] in 1956. That organisation undoubtedly encouraged artistic creativity, writing and publishing among the Kashubs. A change in the quality of Kashubian followed the publication of the *Principles of Kashubian Spelling* (Breza and Treder 1975). This was put together by a committee who integrated the spelling systems of *Klëka* by Roppel (1939) and *Zrzesz* by Bieszk (1956), by narrowing the choice of variants in

phonetics and morphology. The latest changes in orthography occurred in 1996 (introduction of <ã ò ù>) and have been summarised by Eugeniusz Gołąbek in his 1997 *Instructions for Kashubian Spelling* [*Wskôze kaszëbsczégò pisënkù*]. This book was also a forerunner of Gołąbek's normative dictionary, published in 2005. The most recent situation in the domain of language standardisation can be seen in a normalised edition of Ramułt's dictionary published in 2003.

The language of Kashubian literature, which has been under constant development since the mid-nineteenth century, can be located between two extreme opposites:

a) written colloquial (popular) Kashubian with diverse vernacular varieties. This can be seen as a continuation of the *Klëka* attitude and shows no significant assimilation of the Kashubian 'written' input. It has been used by representatives of the older generation such as Bolesław Bork, Stefan Fikus, Bolesław Jażdżewski, Marian Jeliński, Marian Selin, Antoni Pieper and Jan Piepka, with the younger generation displaying a stronger influence from Polish, for example in the work of Stanisław Bartelik, Jerzy Łysk, Roman Skwiercz and Bożena Szymańska-Ugowska.

b) writing according to the *Zrzesz* tradition, in which more neologisms are used and in which standard Kashubian is distanced from dialect varieties. Examples from the older generation include the work of Augustyn K. Hirsz, Stanisław Janke, Alojzy Nagel and Jan Walkusz. This category also includes younger writers with stronger tendencies to use neologisms, such as Jaromira Labudda and Hanna Makurat, and also the language of the journal *Tatczëzna*. A few of these writers also display a substrate of their home vernacular, but most of them depend largely on Trepczyk's *Polish-Kashubian Dictionary* (1994). Some were not speakers of Kashubian in their childhood, and a few – such as Pawel Szczypta, founder of the journal *Òdroda* – are not Kashubian at all.

There are also writers who take an intermediate position in their use of Kashubian. For example, in the work of Bernard Sychta, a local Kashubian vernacular dominates, but Sychta followed his own artistic way. This can be seen in his writing system, for example in the notification of vowel labialisation (e.g. *uekue* 'eye'), consonant palatalisation with *j* (e.g. *mjiłi* 'nice'), and use of <*ö*> and sometimes <*ë*>. Sychta was implementing Majkowski's

views about applying Kashubian only to literature, hence the stage directions in his plays were in Polish. His dramatic works aimed at cultivating
the language of Kashubian, which he viewed as a kind of 'common weal'
and as a link between the main area of Poland and the extinct Polabians.
The language of his works approximated the western dialects of central
Kashubia, with the intensified presence of numerous phonetic and lexical
properties, and he intended it to constitute a reference model for Kashubian. Equally individual in its character is the language used in his prose
and poetry by Stanisław Pestka. Pestka's work is highly intellectualised and
documents local southern lexical fossil forms, combined with the vocabulary of the *Zrzesz* members Aleksander Labuda and Jan Trepczyk (Treder
2008d). Moreover, various further shades of both home vernacular and
literary language can be found in the Kashubian press, in radio and television broadcasts since 1990, and on *Radio Kaszëbë* which was established
in December 2004.

The two main tendencies described above have also been apparent in
the process of translating the Bible into Kashubian. The first tendency can
be seen in Rev. Franciszek Grucza's translation from Latin in 1992, which
distanced Kashubian from Polish. The second can be seen in Eugeniusz
Gołąbek's translation from Polish in 1993, which referred to contemporary
spoken Kashubian as well as to Polish. An intermediate attitude was represented in the translation by Rev. Adam Ryszard Sikora from Greek in 2001
(Treder 2005: 266–86, 287–99). These translations took place in the context
of the introduction of Kashubian to the Catholic liturgy in the mid-1980s,
announced in a 1993 pastoral letter by the Archbishop of Gdańsk, Tadeusz
Gocłowski. Also worth mentioning are two sermon texts by Rev. Marian
Miotk, *Swiętim turę starków* [The holy road of our forefathers] (1991) and
*Séw Bòżégò Słowa na niwie kaszëbsczich serc* [Sowing God's Word in the soil
of Kashubian hearts] (2008), as well as Rev. Jan Walkusz's *Sztrądę słowa*
[Words on the strand] (1996). These include elements of local vernaculars,
but are also partially modelled on the language of the *Zrzesz* circle.

The development of Kashubian literature had a strong influence on
the modernisation of orthography and an indirect influence on the introduction of regional education into schools. As the possibilities for the
traditional socialisation of children within Kashubian families and local

communities narrowed, so parents consigned the teaching of Kashubian to school. The Kashubian-Pomeranian Association, ZK-P, spoke out on this subject only after the changes of August 1980. The current situation has evolved quickly: the first school textbooks and dictionaries have appeared, as well as the first teachers of Kashubian and the first high school graduates, and even the beginnings of language teaching and Kashubian studies at the university level.

Without those past actions, the present significant achievements in the development and maintenance of Kashubian would never have occurred. They have also, of course, been influenced by external factors, such as Poland's attitude to the European Charter for Regional or Minority Languages (2009), and the 2005 'Law on national and ethnic minorities and the regional language'. This law resulted in adoption of the local 'Strategy for protection and development of the Kashubian language and culture' (March 2006) and the creation of the Kashubian Language Board in October 2006, two developments of crucial importance for the future of Kashubian.

After one and a half centuries of evolution, written Kashubian has not developed a unified form. However, a considerable degree of standardisation has been achieved, and a general direction of development assigned. This is due, among other things, to the dictionaries of Labuda and Trepczyk, and to the output of the *Zrzesz* circle. The successive periods and stages of development of literary Kashubian result not only from individual writers upgrading the language status of their native vernaculars, but also from the stratification and synthesis of achievements of the past generations. So we can see Majkowski's original Kashubian from Kościerzyna and Lipusz, modelled after Derdowski, being transformed under the influence of *Zrzesz* into the language of *Remùs*, while the language of the *Zrzesz* circle itself was originally modelled after Majkowski, and later became a model for young contemporary writers (Treder 2007).

The stylistic diversity of Kashubian is considerable. Kashubian dialects have two varieties: 1) colloquial, used in vivid speech, and in contacts with family, neighbours and local people; 2) artistic, characteristic of folklore i.e. songs, fairy tales, proverbs, riddles and wedding orations. Moreover, the properties of individual Kashubian dialects tend to be used for locution and stylistic purposes. Literary Kashubian, striving to meet all the linguistic needs of its users, has developed the following variants:

a) artistic – present in epic and lyric poetry and drama, this variant has been cultivated by several generations of writers: first by Ceynowa, then by Derdowski, the Young-Kashubs, the *Zrzesz* and *Klëka* groups and by numerous modern writers. It is also used in translations from other languages, including Polish.

b) religious – this variant began development between the sixteenth and eighteenth centuries in the so-called Kashubian language antiquities e.g. songs, catechism, prayers and pericopes. More recently it has been developed in translations of the Bible, in prayers and prayer-books, in religious songs and in sermons.

c) journalistic – initiated by Ceynowa's *Skarb Kaszébsko-słovjnskjé mòwë* [Treasure of the Kashubian-Slovincian tongue] (1866–8). The newspaper-style column has been the most frequent medium for this variant; examples include writing by Aleksander Labuda, Alojzy Budzisz, Alojzy Nagel, Stanisław Pestka, Eugeniusz Gołąbek, Stefan Fikus, Augustyn K. Hirsz and Roman Drzeżdżon. This variant is now more and more frequent in newspaper articles, interviews, press notices etc (for example in *Òdroda* or *Pomerania*), as well as in radio and television journalism.

d) scholarly – this includes an academic variant, used in a few humanities texts, mainly in journal papers and articles, a didactic variant (present in textbooks such as the 2000 primer *Kaszëbsczé abecadło. Twój pierszi elemeńtôrz* by Witold Bobrowski and Katarzyna Kwiatkowska), a popular variant, initiated in Ceynowa's *Xążeczka dlo Kaszebov* (1850), and a practical variant used in such things as technical descriptions of embroidery.

Written Kashubian has not developed an official style, although there is a remarkable colloquial written variant of the Kashubian spoken by the intelligentsia assembled in the ZK-P. It is used in private correspondence, particularly by those who did not acquire Kashubian in their family homes, and as yet there has been no research into the range of use and degree of standardisation of these variants. All the above-mentioned variations and sub-variations can be found in abundance in the journal *Òdroda* (Rogowska-Cybulska 2006).

The beginnings of standardisation of Kashubian date back to the birth of its written variety as a potential means of communication, both among the Kashubs themselves and with the outer world. The only Kashub who expressed this aim overtly in the mid-nineteenth century was Ceynowa, creating a grammar, dictionaries and texts, despite the absence of public demand. In the Prussian state there was no institution which could take on and complete such a task. Moreover, Derdowski, Ceynowa's fellow countryman from southern Wiele, did not support his idea, and narrowed the use of Kashubian solely to the domain of belles lettres, to which he contributed significantly with numerous works. He did not believe in the possibility of teaching Kashubian in school, and therefore he used exclusively Polish spelling.

Both at that time and into the twentieth century, the conditions for developing Kashubian were not favourable. A reluctant or even hostile attitude toward its promotion was common among the clergy, both Lutheran clergy in the west (e.g. Rev. G.L. Lorek in Cecenowo), and Catholic clergy in the east (e.g. Rev. G. Pobłocki). For Lutheran clergy, the knowledge and use of German was sufficient; for Catholic clergy, Polish was sufficient, and was implicitly linked to the raison d'état. Even the Young-Kashubs and Majkowski did not take any significant measures in the development of Kashubian. It was only at the end of the interwar period that members of the *Zrzesz* circle, with Aleksander Labuda and Jan Trepczyk, rose to speak on this subject, opposing the actions of the Polish National Democratic Party in Pomerania.


## Characteristics of literary Kashubian and the dialectal substrate


The language of Kashubian writers, which has varied across different periods and also across individual works (for example, take these two extreme examples of Majkowski's work at different periods: *Jak w Koscérznie koscelnygo obrele* ..., written in 1899, and *Żëcé i przigòdë Remusa*, written in 1938), is marked by the use of properties of the writers' native vernaculars. Starting from the time of Ceynowa, it is possible to refer to various degrees of normalisation of literary Kashubian, first on the northern Kashubian dialectal substrate (Ceynowa), then influenced more by southern Kashubian, but with use of some central Kashubian properties (e.g. Derdowski, Majkowski), and followed by a repeated turn both to genuinely northern features (e.g. Budzisz) or to merely allegedly northern features (as in the writing of the *Zrzesz* circle, e.g. Trepczyk, whose features were actually more central in character).

The most apparent domain of unification of literary Kashubian has always been the spelling system, in spite of its numerous changes (Breza 1984: 55–9). Ceynowa changed the spelling system repeatedly, starting from the Polish orthography and moving later to the so-called Slavonic orthography, in order to make Kashubian texts readable for all Slavs. It was partly phonetic: for example, the letter <o> for the vowels [o] and [ô]. Ceynowa also applied the letters <ò> in place of the present-day <a> (e.g. *skôrb* 'treasure'), <é> for today's <ë> (e.g. *Kaszébé* 'Kashubs/Kashubia'). For labialisation he used first <ó> (*Póloch* 'Pole'), later <ò> (*mòva* 'language'); palatalisation was marked with <j>, also in <kj, gj> (*takji dlugji* 'such a long ...'). Derdowski made do with Polish spelling, using <ci, dzi> (*taci dludzi*). The Young-Kashubs initially followed Derdowski (for example in the journal *Gryf*); later, after debates with linguists, they adopted an intermediate spelling. Staying generally within the Polish rules, they used separate diacritics only to differentiate forms e.g. *kôt* 'huts' (Genitive): *kót* 'hoof': *kòt* 'cat'.

Majkowski created his own orthography for his novel *Remùs*, using some features invented by Ceynowa, such as the notation of nasal vowels, and palatalisation marked with <j>, including <kj>, <gj>. Spelling was also influenced by the *Zrzesz* circle, for example Aleksander Labuda (1939), while Roppel encouraged a more Polish-style orthography. This was commonly used until 1975, when it was amended by the *Rules of Kashubian Orthography*, published by the ZK-P. This was amended in turn in 1996, when the obligatory letter <ä> was added, and possible diacritics for labialisation <ò> <ù> were included, as postulated in the *Zrzesz*-oriented spelling advocated by Bieszk (1959). Bieszk wrote: 'What is the progress in the spelling system to be according to our simplification project? (...) elimination of those letters that do not exist in Polish orthography, or make Kashubian spelling strange to the Polish eye, accustomed to the Polish script and not necessarily to the Kashubian one; thus: a) the letter <v> is to be replaced by <w>, what has to be followed by notification of aspiration with a different sign; namely b) with an accent mark <ò> <ù>, as in *ògón* ("tail") or *ùzdrzec* ("see")' (Treder 2005: 256).

A survey of Kashubian literature reveals that the process of language normalisation has been marked by a tendency to foreground the following features:

1. phonetic: a) type *cwiardi* and *môłczëc* as opposed to *cwardi/twardi*, *milczec* ('hard, tough', 'be silent, hush'); b) type *klic, wzyc* as opposed to *kląc, wząc* ('to curse', 'to take'); c) type *kòtk* and *kùńc* as opposed to *kòtek, kùniec* ('kitten', 'end'); d) range of use of *ń* instead of *n* in e.g. *gruńt, hańdel* ('soil', 'commerce'); e) pronunciation of *rz* in e.g. *rzéka, mòrze* ('river', 'sea'), and the following notation of <rs> as <rz> as in *gbùrztwò, mòrzczi* ('farmers', 'maritime');

2. inflectional: a) type *anatomijô, pòstacëjô* as opposed to *anatomiô, pòstacjô* ('anatomy', 'figure'); b) instrumental singular of masculine and neutral nouns with final *-ę* instead of *-em* e.g. *Bogę, miodę* ('God', 'honey'); c) instrumental plural with *-ima/-yma, -ama: taczima bòsyma knôpama* ('with such barefoot boys'); d) locative plural *-ëch/-ich: swòjich dobrëch* ('own good ...'); e) adjectival inflection of nouns e.g. *wieselé, -égo, -im* ('wedding'); f) inflection of the Genitive Singular: *-égò* or *-éhò* next to *éwò*, e.g. *dobrégò* or *dobréhò* ('good'); g) the Accusative form of pronouns with *–ā*, such as *jā, naszā*, or with *-ą: ją, naszą* ('her', 'ours'); h) verb conjugation forms, as *pitaję, pitajesz* opposed to *pitóm, pitôsz* ('I, you ask'); i) imperative ending *-i/ë* in *niesë, robi* as opposed to *nies, rób* ('carry!', 'do!'); j) past tense forms such as *jem pisôł, jes pisôł* as opposed to *jô pisôł, të pisôł* ('I, you wrote'); k) abbreviated past forms of third-person singular, such as *da, zaczā* opposed to *dała, zaczāła* ('she gave', 'she began');

3. word-formation: a) compounds, as *òchlëdëtk* ('cooling-off'), *kùmméster* ('crib-maker'), *stalata* ('century') – both authentic and neologism; b) type *bòlącé* ('painful'), *lëstowi* ('foliage'); c) type *adresa* ('address') and

*rozwij* ('development'); d) productivity of certain affixes: i) prefixes *òt-*: *òtmiana* ('modification'); *s-*: *smrok* ('dusk'); ii) suffixes: *-unk/-ënk*: *ratënk* ('rescue'); *-ota* and *-osc*: *mòdrota/ mòdrosc* ('wisdom'); *-izna/ -ëzna*: *słabizna* ('weakness'); *-itwa/-ëtwa*: *grzëbitwa* ('mushrooming'); *-ba*: *ùczba* ('learning'); *-ā*: *swiniā* ('swine'); *-iszcze/-szcze* and *-iskò/ -skò*: *kalëszcze* ('puddle'); *-éra*: *garnéra* ('garnishing'); *-érowac*: *badérowac* (to research'); *-iwac/-ëwac* and *-owac*: *wësëpëwac/wësëpòwac* ('pour out'); iii) verb diminutives, e.g. *róbkac, róbkôj* ('to do/do a bit'); iv) iterative verbs, as *derac, derowac* ('to make a gift');

4. syntactic: a) participles *piszãc(ë), zrobiwszë* ('writing', 'having done') – absent in dialects; b) frequency of passive voice, e.g. *móm zrobioné* ('I have done'); c) conjunctions: *abë* ('in order to'), *chtëren* ('which one'), *co* ('that, what'), *jaczi* ('which'); *ë* ('and'), *ëż(le)* ('if'), *jiże* ('that');

5. lexical: a) balance between authentic vocabulary and neologisms; b) specifically folk versus abstract vocabulary, borrowed from literary Polish; c) attitude toward German features: these are common in spoken Kashubian (predominantly from Low German dialects) or elsewhere are borrowed from literary (High) German.

The developing Kashubian language, characterised by significant standardisation of at least some of the above-mentioned attributes – and lacking obviously local, dialectal features – will reveal a greater distance from spoken Kashubian and its individual dialects and a closer approach to Polish. In the history of literary Kashubian, Polish has played a similar role (both positive and negative) to the role which Latin used to play in the formation of the Polish language. Its unifying influence has been strengthened by such institutions as the Catholic Church, the administrative system, the schooling system and printed literature.

## The history of Kashubian studies

Kashubian scholarship has been slow to develop, and academic research started only in the nineteenth century. The first indirect attempts originate from the sixteenth and seventeenth centuries, in the ancient chronicles (e.g. Thomas Kantzow's *Pomerania* from 1536), in descriptions of journeys (e.g. Johan Bernoulli's *Reisen durch Brandenburg, Pommern, Preussen, Kurland, Russland und Polen in den Jahre 1777 und 1778*, published in 1779) or in the writings of pastors from Western Pomerania. The oldest known features of the Kashubian language were reconstructed only in the eighteenth century from Michał Pontanus' translation *Maly Catechism D. Marciná Lutherá Niemiecko-Wándalski ábo Slowięski to jestá z Niemieckiego języka w Slowieski wystáwion ...* (1643) and in the nineteenth century from Szimon Krofej's translation of Luther's *Duchowne piesnie D. Marcina Luthera ... Zniemieckiego w Slawięsky ięzik wilozone* (1586). Pontanus' text (or actually its second edition) was known to Krzysztof Celestyn Mrongowiusz, and was discovered by Franz Tetzner in 1896. The titles indicate that Krofej and Pontanus defined the language of their translations, and indirectly the language of their readers, as *slawięsky, słowięski* ('Slavonic'); this is what the language of Kashubs in Western Pomerania was called at that time. These texts were referred to later in the writings of Christian W. Haken, a pastor from Słupsk. A lot of useful data can be found through analyzing other relics of literature, such as *Perykopy smołdzińskie, Śpiewnik starokaszubski, Przysięgi słowińskie z Wierzchocina* etc. These have been thoroughly researched and described in recent decades (Popowska-Taborska 1996).

Research into Kashubian intensified with the genesis of Slavistics at the turn of the nineteenth century. Kashubian even attracted the attention of the harbinger of Slavonic studies, Karl Gottlob Anton (1751–1818), who gathered some 300 words from Western Pomerania (also taken from the work of Haken, and partly listed in Anton 1783), including the name of the Slovincians: *Słowińcy*. This material was familiar to the Russian researcher Izmail Ivanovich Sreznevskiy in 1840. A scholarly interest in the Kashubs among the Russians coincided with the publication of a description of a journey to Prussia, Russia and Poland undertaken in 1777–8 by Johan Bernoulli, a Swiss scholar. Among other things, this publication described the language situation in the Kashubian (Slovincian) village of Szczep-kowice. Bernoulli's work may have influenced the contents of a work of 1787–9 entitled *Sravnitelnye slovari vsekh yazykov i narechiy* ... [Comparative dictionaries of all languages and dialects], which also contained a lexicon recorded by pastors among the Slovincians (Popowska-Taborska 1996: 12–14). G.L. Lorek, a pastor from Cecenowo (1760–1845), wrote a description of the Łeba Kashubs printed in 1821, as well as handwritten Kashubian-German-Polish glossaries from 1835 and 1836, Kashubian translations of German-language readers and Kashubian sermons. He claimed that the Kashubs 'have no original proverbs or songs – that is why they never sing'.

The works of Slavicists such as the Czech Josef Dobrovský (1763–1829) or the Slovak Pavel Jozef Šafařík (1795–1861) indirectly provided a lot of information on the Kashubs and their language to Krzysztof Celestyn Mrongowiusz (1764–1855), who lived in Gdańsk from 1798. In his 1823 dictionary Mrongowiusz compiled over 170 Kashubian entries (some also taken from Pontanus' work) and appealed for their further recording. In the introduction he states that Kashubian is similar to Russian with regard to stress, which was misquoted as a statement of general analogy between the two languages. At the request of the Russian count Nikolay Rumiantsov (1754–1826), Mrongowiusz initiated field research among the Kabatks in 1826–7. This resulted in the recovery of Pontanus' manuscripts of *Słowniczek kaszubski* and *Katechizm* and their publication in 1828, as well as a conceptualisation of Mrongowiusz's further research programme for Kashubian. The programme included: 1) compiling a Kashubian glossary; 2) creating a list of Kashubian place-names; 3) establishing the correct categorisation of Kashubian either within the western or eastern branches of Slavdom, according to Dobrovský's scheme; 4) recording the names of the months; 5) compiling the available literature on Kashubia; 6) recording Kashubian proverbs; 7) recording legends and fables common to the Kashubs and the Poles; 8) describing ancient pagan worship, folk festivals and seasonal rituals; 9) recording nicknames (Treder 2000).

Mrongowiusz stated that 'Kashubian used in Western Pomerania constitutes only a dialect of literary Polish (*Hochpolnisch*), even closer than Bavarian or Saxonian dialects in relation to literary German (*Hochdeutsch*)'. This opinion was repeated later by the Russians P.I. Preys and Aleksandr Hilferding (Treder 2003). When Mrongowiusz later came to know the Lusatian languages (the languages of the Sorbians), he declared Kashubian to be an Old-Pomeranian sister of the 'Windic tongue', closely related to Polabian.

Through the work of the Czech scholars František L. Čelakovský and Jan E. Purkyně and the Russian Izmail Sreznevskiy, the debates on Kashubian reached Wrocław, where Ceynowa moved to continue his studies after living in Chojnice. He became familiar with Šafařík's book *Słowiański narodopis* (1843), which contained a short list of the characteristics of the 'Kashubian sub-dialect' as well as remarks on the 1643, 1758 and 1828 editions of Pontanus' *Katechizm*, presumably based on Preys' widely known *Doneseniye* of 1840. Mrongowiusz's *Słowniczek kaszubski* was mentioned in *Doneseniye*, although without proper information being provided on the author, whom Preys visited in Gdańsk.

In 1843, Purkyně's proposal to continue Mrongowiusz's programme was taken up by Ceynowa, who added a practical dimension. He aimed to create a Kashubian literary language, consequently including Kashubian on an equal basis with the family of Slavonic languages; it was in this field that Ceynowa made his most important and successful contribution. He knew the opinions held by Mrongowiusz, Šafařík, Sreznevskiy, Hilferding, Franz Miklosich and August Schleicher, and even as a non-philologist he was aware that his native Kashubian could only escape from its transitory position between Polish and Polabian by creating a literature. He wrote: 'It is quite normal that a people without books printed in their language cannot speak identically everywhere, but various dialects arise and differentiate'; also 'We, the Kashubs, speak a Slavonic tongue, i.e. similar to that spoken by Poles or Sorbs known as Lusatians' (1850). His 1879 *Zarés do Grammatikj* ... was prefaced by a proverb: 'Everybody praises God as he is able to'. Basing his work on his native dialect of Sławoszyno, Ceynowa created an alphabet, a spelling system, glossaries, a grammar and numerous texts across various genres: spiritual, literary, political, philosophical, historical, ethnographic and medical.

A theoretical rationale for these ideas and activities was provided later by Ramułt. Ceynowa's work on Kashubian deepened and intensified after contact with Hilferding, who came to Kashubia in 1856 by order of the St Petersburg Academy of Sciences; his aim was to study the diversity of Kashubian, as the information on this provided by Ceynowa was still too limited. In his 1862 book *Ostatki slavyan na yuzhnom beregu Baltiyskogo morya*, Hilferding described various linguistic features, recorded numerous texts and compiled a glossary indicating the most common Kabatk, Kashubian and Slovincian forms. He divided the texts gathered during fieldwork into Slovincian, Kabatk, Pomeranian (from the Leba lake and the area west of it, and from Bytów) and Kashubian (from West Prussia). The volume also contained a detailed description of the endangered Kashubian spoken by the Slovincians and Bytówians, the dialect spoken by the Kabatks, and the well-preserved Kashubian from Gdańsk Pomerania.

As the first scholar to investigate the entire linguistic area of Kashubian, Hilferding extended the summary of the language written by Preys (who had taken over this task from Mrongowiusz):

> The dialect spoken by those remnants of the Baltic Slavs indicates most similarities to the Polish language. In various old literary texts, we can also find some remains of a Slavic dialect, spoken by the tribes who inhabited the banks of the Elbe river and the western part of Baltic Pomerania, which can indicate that the language of the ancient populace of Mecklenburg, Brandenburg and Lüneburg *Wendland* was close to the Polish language, but also had its own characteristics. The attested linguistic features, supported by various historical facts, imply that Polish and the language of Baltic Slavs composed a common language branch of the Slavs – which could be called a Lekhitic branch, which divided into two sub-branches: Polish and Baltic. The language of the Kashubs and Pomeranian Slovincians are the last living remnants of a Baltic sub-branch, which during the Middle Ages occupied an area at least equal to that of the Polish sub-branch. (Hilferding 1862: 98)

Besides the dialect texts, the book itself constituted a sort of synthesis of Hilferding's own rich materials with those of Ceynowa and Preys. This was the first ever fully scientific work on Kashubian, and it led to the scholarly world becoming interested in Kashubian matters. Lucjan Malinowski (1875) and later Aleksander Brückner (1894) introduced the ideas of Sreznevskiy (of St Petersburg) and Miklosich (of Vienna) to Polish scholarship. The

Polish dialectologist Kazimierz Nitsch (1905) in principle supported their views, especially after his own research in the Kashubian village of Luzino (in 1901); he stressed the remarkable separateness of Kashubian from other dialects spoken in Poland. This idea of the transitory nature of Kashubian was further developed by Zdzisław Stieber, and documented in the *Atlas językowy kaszubszczyzny* (1964), compiled and published by a team from the Polish Academy of Sciences, including researchers such as Hanna Popowska-Taborska, Kwiryna Handke, Ewa Rzetelska-Feleszko and Jadwiga Zieniukowa (cf. Majowa 1978).

After meeting Hilferding personally, Ceynowa intensified his work on the Kashubian glossary (1861) and grammar (1879), focusing however on the variant spoken in so-called 'Kashubia proper', i.e. Gdańsk Pomerania, in particular his native region of Puck. He did not research the Kashubs of Western Pomerania because he had great respect for the research of Hilferding. Hilderding's general conclusions concurred with Ceynowa's assumptions, apart from his opinion on the status of Kashubian, which he declared as the 'most similar to the Polish language'. Ceynowa had declared it in 1850 to be a separate Slavonic language, and as such he had pronounced it necessary to develop a written version of Kashubian; furthermore, he directly endorsed a programme for the separateness of the Kashubs as a nation (Ramułt 1893: XXXVII).

Ceynowa probably identified Kashubia with historical Pomerania and proposed his literary Kashubian as appropriate for all Pomeranians. His *Zarés do Grammatikj ...* (1879) is not an exact description of his native dialect, from Sławoszyno near Puck. At this time, numerous features of Kashubian differentiated it (descriptively) from Polish, especially in its literary form. Since the Middle Ages the Lekhitic group of languages had been subject to a constant process of differentiation; for example, conflation of consonants into *ôł* (as in *pôłnié* 'midday'), change of *\*ę* into *i* || *y* (e.g. *cąc* next to *cyc* 'to cut'), replacement of *ś ź ć dź* by *s z c dz* (e.g. *sedzec* 'to sit'), emergence of a peculiar *schwa* vowel i.e. development of short *ĭ, ў, ŭ* into *ë*, as in *Kaszëbë* ('Kashubia, Kashubs'). After the extinction of Polabian, *ķ ǵ* developed into *ć dź* or *cz dż*, e.g. *tacé nodżi* ('such legs'), the latter features being nowadays of constitutive nature. As the evolution of Kashubian continued, so its internal diversity increased, including replacement of *ł* by *l* (so-called *bylaczenie*: as in *bél, bëla* instead of *bél, bëła* 'he, she was'), dispalatalisation of *ń* into *n* (e.g.. *òdżin* 'fire'), and development of the regional dialect of Luzino and Szemud, with pronunciation patterns as in *szła krjewa dje Przetjeczëna i złóma sje njegã* ('a cow went to Przetoczyno and broke its leg').

After publication of Derdowski's poem *O panu Czorlińscim co do Pucka po sece jachoł* in 1880, Alfons Parczewski (1849–1933), a lawyer and ethnographer from Poznań, made two journeys (1880, 1885) to visit the Slovincians and Kashubs in the vicinities of Lębork and Bytów. He published the results in his book *Szczątki kaszubskie w prowincji pomorskiej* (Poznań 1896). It contained a review of Hilferding's book, followed by his own ethnographic, statistical and linguistic data, as well as a collection of texts and vocabulary. Most of his linguistic data was collected in Wielka Gardna, Smołdzino, Cecenowo, Główczyce, Izbica, Żarnowska, Łeba and Sarbsko.

Ramułt's interest in Kashubia originated in his fascination with the work of Ceynowa. He advanced Ceynowa's ideas about the Kashubs' linguistic and ethnic separateness, and was himself a disciple of Antoni Kalina (1846–1906), a Slavicist from Lemberg/Lwów, who from the beginning claimed Kashubian as a separate language. In the introduction to his *Słownik języka pomorskiego, czyli kaszubskiego* (1893), Ramułt published his statistics on the Kashubs (he counted 170,000, including 19,000 in Puck county, 29,000 in Wejherowo county and 50,000 in Kartuzy county). He also presented the 'dialects of the Pomeranian language', which he divided into northern, central and southern, writing: 'the first group includes varieties spoken by the Slovincians and Kabatks in the county of Słupsk, that of the Kashubs on the Łeba lake in the north-eastern part of Lębork county, that from Żarnowiec in the north-eastern part of Lębork county and north-west of Puck county, the variety spoken by the Bylaks in the holms of Swarzewo, Puck and Oksywie, as well as the variety spoken by the Rybaks [fishermen] in the Hel peninsula' (Ramułt 1893: XXX). He also wrote 'Pronunciation of the sound *l* divides the northern Kashubs into two subgroups: the Slovincians and Bylaks, even if not direct neighbours, having a hard *l*, while the rest of the Kashubs in those vicinities pronounce *l* clearly in the same way as the Russians, Ruthenes[3] or Lithuanians. The vernacular spoken

3    A former designation of the Belarusians and Ukrainians.

by the fishermen is closest to that of the Bylaks, although they differ in many respects, mainly as far as the vowel quantity and stress is concerned' (Ramułt 1893: XXX).

He identifies further northern features through examining other dialects: 'The northern accentuation patterns change into southern ones in the southern part of Kartuzy county, where stress follows the Czech pattern, falling on the first syllable of the word' (Ramułt 1893: XXXI). He also claimed the stress in the north to be free, and wrote that 'There are also some differences between individual dialects in Pomerania, which can be defined as quantitative. Linguistic phenomena which are of regular character in the north can become accidental in the south and appear solely in some forms. This is for instance the case of the change of *u* into *ë*, which takes place in Kashubia even in close syllables, e.g. *ced, cede* (in contrast [to Polish] *cud, cudu* 'miracle' (Nominative/Genitive)) (Ramułt 1893: XXXI). His general opinion on foreign influence is quite accurate: 'To the general characteristics of Pomeranian dialects, one should add that the northern varieties have suffered much more than the southern ones from the contiguity of Germany, both in the lexical and syntactic respect, whereas in the south the influence of not only bookish Polish, but also folk dialects of Kociewie and Bory is more remarkable'. It is also worthy of note that literary Polish strongly affected the northern dialects, through the influence of the Church.

In the introduction to his book, Ramułt justified his view (also apparent in the title) that: 1) the idiom spoken by the Kashubs and Slovincians is a separate Slavonic language; 2) the individual varieties spoken by the Polabians are also separate Slavonic languages; 3) 'the group of dialects represented by the tongues of the Polabians, Slovincians and Kashubs should be called Pomeranian'; 4) 'the group of Pomeranian languages belongs to the West Slavonic family'; 5) that family is divided into four groups: Czecho-Slovak (Moravian), Sorbian (Lusatian Sorbian), Polish and Pomeranian; 6. 'the Pomeranian language has a place between Polish and the group of Sorbian dialects' (ibid.: XLII). He thus questioned the division of West Slavonic languages recently proposed by August Schleicher (1821–68).

Ramułt's concept was logical and made efficient and competent use of ideas about the separateness of Kashubian which had been emphasised since Mrongowiusz's time and practically realised by Ceynowa. Kashubian has so many clearly distinct features that it is easier to justify closer relations between the Kashubs and the Polabians than between Kashubian and the dialects of continental Poland, so they can be regarded as a Pomeranian group in transition between Polish and Sorbian dialects. However, the classification by Schleicher, who had placed Kashubian in a transitional position between the Polish and Polabian dialects, seems to be supported by arguments put forward in 1897 and 1904 by the Polish linguist Jan Baudouin de Courtenay (1845–1929). Baudouin de Courtenay claimed that Kashubian had shared more common processes with Polish, such as preserved nasal vowels (absent in Sorbian), umlaut, supplementary lengthening, and diversification of continuants of ancient long and short vowels. Baudouin de Courtenay therefore did not accept the hypotheses of Ramułt and Lorentz. He accomplished a modern synthesis of Kashubian, explaining such features as the origin of the Genitive ending -*ewò* or the rules for the change of short *ĭ ў ŭ* into *ə*, thereby formulating his famous statement that Kashubian is 'plus polonais que le polonais même'.

The Finnish researcher Josef J. Mikkola (1866–1946), intrigued by Hilferding's sensational reports, travelled to Kashubia in 1896 and stayed in Kluki and Wielka Gardna, as well as in the vicinities of Puck and Jastarnia. He published the results of his research in the works *K izucheniyu kashubskikh govorov* (1897) and *Betonung und Quantität in der westslavischen Sprachen* (1899), highlighting prosodic phenomena, including intonation. In 1891, the Sorbian Gotthelf M. Bronisch (1868–1937) took up Kashubian studies, inspired by August Leskien (1840–1916), and in 1896 and 1897 he published in Leipzig the two-volumed *Kaschubische Dialectstudien*. In the first volume he describes the varieties of Kashubian spoken in the Puck holms and the dialect of Luzino and Szemud, as well as the Bytów region, his work continuing that of Hilferding and Mikkola. He made use of Ramułt's dictionary, although misinterpreting it as a description of central dialects. The second volume contains texts from these dialectal areas.

As a Slav, Bronisch paved the way for the German Friedrich Lorentz (1870–1937), who started his exhaustive research in Kashubia from a study of Slovincian (1897), compiling its grammar (1903), numerous texts (1905) and a dictionary (1908, 1912). In his *Slovinzische Grammatik* Lorentz wrote: 'When 6 years ago I met the Slovincians for the first time, I was astounded to discover that their tongue, being doubtlessly the most ancient in the entire western Slavdom, could have died out without a detailed description and analysis'. The comprehensive *Przyczynki do gramatyki i słownika narzecza słowińskiego* published in 1913 by Mikołaj Rudnicki (1881–1978) completes and partly verifies Lorentz's work.

After studying Slovincian, Lorentz comprehensively researched the territory of Kashubia, on a scale that had never occurred before. He recorded over 1,000 Pomeranian texts (*Teksty pomorskie*), representing all the villages divided according to twenty-one dialectal groups, with seventy-six sub-dialects shown on the map. He compiled a dictionary, published posthumously in 1958 (letters A–P), also containing a lexicon of Kashubian literature. He researched the Slavonic toponymy of medieval Pomerania (cf. *Slavische Namen Hinterpommerns*, 1964), and also examined other fragments of old literature, such as the translations of Krofej and Pontanus. He wrote *Geschichte der pomoranischen (kaschubischen) Sprache* (1925) and *Geschichte der Kaschuben* (1926). He was the author of *Zarys etnografii kaszubskiej* (1934), which declared the identity of Kashubian and Polish folk cultures and observed the progress of Germanisation and the decay of Slovincian, as well as describing bilingualism among the northern Kashubs, and perceiving their attachment to their forefathers' traditions and language. Lorentz sympathised with the advocates of writing in Kashubian, described the stages of the evolution of literary Kashubian (Ceynowa, Derdowski, the Young-Kashubs and the *Zrzesz* circle), worked on orthography and compiled the *Kaschubische Grammatik* (1919).

In his *Gramatyka pomorska* (1927), Lorentz proposed 'northern Pomeranian as distinguished from southern by preserved constant vowel quantity differences', and divided the language into:

A. Eastern Slovincian (Smołdzino parish and Stojęcino) and western Slovincian (Gardna parish), at the edge of extinction.

B. Northern Kashubian – at the edge of extinction or endangered. This included: 1) the western sub-dialects of Główczyce, Cecenowo, Charbrowo and Łeba, Osiek, Gniewino and Salino, Tyłowo, Góra, Luzino and Wejherowo, and Szemud, with the dialects of Luzino, Wejherowo and Szemud described as being under the influence of neighbouring varieties; 2) the eastern sub-dialects: a) the Bylaks' vernaculars of Jastarnia, Kuźnice,

Chałupy, Swarzewo and Strzelno, Starzyno and Mechowo, and Oksywie; b) non-Bylak vernaculars of Żarnowiec, Puck, Reda and Wielki Kack; c) the mixed sub-dialects of Rumia, Chylonia and Witomino.

C. Eastern Kashubian, comprising some dull sub-dialects of more recent origin, from Leśno, Kielno, Warzewo and Kłosowo, Chwaszczyno, Mały Kack and Sopot.

D. Northern Pomeranian sub-dialects from Tępcz and Głodowo in the parish of Strzepcz.

Lorentz's theory of an independent Kashubian language, with Slovincian at that time regarded as a separate variety, originates from his acceptance of Ceynowa's viewpoint, strengthened theoretically by Ramułt. At the end of his *Gramatyka pomorska*, however, Lorentz stated: 'I had agreed with Ramułt, but in the meantime I came to the conclusion that I was wrong; I have not, however, come closer to a final conclusion' (Lorentz 1927: 25). This happened under the influence of the polemics between Baudouin de Courtenay and Nitsch, who considered that Kashubian held a transitional position within the Lekhitic area, between the Polabian language and dialects of continental Poland. This theory had already been put forward by Lucjan Malinowski (1839–98).

Kazimierz Nitsch (1874–1958), a Polish linguist, started his career as a dialectologist in 1901 by researching the dialect of Luzino. His study, published in 1903, contained texts from Luzino and Robakowo as well as a glossary containing a different lexicon from that compiled by Ramułt. Nitsch also talked to Bronisch's informants. Later he researched other regions of Kashubia, preparing relevant descriptions accompanied by texts and glossaries (including the names of fields, lakes etc) from the villages of Borzyszkowy and Brzeźno, Brusy, Swornegacie in Chojnice county and Grabowo and Wdzydze in Kościerzyna county (in *Dialekty polskie Prus Zachodnich*, Vol. 1, 1907). His first general conclusions concerning Kashubian were announced in *Stosunki pokrewieństwa języków lechickich* (1905), polemising with Lorentz's theses in *Das gegenseitige Verhältniss der sogenannten lechischen Sprachen* (1902), and in the works *Mowa Kaszubów* and *Mowa ludu polskiego* (1911). In these, he wrote about the so-called 'Kashubian issue', about the separateness of Kashubian from the Polish dialects and about Kashubian literature, quoting the work of Ceynowa,

Derdowski and Karnowski. As far as Kashubian linguistic peculiarities are concerned, he emphasised that some of these were to be found solely in the northern variety (from areas north of Kartuzy), making it less comprehensible to Poles e.g. mobile stress, and word-types such as *warna* ('crow'), *wôłk* ('wolf'), *Stôłp* ('Słupsk'), *pisc* ('fist'), *klëcec* ('to kneel'), *bél* ('he was'), *robil* ('he did') and *zómkòwiszcze* ('castle'). He stressed the role of the process of advanced pronunciation with a tendency to de-labialise the rounded and back vowels in the sub-dialect of Borzyszkowy, in comparison with the conservative variety of Kashubian spoken in Swornegacie. He argued that the process was extremely advanced in western Kashubia, in particular in the sub-dialects of Sulęczyno and Sierakowice (Górnowicz 1965). Nitsch's position was assimilated by the Young-Kashubs and expressed by Karnowski in his study *Zdanie o stosunku językowym ludności kaszubskiej do polskiej* (1910). This was of particular importance as a complete presentation of the scholarly output on Kashubian and the discussion of its status up until that date, written by a competent Kashub who knew the entirety of the relevant literature in depth.

Fifty years after Nitsch and forty years after publication of Lorentz's work, a new stage in Kashubian studies started, following the preparation of the *Atlas językowy kaszubszczynzy* (1964). This project was initiated in 1954 by Zdzisław Stieber, the author of numerous works on Kashubian, including *Zagadnienie iloczasu kaszubskiego* (1950) and *Stosunek kaszubszczyzny do dialektów Polski lądowej* (1954). The Atlas summed up the views on the status of Kashubian from Baudouin de Courtenay to Nitsch, and adopted a concept of two Lekhitic poles, north-western (Polabian) and south-eastern (Polish), with 'transitional' Kashubian in between. It contains 750 maps, which display phonetic, inflectional, morphological and lexical phenomena, accompanied by excellent commentaries, with references to materials compiled in Lorentz's and Sychta's dictionaries. This impressive publication confirmed Stieber's thesis that Kashubian had developed together with the entire Polish linguistic area over a long period, being subject to a few late phonetic and morphological changes, yet preserving numerous features of the north-western axis as well as archaisms absent from Old Polish.

The Atlas project was accompanied by more detailed research carried out by members of the team, as well as by auxiliary researchers, including Bogusław Kreja, Hubert Górnowicz, Janusz Siatkowski, and Paweł Smoczyński. They often used the same materials, or complemented and verified their work using the Atlas informants. Worthy of note are the new arrangements concerning the internal dialectal divisions in Kashubia drawn up by Kwiryna Handke. These indicate that the northern dialects can be divided into: 1. the lesser complex, limited to the county of Puck with: a) Hel peninsula b) the eastern area, often regarded as including the Hel peninsula c) the western area, in particular the vicinity of Żarnowiec lake; and 2. the greater complex, including the rest of Puck county and the county of Wejherowo.

Hanna Popowska-Taborska, a member of the Atlas team, wrote the monograph *Centralne zagadnienie wokalizmu kaszubskiego. Kaszubska zmiana ę ≥ i oraz ĭ, ў, ŭ ≥ ə* (1961). She also researched the pronunciation of nasal vowels in Bór and Jastarnia, analysed the internal geography of words and their range in Slavonic languages (e.g. peripheral archaisms), studied the literary relics of Pomeranian (e.g. the seventeenth- and eighteenth-century psalm books) and Kashubian (e.g. the 1402 *Dutki brzeskie*; the language of the translations by Krofej and Pontanus; and Slovincian oath texts from Wierzchocino), and the history of Kashubian lexicography since the end of the eighteenth century. One of her books, published in 1996, was devoted entirely to the Kashubian lexicon. Together with Wiesław Boryś, she initiated and co-authored the *Słownik etymologiczny kaszubszczyzny*, differentiating it from literary Polish and referring to all known lexical collections, both historical (e.g. Slovincian) and contemporary, in particular the Atlas and Sychta's dictionary. She has also published a popular outline of Kashubian studies (1980), and (together with Ewa Rzetelska-Feleszko) an important contribution to historical dialectology entitled *Dialekty kaszubskie w świetle dziewiętnastowiecznych materiałów archiwalnych. Prezentacja i opracowanie kaszubskich materiałów językowych zebranych przez Georga Wenkera w latach 1879–1887* (2009). The Warsaw centre of Slavonic studies has also carried out comparative research on Kashubian and other Slavonic languages, especially Sorbian, as well as on the history of Kashubian-Prussian relations.

Paweł Smoczyński (1914–79) was the author of a comprehensive monograph entitled *Stosunek dzisiejszego dialektu Sławoszyna do języka Cenowy* (1956); his other publications included *O socjologicznym podłożu nowszych zmian w kaszubskim dialekcie wsi Kętrzyno* (1964), *W sprawie zmian k'-g' na Kaszubach i w zachodnich dialektach północnopolskich* (1958), and *Zmiany językowe w Luzinie w ostatnich pięćdziesięciu latach* (1955). The latter presented a comparative diachronic approach to Nitsch's report, simultaneously confirming its findings and broadening its application, while severely criticizing Lorentz's dictionary. The relics of vernaculars spoken by the Slovincians from Gardna Lake have been gathered and edited by Zenon Sobierajski (1917–2007), who started publishing the *Słownik gwarowy tzw. Słowińców kaszubskich* in 1997 (Vol. 1, A–C).[4]

Zuzanna Topolińska has written about the problems of prosody, stress, quantity and duration, as well as other crucial problems of phonetics and phonology. He book *A Historical Phonology of the Kashubian Dialects of Polish* was published in 1974, focusing on the chronological evolution of the Kashubian phonemic system. Kashubian stress has also been researched by Tadeusz Lehr-Spławiński and Jerzy Kuryłowicz. Sychta's monumental *Słownik gwar kaszubskich na tle kultury ludowej* (1967) contains a rich collection of vocabulary from the entire territory of Kashubia, with special focus on the lexical geography. It has constituted a research base for numerous detailed studies in linguistics, including Jerzy Treder's work on phraseology, Ewa Rogowska's work on phytonomy, Marek Cybulski's work on syntax and morphophonemic alternations, and Justyna Pomierska's work on proverbs.

Recent years have seen particular development within Kashubian literary studies, a field which was initiated by Lorentz and intensively continued by Treder, who has researched the language of works by Ceynowa, Derdowski, Majkowski, Heyke, the *Zrzesz* circle and translations into Kashubian (2005); the language of Sychta's dramas (2008b); Pestka's poetry (2008d); and the theory and practice of the standardisation of Kashubian (2007). Treder recently published the first ever Kashubian-language compendium

---

4    The next volumes have not been published yet.

of Kashubian language studies (Treder 2009). New sociolinguistic research has been carried out by Niamh Nestor in Ireland, Agnieszka Meinartowicz in Barcelona and Marlena Porębska in Erlangen, Germany. Hanna Makurat, based in Gdańsk, studies Kashubian-Polish and Polish-Kashubian interferences. Also of international significance are works by the Poznań-based linguists Alfred Majewicz and Tomasz Wicherkiewicz.

Kashubian has attracted scholarly interest for a long time, particularly since the end of the eighteenth century. However, the second half of the twentieth century has witnessed some radical changes of both a quantitative and a qualitative character. For more than two centuries Kashubian linguistics have set the tone and direction of Kashubian studies in general; its accomplishments can be attributed in some measure to the spectacular fieldwork achievements of Lorentz and to the empirical and methodological works of Nitsch, who started his career in dialectology in 1901 with Kashubian Luzino. After 1945, and especially after 1954, this legacy has been continued and enriched, with the achievements of the Atlas team of particular importance, as well as the work of Gdańsk-based researchers, first at the Higher School of Education (since 1948) and later at the University of Gdańsk (since 1970). The Gdańsk academic centre of Kashubian studies can be regarded as a continuation of the Cracow research school, through the influence of Nitsch and Stieber on Górnowicz, and Górnowicz's subsequent influence on Edward Breza and Jerzy Treder (Treder 2008a). It is also worth noting that linguistic investigations have become important in the research of the outstanding Polish medievalist Gerard Labuda, a Kashub himself.

Recent decades have brought numerous works on Kashubian, which are also of wider importance for Slavonic studies. Some of these have put forward new syntheses to be based on existing reliable materials; other modify, specify or clarify previous judgements or re-examine them using new research methods. The majority of these research initiatives were initiated by the once buoyant centre of Slavonic studies in Warsaw (in particular the Institute of Slavistics), whose representatives continue to collaborate actively with the University of Gdańsk. The University of Gdańsk also has a lively co-operation with the Berlin-based Friedhelm Hinze, a continuator of Lorentz's work who has been crucial in informing the Slavistic world of the research results from Warsaw and Gdańsk.

Detailed information on the history of this research can be found in a comprehensive bibliography by Górnowicz compiled in 1965, which follows the survey by Kamińska and Pałkowska published in 1958. A further bibliography was compiled by Treder 1991. A rich and up-to-date source of references is the encyclopaedic handbook *Język kaszubski. Poradnik językowy* (Treder 2006). Kashubian studies has come a long way since its origins in Ceynowa's manifesto of 1843, which took up the research programme of Krzysztof Celestyn Mrongowiusz, a Mazurian living in Gdańsk.

JERZY TREDER AND CEZARY OBRACHT-PRONDZYŃSKI

# Kashubian Literature: The Phenomenon, its History and its Social Dimension

## Introduction

Kashubian literature is a cultural phenomenon which has attracted scholarly interest from its very beginning, or in other words since the commencement of a public debate on the so-called 'Kashubian issue' (Bukowski 1950; Drzeżdżon 1973; Drzeżdżon 1986; Neureiter 1982; Neureiter 1991; Samp 2000; Treder 2005; Zielonka 2007). Florian Ceynowa reflected publicly on whether such a literature was to come into being, asking whether Kashubian was able to give birth to literature that went beyond fireside tales and legends, and whether the Kashubs' tongue would be able to express deep emotions and experiences. It was a long time before Kashubian literature became recognised as autonomous and independent, and before its scope extended beyond the stage of popular culture consisting of folkloric stories, simple rhymes and fables. Kashubian literature not only had to develop a circle of recognised writers (in that respect, a breakthrough came with publications by the Young-Kashubs at the beginning of the twentieth century), but also a group of researchers, commentators, critics, interpreters, even chroniclers, who have studied and popularised works created in Kashubian.

From its very beginning, Kashubian literature has also had to cope with the problem of public reception. As a 'minor' literature (although the term is merely conventional, as all such classifications must be arbitrary – the opposition 'minor' versus 'great' simply refers to the size of the group speaking the language in which the literature in question is written) it has functioned differently from the 'great' literatures, which are not constantly questioned and doubted, and which are received by a substantial circle of

educated readers. Common opinion judges Kashubian literature to be
directed at two circles of readers: the Kashubs themselves and researchers
(i.e. linguists dealing with Kashubian and literature specialists studying the
writing of minor ethnic groups). Who exactly makes up the first group, the
Kashubs? Is Kashubian literature a 'literature without people' (Samp 1983),
without readers and audience? And if the Kashubs do read the writings,
what are they looking for and why? What evidence is there of the vitality
of the literature? Why does it continue to develop, with new generations
of writers springing up, and evidence of yearly growth in literary output?
And to what extent has the literature developed, if we compare its present
condition with its origins?

## The origins of Kashubian literature

The origins of Kashubian literature can be found in two translations from
German. The first was *Duchowne piesnie Dra Marcina Luthera i inszich
naboznich mężow. Zniemieckiego w slawięsky język wilozone* by Simon
Krofey, a Lutheran pastor from Bytów, published in Gdańsk in 1586
and re-discovered in 1896 in Smołdzino by Franz Tetzner. In addition to
psalms, this edition also included basic prayers such as the Apostles' Creed
and the Lord's Prayer. The second work was *Mały Catechism D. Marciná
Lutherá Niemiecko-Wándalski ábo Słowięski to jestá z Niemieckiego języká
w Słowięski wystáwion ...*, published in 1643 by Michał Pontanus, alias
Mostnik, a preacher from Smołdzino. This volume, printed bilingually
in German and Kashubian, included the Passion and the psalms, and was
aimed at Lutheran pastors. The second edition in 1758 was reworded and
Polonised, and was the basis for another edition, by Krzysztof Celestyn
Mrongowiusz (Szczecin, 1828). This was in turn re-Kashubised by Cey-
nowa in 1861 as *Pjnc głovnech wóddzałov Evangjelickjeho Katechizmu z
Njemjeckjeho na Kaśebsko-Słovjenskj język ...*, with a supplement entitled
*Spóvjedz e Nobóżenstvo codzenne.*

The titles of both of these literary milestones emphasise the translations' linguistic distinctness from the official Polish Church language, although some scholars claim that the language used is a northern variety of Polish, with numerous Kashubian features which manifest themselves in phonetics, inflection and lexicon. There are similar arguments with regard to the language of other so-called landmarks of Kashubian literature, such as *Perykopy smołdzińskie* (1770), and *Przysięgi słowińskie z Wierzchocina* (1725).

Simon Krofey can be said to have assumed a practical position, conducting his evangelisation according to the principles of the Reformation – in the language of the congregation, i.e. Kashubian. This later also prompted 'more books to be translated into the tongue' (cf. Krofey 1586, 1958). Ceynowa continued that pragmatic attitude, although operating in partitioned Poland and in the context of the Slavicists' reflections on Kashubian. The Slavicists referred to Kashubian at that time as a 'transitional' dialect, in the absence of an autonomous literature and a translation of the Bible.

When Ceynowa tried to revive the early Kashubian writings, those for whom they were published (the Protestant Kashubs of West Pomerania) were just in the process of undergoing intense Germanisation. Literature became a symbol of the disappearing Kashubian-speaking Protestants, whose coffins were furnished with their old psalm books. Along with the people, the language and the books were passing away. Despite everything, though, written Kashubian survived – not among the Lutheran Kashubs but thanks to the genius of their Catholic compatriots in Gdańsk Pomerania: Ceynowa and Derdowski.

# The originators of Kashubian literature:
# Florian Ceynowa and Hieronim Derdowski

The beginnings of literary Kashubian should be sought in the work of Florian Ceynowa (1817–81), from Sławoszyno near Puck. The inspiration to write in Kashubian probably came from the previously mentioned works of Pontanus. Ceynowa also pretended to have found an eighteenth-century manuscript, *Rozmòva Pòlôcha s Kaszébą* by Reverend Szmuk (or Szmuda) of Puck, in fact written by Ceynowa himself, in this way deliberately 'aging' the history of Kashubian literature. That attempt to age the literature was also expressed in use of the dialogue form, which in the mid-nineteenth century was already an anachronism, but in this case was used on purpose to give the text an impression of antiquity.

Ceynowa's unquestionably great contribution was the commencement of and justification for writing in Kashubian, along with the creation of an alphabet and spelling system, vocabularies and grammatical descriptions, as well as sample texts in Kashubian. Some of these were ethnographic e.g. *Wiléjá Noweho Roku* (1843), *Zvéczaje é wóbéczaje Kaszébsko-słovjnskjeho narodé* (1862); some were historical e.g. *Kile słov wó Kaszebach e jich zemi* (1850). He also wrote journalistic pieces e.g. *Kaszebji do Pólochov* and *Wó narodowoscé, a wó móvje* (1850), and used Kashubian in translations, for example of Pushkin's fables and Tyutchev's poems. The primary goal was to reveal the potential of Kashubian to express emotions and thoughts, thus fighting against the inferiority complex of a 'polluted tongue', so strong among the Kashubs. Hence, the message of his activities could be his often-repeated catchphrase: 'It's high time no Kashub was ashamed to speak Kashubian'.

Much of Ceynowa's writing was published in his self-edited quasi-periodical *Skôrb kaszëbsko-słowinsczi mowë* (1866–68), considered to be the first Kashubian journal. His most important journalistic works are two 'discourses': *Rozmova Pólocha s Kaszebą* (1850; 2nd edition published 1865) and *Rozmòva Kaszébé s Pòlôchę* (1862; cf. Ceynowa 2007). These are quite autonomous and are different from one another in literary form (though not in spelling); they were written under very different circumstances. Both were written as dialogues: the first one aimed at persuading a Polish nobleman to become a Kashub, because of the beauty and the biblical origin of Kashubia, its language, and the honesty of its people; and the second one aimed at persuading a Kashub to become a Pole, because of the antiquity of the Polish nation and the idea of a life free of work. The first of these discourses presented in an attractive way a basic knowledge of Kashubia, expressed in Kashubian (through idioms and proverbs), and arranged around the following themes: the appellation of the Kashubs and their sub-groupings; the location and borders of Kashubia; old Kashubian documents and writings; the history of Kashubia (the image of Kashubia as Palestine, i.e. the Promised Land, and as Paradise); names (with origins) of Kashubia's forests, swamps, rivers, lakes and seas; the status of Kashubian in comparison with other Slavonic and Indo-European and even Semitic languages; the originality of the Kashubian language and the ease of acquiring it; and the relationship between the Kashubs and the Poles. The parable of Kashubia as Palestine was well planned and executed, with various elements probably referring to a folk tradition, and the discourse is written in a robust but harmonious language and a casual conversational tone.

The second discourse contains reflections on the experience of an uprising and on the imprisonment of the author (1846–7). It examines the political and social situation, including criticism of the Church and the nobility. As an avowed democrat, Ceynowa severely criticised both the Church (as a contributor to the Kashubs' Germanisation) and the nobility (for their self-Germanisation, leading to the downfall of the whole Kashubian community, and its very low morale). Particularly noteworthy is the statement that 'peasants are the base of every state'.

Ceynowa's writings therefore displayed various elements: a belief in democracy, the beginnings of positivist ideas, but also strong Slavophile tendencies, since he believed the Slavs were the appointed defenders of a morally and socially wholesome Europe, showing the influence of Romantic ideas. Altogether, the second discourse is of a less literary and metaphorical character; it is more literal and intellectual, and written in a correct, standardised, robust and sharp language.

The revolutionary nature of Ceynowa's views on the autonomous character of Kashubian and his criticism of the clergy and nobility, as well as his pan-Slavic ideas, made him enemies. Ceynowa died convinced that he had no successors. Before his death he met Hieronim Derdowski, to whom he offered his publications, although expressing regret at his ideological differences. Derdowski, even if he didn't agree with Ceynowa's ideological programme, paid tribute to his devotion to the Kashubs and their culture in the poem *Wojkasyn ze Słowoszena – Dr Florian Ceynowa* (1881).

Derdowski (1852–1902), from Wiele in southern Kashubia, should be regarded as the first authentic Kashubian man of letters. Having accepted and continued Ceynowa's commitment to writing in Kashubian, he nonetheless saw the relationship between Kashubian and Polish quite differently. This resulted in differences from Ceynowa's spelling and wording. Derdowski's most important work, still probably the most popular Kashubian poem, was *O panu Czorlińscim co do Pucka po sece jachoł* (1880), which contained the essence of his ideological programme, and was to become the motto of the Kashubian movement: 'There is no Kashubia without Poland; and no Poland without Kashubia'. Derdowski certainly had the gift of formulating ideological slogans. It is from a fragment of his work that the lyrics of the Kashubian anthem *Tam, gdze Wisła*, were taken, with the melody composed later by Feliks Nowowiejski:

| | |
|---|---|
| *Tam, gdze Wisła òd Kraköwa* | *Where the Vistula from Cracow* |
| *W pòlsczé mòrze płinie,* | *Flows into the Polish sea,* |
| *Pòlskô wiara, pòlskô mòwa* | *The Polish faith, the Polish tongue* |
| *Nigdë nie zadżinie.* | *Shall never perish.* |
| *Nigdë do zgùbë* | *Never to extinction* |
| *Nie przińdą Kaszubë,* | *Shall the Kashubs come,* |
| *Marsz, marsz za wrodżem!* | *March, march, follow the enemy!* |
| *Më trzimómë z Bòdżem!* | *We remain with God!* |

'Never to extinction the Kashubs shall come' and 'We remain with God' have become slogans, the former found written and displayed in many Kashubian locations, the latter heard at each major Kashubian meeting.

Derdowski was quite a colourful personage: a restless globetrotter, a fervent Polish patriot simultaneously devoted to Kashubian culture, having been brought up with Romantic literature. Throughout his life he strove to gain some financial stability, which brought him eventually to America – to Winona, Wisconsin, where he published his journal *Wiarus* and where he died and was buried. Derdowski's works have been extremely popular, including those written in Kashubian, such as *Kaszube pod Widnem* (1883 and 2002; English translation 2007), about the Kashubs' participation in the 1683 Relief of Vienna. The leitmotif of a travelling nobleman-fisherman allowed Derdowski in his writings to present the history and geography of Kashubia and types and characters of local people. He wrote about their religious and superstitious nature, their robust tongue, and local legends (for example, a lullaby about the 1308 massacre, supposedly organised by the Teutonic Knights after their conquest of Gdańsk, and a couplet on the legendary figure of Wanda, who refused to marry a German)[1]. He also wrote about Kashubian myths (e.g. about the giants' stones); superstitions and beliefs (e.g. the last witch-ducking in Chałupy in the Hel peninsula in 1836); mythology and demonology (e.g. devils, imps and witches); and folk catechism (including an 'examination' on knowledge of the Bible). Moreover, Derdowski should be regarded as the first Kashubian marine writer, for his effective description of a sea voyage during a storm.

He had a splendid command of his native Kashubian and used his natural sense of humour in a masterly way. In comparison to Ceynowa he was a talented writer, although his material was derivative. He also adopted ideas from Adam Mickiewicz's *Pan Tadeusz* and from Fritz Reuter's Low-German humorous tales. His works have been published in numerous editions – for example, *O panu Czôrliśczim* ... was republished in its original form in 1911, 1934 and 1990, in another spelling in 1960 and 1976, and in its current orthography in 2007 – which is a strong indication that his writings teach Kashubs to read in Kashubian.

---

[1]    One of the founding myths of the town of Kraków (Cracow).

# The Young-Kashubs and Bernard Sychta

The beginning of the twentieth century brought crucial changes within the Kashubian community, and this was reflected in the situation of Kashubian literature. Young members of the intelligentsia formed a group called the Young-Kashubs. They had studied in German grammar schools, while at the same time discovering Polish culture, including its Romantic literature (particularly the works of Adam Mickiewicz and Juliusz Słowacki), and had continued to learn the history of Poland during clandestine Philomath classes. Educated at German universities, they were familiar with contemporary ideologies and literary trends (for example, evolutionism, positivism, modernism and neo-Romanticism). They had a good grasp of the modern arts and sciences, and brought a totally new spirit to Kashubia. They articulated a programme which underlay the Kashubian-Pomeranian movement for decades, and which still provides inspiration for new generations of Kashubian writers, journalists and activists.

A young physician from Kościerzyna, Aleksander Majkowski (1876–1938), having returned from studies in Greifswald, Berlin and Munich, in 1905 started editing *Drużba. Pismo dla polściech Kaszubów* as a supplement to *Gazeta Gdańska*. In 1906, a teacher called Izydor Gulgowski founded the first open-air museum in (partitioned) Poland, in Wdzydze. At the same time, in the theological seminary in Pelplin, the Circle of Kashubologists was founded by Jan Karnowski (1886–1939), from Brusy in southern Kashubia. Another member of the Circle was Leon Heyke (1885–1939) – later a priest, physician, poet and teacher of Kashubian youth.

These people were soon to gather around the *Gryf* journal, established by Majkowski in 1908, which became a phenomenon on a regional scale and attracted extensive feedback from Polish and German opinion-formers. Before long, in 1911, the first Kashubian ethnographic exhibition was set up in Kościerzyna, and finally in 1912 the first strictly regional organisation in Pomerania was established in Gdańsk: the Young-Kashubs' Association. As early as 1913, the group accomplished the foundation of the Kashubian-Pomeranian Museum in Sopot (Zoppot).

The Young-Kashubs also formed the first Kashubian literary group. At first they wrote mainly poetry, the first volumes being Majkowski's *Spiewe i frantówci* (1905) and Karnowski's *Nôwotnê spiéwǎ* (1910), but later they developed other forms. The greatest achievement of that generation was surely Majkowski's novel *Žëcé i przigodë Remusa* (1938). He wrote it over many years, first in versified Polish and eventually in his own literary variety of Kashubian. The novel could be called an idiosyncratic guidebook to the Kashubia of the second half of nineteenth century; its hero is a travelling dealer in books and devotional articles. Besides some autobiographical threads, the plot is interspersed with many legends (e.g. a legend about a ghostly army) and with fairy-tales, particularly a tale about a sunken castle, which acts as a symbol of Kashubia, and a princess under a curse, together with various phantoms called Fear, Pain and Worthless (Remus himself embodies the idea of freedom). The novelist derived some of his ideas from works such as *Don Quixote*, Reuter's *Ut mine stromtid*, Goethe's *Faust*, Lagerlöf's *Gösta Berling*, and from Nietzsche, whose writings Majkowski read passionately. There are a lot of syncretic examples of various art disciplines. In comparison to Derdowski's 'folk' *Czorlińsci*, which was designed solely to entertain, Majkowski's prose performed obvious didactic functions, urging readers to protect their forefathers' heritage and to liberate Kashubia from satanic despair. As Andrzej Bukowski wrote: 'the author upgraded a daily, common Kashubian vernacular to a ceremonial, dignified, solemn form, thus creating a model for the Kashubian literary language'. Majkowski's masterpiece has been published in several editions and translations: translated into Polish by Lech Bądkowski (1966), German by Eva Brenner (1988), French by Jaqueline Dera-Fischer (1992) and English by Blanche Krbechek and Katarzyna Gawlik-Luiken (2008). A passage from the novel – in the Kashubian original and in English translation – is reproduced at the end of this book.

The Young-Kashubs developed Kashubian regional literature extensively, seeing literature as a spiritual guide of the greatest importance throughout the region. Their writings show many typically Kashubian features, and they made use of various literary genres, e.g. lyrical poetry, rhyming and blank verse, epic poems, ballads, reflections, memoirs, religious and scholarly prose, stage dramas, feuilletons and humorous tales.

The Young-Kashubs' views were highly influential for a member of the younger generation, Bernard Sychta (1907–82) from Puzdrowo near Sierakowice, a priest, ethnographer, lexicographer and writer. In Sychta's life, as well as in his writings, he invariably held to the declaration: 'Kashubia does not belong to Poland, it constitutes Poland!' Influenced by Karnowski's dramas, he wrote stage plays of a historical nature (e.g. *Òstatnô gwiôzdka Mestwina*) as well as plays drawing on ritual and custom, including his best-known drama *Hanka sę żeni. Wesele kaszubskie* (1935, printed in 1937). Sychta's dramas draw strongly on folklore traditions such as wedding ceremonies, and frequently blend realistic scenes with fantasy. To this day they are very popular among amateur actors in Kashubia, always evoking lively reactions from the audience. Sychta was also the author of the monumental seven-volume *Słownik gwar kaszubskich na tle kultury ludowej* (1967–76).

## The *Zrzesz* circle and their followers

The literary platform of the Young-Kashubs was established over the final years of the existence of Prussia, during a period of tough Polish-German confrontation in Pomerania. In their ideological choices the Young-Kashubs opted for Polishness, but under the banner 'everything Kashubian is Polish'; they were profoundly convinced that the Kashubian culture deserved equal treatment based on partnership with Polish culture. In their opinion, the Polish national identity could spread in Kashubia only through using the resources of the native Kashubian culture.

Regaining Poland's independence (and access to the sea) in 1920 was a joyful event, but the first years of liberty brought so many disappointments to the Kashubs that their leaders' political attitudes radicalised significantly. These attitudes were given their most prominent expression within a circle of young Kashubian intelligentsia who commenced their adult life at the end of the 1920s. This group gathered around the Kashubian Association (established in 1920) and around the journal *Zrzesz Kaszëbskô* (1933–9).

Like the Young-Kashubs they put forward an ideological and literary platform, and the majority of their members made their names in the history of Kashubian literature, including Aleksander Labuda (1902–81), Jan Trepczyk (1907–89), Jan Rompski (1913–69), Franciszek Grucza (1911–93) and Stefan Bieszk (1895–1964).

The root of their ideology was Ceynowa's view of Kashubian as a separate Slavonic language. They were also convinced of the great artistic potential of Kashubian. The first writings of the *Zrzesz* circle appeared at the beginning of the 1930s, setting the direction for the evolution of Kashubian literature until the end of the 1980s. They produced a number of very significant works, including Labuda's collection of popular sociopolitical feuilletons *Guczów Mack gôdô*, Trepczyk's melodious songs and fine poems, Grucza's 1992 translation of the New Testament (from the Latin), and Bieszk's sonnets.

Their literary activity was strictly governed by their idea of Kashubian culture and history – a good example would be Rompski's dramas, which addressed three main topics: the Kashubs' history and tragic fate; the role of the Kashubian language as the paramount marker, the foundation of the Kashubs' identity; and the Kashubs' main treasure, their love of their native land.

The *Zrzesz* circle commenced their artistic activity in the interwar period, but continued after the Second World War, when their major works appeared. It is important to note not only the controversy which their attitudes caused, but also the followers they attracted and the influence they have had upon subsequent generations of writers.

## Diversity of literary activity during the interwar period

There was a boom in Kashubian literature during the interwar period. In spite of a difficult economic situation and a sense of discrimination among many circles in Kashubia and Pomerania, as well as problems in obtaining an adequate education, a significant number of young Kashubian writers appeared. They did not belong solely to the Young-Kashub and *Zrzesz* circles; in the mid-1930s, a group gathered around the journal *Klëka*, published in Wejherowo (1937–9). This group included Leon Roppel (1912–78), from northern Kashubia, and the much older poet Franciszek Sędzicki (1882–1957), from the south. These two prolific writers made their debut in the 1930s in clear opposition to the *Zrzesz* ideology, addressing both political and national questions (the *Klëka* circle stressed the Polish character of Kashubia) alongside linguistic matters. They viewed Kashubian as a dialect, and wrote without neologisms, embracing numerous Polish forms. Roppel's abundant literary output included poetry, stage plays, short stories, collections of songs, sayings, proverbs and riddles. He also carried out other work editing and promoting Kashubian literature, for example producing an anthology of marine poems.

Northern Kashubia produced other writers with very different life stories, one of them being Alojzy Budzisz (1874–1934), neglected and forgotten for many years, mainly because he published in journals edited by the German linguist Friedrich Lorentz such as *Przyjaciel Ludu Kaszubskiego* (1928–9), *Vjérni Naszińc* (1930) and *Bënë ë buten* (1930). These journals were treated with animosity in Kashubian circles, and Budzisz was even accused of being a German lackey and having a hostile attitude to the Polish state. This example illustrates the dependence of the development and reception of Kashubian literature upon political circumstances. Budzisz was an important influence on Labuda and Trepczyk, and on representatives of the younger generation such as Jan Drzeżdżon, who translated Budzisz's works into Polish and placed him among the most eminent Kashubian authors. His writing has become more widely known only since 2007, when his collected works were published in modern spelling, including all his short stories, sketches, fairy-tales, humorous pieces, jokes, poems and historical essays. Budzisz wrote in a north-eastern Kashubian dialect, reminiscent of the language used by Ceynowa, and used archaisms and neologisms, as well as loan-words from German and Polish.

Other noteworthy Kashubian writers from the north were: Jan Bilot (1898–1940), strongly influenced by Budzisz and the author of stories, humorous sketches, folk tales and legends written in the sub-dialect of Puck, but also containing neologisms and loans from Polish; Jan Patock

(1886–1940), from Strzelno, who focused mainly on folklore and collected tales, legends, anecdotes, riddles, proverbs, ditties, predictions and healing charms; Augustyn Dominik (1915–87), who wrote legends and tales; and Józef Klebba (1860–1931), a blacksmith from Kosakowo, the author of an epic satirical poem and ballads on the heroic deeds of Kashubian fishermen.

Altogether, allowing for the political circumstances, the interwar period was relatively rich in literary debuts, although most of the above-mentioned writers expanded their activities after 1945. Many originated from north Kashubia and they represented various ideological schools, with differing opinions on the status of Kashubian, its artistic potential, and the function of Kashubian literature.

## Literary activities and new phenomena after the Second World War

The Second World War slowed down the development of Kashubian literature and fractured publishing activities. Majkowski died a year before the outbreak of war, Karnowski one month afterwards; Heyke was murdered by the Nazis. Sychta actually stopped writing in Kashubian after the war, devoting himself to ethnographic and lexicographic work, with the exception of *Wesele kociewskie* (1959), written in the Kociewie dialect.

However, this did not mean that literary life came to a standstill. After 1945 many pre-war authors continued writing, predominantly members of the *Zrzesz* circle and also some of the *Klëka* circle. New writers also appeared, such as Antoni Pepliński (first work published in 1946), Jan Piepka (first work published in 1952), Alojzy Nagel (first work published in 1953), and Anna Łajming (first work published in 1958). Pepliński, Piepka and Nagel all began their artistic work after the war, or in the difficult Stalinist times.

In order to understand the phenomenon of Kashubian literature, it is necessary to understand the conditions of post-war literary life, particularly the fact that all the literary initiatives of 1956–89 were inspired within the Kashubian community itself, with hardly any support from state institutions. The state treated many Kashubian cultural activities with animosity and tried to block them. In fact, it is worth emphasising that all Kashubian writers, until quite recently, have been self-taught amateurs. There was no possibility of learning to write in Kashubian, as it was absent from schools.

When analyzing the instruments of development of post-war Kashubian literature, one should begin with the press, and in particular literary supplements, as they constituted the main forum for Kashubian writers. Research shows that post-war Kashubian literature was published almost exclusively in the literary and socio-cultural publications issued by the Kashubian community, such as *Chëcz*, the supplement to *Zrzesz Kaszëbskô*. The small number of 'general' literary publications edited in Gdańsk after the war seldom published Kashubian poetry, and it was even less common for them to publish Kashubian prose pieces. An exception was Gdańsk's first literary paper *Wiatr od Morza*, which printed a few poems by Sędzicki and Roppel. In the years to come Kashubian writing found its way into *Rejsy*, a supplement to *Dziennik Bałtycki*, and to a lesser extent into the monthly *Litery* (where the editor Tadeusz Bolduan was responsible for Kashubian issues). Other publications have continued to ignore Kashubian-language literature to this day, fostering the opinion that it is addressed only to a narrow, limited circle of readers. This resulted in the literature functioning indeed within a small community, with no way of reaching the general public, or even specialists in literary studies or in the history of Pomeranian regional literature.

The biweekly *Kaszëbë*, with its literary-artistic supplement *Pomerania* edited between 1957 and 1961 by Stanisław Pestka (1957–61), was enormously important to the development of modern Kashubian literature. *Pomerania* became an independent monthly publication in 1963, and almost all post-war Kashubian-language writers have published there at some stage. This journal is still an important forum for Kashubian writers; between 1995 and 1999 almost 150 texts in Kashubian appeared in *Pomerania*, by over fifty authors, including five plays, more than seventy poems and a few short prose pieces.

For many years after the war, new talent appeared sporadically. There were no Kashubian classes within schools; no writing courses, workshops or literary societies; no publishing houses interested in modern or classical Kashubian literature. Therefore, the press had a vital role to play; the editors were almost always writers themselves or actively encouraged others to write and encouraged novices. If not for the endeavours of these editors, under the auspices of the ZK-P Association, the condition of Kashubian literature would have been much worse. They initiated writing competitions, the first ones (organised in 1976 and 1977) paving the way for next generation of Kashubian writers. The winners of the first competition were Jerzy Stachurski for poetry and Stefan Fikus for prose. The winners of the second competition were Krystyna Muza for poetry and Jaromira Labudda for prose. Participation in those events ensured sustained writing activity among new authors.

In 1984 a competition was organised for 'poetry, short prose works, or stage plays written in the Kashubian dialect or Kociewie sub-dialect', and more than sixty works were submitted. The following years saw many similar events: for example, since the 1980s a 'Literary Contest' has been held in Lębork with a special award for a Kashubian-language text. In the 1990s the journal *Pomerania* organised an annual contest named after Izabella Trojanowska, to honour her contribution to the development of Kashubian publishing. There have also been a great many local, youth and children's literary competitions, the most important announced in 1996 and named after Jan Drzeżdżon. This competition has enjoyed high prestige on a national scale, and the entries are judged within two categories: Polish-language literature and Kashubian-language literature. Kashubian literary circles have also created their own awards, granted to persons writing in Kashubian or about Kashubia. The oldest (awarded by the *Pomerania* editors since 1984) and most prestigious prize is for young writers and is named after Roman Wróblewski.

Any circle of writers needs a place to meet, the opportunity to talk, exchange experiences and techniques, listen to or read a poem. This is particularly important for small groups which have been formed slowly and painfully. A young Kashubian writer has an incomparably more difficult path to an artistic career and to publication than a Polish author, often facing the unassisted study of the history of Kashubian literature and its traditions, searching out scattered and inaccessible publications, mastering the spelling rules and coping with the dialectal diversity of Kashubian. Therefore enormous importance is attached to the meetings of Kashubian-writing authors which have taken place since 1978 in the rural heart of Kashubia, in Łączyńska Huta. Originally these meetings were held in the hut (the *Chëcz*) of the students' club *Pomorania*; later in a historic country farmhouse belonging to Józef Borzyszkowski (future professor in the University of Gdańsk, Pomeranian politician, president of the ZK-P Association and founder of the Kashubian Institute). The meetings have contributed to the development of a sizeable, generationally and socially diversified group of Kashubian writers, eager to discuss creative writing in Kashubian. The first meeting was dedicated to the new Kashubian literature. New organisers came on board in 1997, and the meetings moved to Wejherowo. Since 2001, a new writers' group has gathered around the annual publication *Zymk*.

These meetings of Kashubian-language authors were in some ways a continuation of the conventions which took place in Kościerzyna from October 1971, on Lech Bądkowski's initiative. The theme of the first gathering was 'Paths of development for Kashubian-Pomeranian literature', presented by Jan Drzeżdżon, himself not only a researcher but also a Kashubian and Polish-language writer. These conferences continued to take place until the end of the 1990s, first under the name 'Meetings of Kashubian-Pomeranian Literati', later shortened to the 'Meetings in Wdzydze'. They became one of the main points of contact for those interested in literary development within Kashubian-Pomeranian circles. Crucially, they were attended not only by Kashubian-language writers, but also authors with no Kashubian or Pomeranian roots, who actively supported regional literature and enriched the artistic production of the region from a new, wider perspective. Together, the 'Meetings in Wdzydze' and the meetings in Łączyńska Huta have created the germ of a Kashubian literary community. It is worth reflecting now on the geography of that community, and considering where its main centres lie and from which parts of Kashubia its members originate.

## The geographical and ideological diversity of the Kashubian literary community

One of the characteristics of Kashubian literature, particularly in the immediate post-war period, has been the disparate location of writers and their milieux. Only since the 1960s (and more definitely in the 1970s) has Gdańsk became an obvious hub, for a number of reasons. Firstly, it is there that the main media publishing Kashubian literature have been located (*Kaszëbë* and *Pomerania*). Secondly, the ZK-P Association has increased in strength as a regional organisation initiating literature-promoting activities. Thirdly, new scholarly circles specialising in literary studies have grown up there, and finally, a number of Kashubian writers such as Roppel, Pestka, Drzeżdżon, Stachurski and Nagel have settled or started work in Gdańsk (or more accurately in the Tricity).[2]

Another lively centre of a developing literary life has been Wejherowo; to a lesser degree also Słupsk, Kościerzyna and Kartuzy; and more recently Puck and Bytów. In Wejherowo, the most famous literary figure has been Trepczyk, but other writers have also been active there, such as Klemens Derc, Paweł Szefka and Stanisław Janke. Significantly, Wejherowo also hosted the journal *Zrzesz*, published there after the war together with its supplement *Chëcz*. In later years, the Museum of Kashubian-Pomeranian Literature and Music in Wejherowo has become not only the main centre for documents on Kashubian writing, but has also organised meetings, conferences, seminars, exhibitions, competitions and other initiatives to support the development of Kashubian literature. Wejherowo has thus developed an interesting literary circle, whose members are, however, mainly Polish-language writers.

In Słupsk, the most eminent author has unquestionably been Anna Łajming, although the activity of the local branch of the Union of Polish Writers has also been important, promoting and reviewing the activities of Jerzy Dąbrowa-Januszewski, himself a journalist and writer, as well as supporting the creation of mise-en-scènes of Kashubian literature in the *Tęcza* Puppet Theatre.

---

2    Tricity – urban agglomeration consisting of the cities Gdańsk, Gdynia and Sopot.

Kościerzyna will go down in the history of post-war Kashubian literature mainly as the location of the 'Meetings in Wdzydze', organised as a joint effort by the municipal authorities and the local branch of the ZK-P Association. Kościerzyna has also been the home of the poet Bożena Szymańska-Ugowska, as well as the late Bolesław Jażdżewski.

Kartuzy's is important mainly for the artistic output of Feliks Marszałkowski, whose greatest contribution was preserving and editing the legacy of Karnowski. The 1990s saw the growing importance in Kartuzy of *Gazeta Kartuska*, in which writers of both the older and the new generation, including Augustyn K. Hirsz, Wanda Kiedrowska, Dorota Ulenberg and Ida Czaja, have published their work.

Another important area for Kashubian literature has been the Hel Peninsula, attracting such writers as Krystyna Muza, Marian Sellin, Antoni Pieper, and above all Augustyn Necel. Northern Kashubia was also home to Drzeżdżon and Dominik, and to a sizeable group of younger-generation authors, including Michał Pieper, the brothers Artur and Łukasz Jabłoński, Piotr Ciskowski and Tomasz Fopke.

The post-immigration territories of western Kashubia[3] have also produced important writers, such as Stefan Fikus of Lębork, Anna Łajming of Słupsk, Marian Majkowski of Ustka, Robert Żmuda-Trzebiatowski of Miastko, and more recently Piotr Dziekanowski of Bytów, who has initiated an original stream of Kashubian-language science-fiction and comic-strip literature.

The case of western Kashubia shows that 'birth-place geography' does not always coincide with the 'geography of creative work'. Some writers have left their home regions and moved to Gdańsk, to other regions of Kashubia or even out of Pomerania altogether. For example, Zygmunt Narski and Jan Rompski have lived in Toruń, Stefan Bieszk in Chełmno, and Bernard Sychta in Pelplin. Marian Jeliński settled in Swarzędz in Greater Poland, and Stanisław Bartelik in Kielce. Literature in Kashubian has also been created in exile, for example by Danuta Charland (née Byczkowska), from Boston, Massachusetts.

---

3    Bytów/Bütow and Lębork/Lauenburg, which belonged to Germany before the Second World War.

The circle of Kashubian writers still welcomes new members of various generations (some even as late debutants). The level of education of these writers is increasing, resulting in the gradual disappearance of the popular folk trend in Kashubian literature. The dominant genre is still poetry – the 1990s saw the highest ever publication of poetry collections. Kashubian literature is a lively phenomenon in constant development, exploring new territory, both in the geographical and thematic sense, with a growing number of writers, various forms of organised literary activity, increasing numbers of publications, and a growing number of translations.

As described earlier, the first translations into Kashubian were made by Florian Ceynowa. The Young-Kashubs translated Goethe's and Eichendorff's works from German, Horace's from Latin, and Krylov's from Russian. Recent years have seen a real blossoming in this area: examples include translations from English (A.A. Milne's *Winnie the Pooh* and fragments of Shakespeare's *Romeo and Juliet* and *Hamlet*) and from Russian, including Krylov's fables and the poetry of Bunin and Pushkin. There have also been translations from Belarusian, Dutch, Frisian, Greek, Italian, Latvian, Serbian, Slovene and Ukrainian. Translations from Polish into Kashubian are particularly interesting, for example Janke's translation of *Bogurodzica*,[4] and editions of Adam Mickiewicz's *Crimean Sonnets*, *The Ode to Youth* and the *Invocation* to *Pan Tadeusz* (the latter has just been translated in its entirety). Other translations of Polish poets and novelists include the works of Jan Kochanowski, Juliusz Słowacki and Henryk Sienkiewicz; Pope John Paul II's *Roman Triptich*; and the popular Polish comic-strip *Kajko i Kokosz* (*Na latowiskù*, 2005).

There are also translations of religious texts. Eugeniusz Gołąbek was the first translator of the New Testament from Polish (*Swięté Pismiona Nowégo Testameńtu*, 1993), and he also translated the *Psalms* (*Knéga Psalmów*, 1999) and put together a lectionary entitled *To je słowò Bòżé* (2007). Franciszek Grucza has translated part of the New Testament from Latin (*Kaszëbskô Biblëjô. Nowi Testament. IV Ewanjelje*, 1992), while Adam Sikora has translated the four *Ewangelie* (2001–9) from Greek. These translations are highly

---

4   *Bogurodzica* or 'The Mother of God' is the oldest Polish religious hymn, composed between the tenth and thirteenth centuries.

valuable and prestigious among the Kashubian community, who are strongly devoted to the Catholic Church and see the introduction of Kashubian into religious services as an important step in upgrading their language status.

Translations have also taken place in the opposite direction, with Kashubian literature being published in foreign translation (mainly in Polish). The first example was Majkowski's novel *Remùs*, and the 1996 translation by Lech Bądkowski initiated a fierce debate about how a dialectal literature (as Kashubian was regarded at that time) can be translated into standard literary Polish. There have also been translations of Kashubian literature into German, including Majkowski's *Remùs* (which also went into French- and English-language editions), and the poetry of Karnowski and Trepczyk. Derdowski's works have also been translated into English, and those of other authors into Belarusian, Russian and Sorbian. All this testifies to the international dimension of Kashubian literature, even if still to a modest degree. Moreover, the translations provide evidence of an external interest in Kashubian literature and its creative and stylistic possibilities.

The criteria which until recently differentiated the various Kashubian literary circles was of course their attitudes to the status of the Kashubian language. After the war, the diversity of opinion on this matter was more or less reduced to two ideological schools, heavily polarised and even conflicted, and expressed by the circles of *Zrzesz* and *Klëka* (including Sędzicki and Sychta). However, a third perspective has evolved in recent years, represented by writers who are not directly involved in any ideological disputes. For these writers, all that counts is the fact of writing in Kashubian, without necessarily making any ethnic or linguistic self-identification. For contemporary Kashubian writers, the dispute has actually lost its raison d'être.

The debate had focused principally on the question of the status of Kashubian: as an independent language or as a dialect (of Polish). In the new socio-political reality after 1945, the vehemence of the debate lessened. For all Kashubian-language writers, the most valuable aspect of the postwar years has simply been the cultivation of Kashubian, whether it is called a dialect, a language, a tongue or a vernacular. However, if we continue to use the criteria which were so important up until 1939, it is possible to divide post-war writers into three categories:

1. Regarding Kashubian as a separate language. Following the views of Ceynowa; the *Zrzesz* circle, e.g. Stefan Bieszk, Franciszek Grucza, Aleksander Labuda, Jan Rompski and Jan Trepczyk (former *Zrzesz*-members); and new writers August Chrabkowski, Augustyn K. Hirsz, Marian Jeliński, Jaromira Labudda and Eugeniusz Pryczkowski.

2. Regarding Kashubian as a dialect. Following the views of Derdowski; the Young-Kashubs (not including Majkowski in his later years); Franciszek Sędzicki; Bernard Sychta; the *Klëka* circle, e.g. Józef Ceynowa, Leon Roppel, Paweł Szefka; and new writers Bolesław Bork, Stefan Fikus, Benedykt Karczewski, Anna Łajming, Marian Majkowski, Alojzy Nagel, Zygmunt Narski, Stanisław Okoń, Jan Piepka, Marian Selin and Jan Szutenberg.

3. Neutral or ambivalent to any categorisation of Kashubian. Includes writers from a number of different generations, e.g. Stanisław Bartelik, Ida Czaja, Henryk Dawidowski, Jan Drzeżdżon, Roman Drzeżdżon, Tomasz Fopke, Henryk Hewelt, Stanisław Janke, Bolesław Jażdżewski, Wanda Kiedrowska, Jerzy Łysk, Stanisław Pestka, Roman Skwiercz, Jerzy Stachurski, Jan Walkusz and Robert Żmuda-Trzebiatowski.

Ascribing a writer to any of these categories is subjective and risky. Besides the writer's own declaration of their attitude to the status of the language, additional arguments can be made based on an author's extra-literary utterances or opinions. But these factors can by no means be decisive, and should lead only to some provisional classification, supplementing other equally fallible means of categorising writers, such as by genre, content or theme.

Affiliation to the third category may perhaps be said to indicate some unaffectedness in the literature itself: the language of writing is simply as it is, and creating literature in a particular language does not exclusively mean manifesting the author's language attitudes. Pre-war Kashubian literature focused disproportionately on the status of the language: worshipping it, creating it, and also teaching it to others. And of course the literary language of contemporary Kashubian writers very often reveals not only general Kashubian characteristics, but also various local dialectal features. It is no accident that the third of the above categories is the largest one and the most diversified: artistically, generically, thematically and generationally.

Orality, literacy and the internet:
the anthropology of Kashubian literature

One of the most striking elements of Kashubian literature is that it could
easily never have been created. The transition of an ethnicity or culture to
the stage of literacy is by no means a common trend, and the majority of
cultures have not worked out written versions of their native language. In
addition, the Kashubs could well have put down permanent roots in an
alien literary tradition such as German or Polish; however, this has never
happened.

The Kashubs' transition from orality to literacy took many years and
was full of turning points, crises and slowdowns. As described earlier, the
beginnings of the Kashubian literary tradition can be found as long ago
as the sixteenth century, and these were strongly connected to a religious
tradition (i.e. Protestantism) which was later to be responsible for the
decline of a considerable part of the Kashubian population. It was only at
the turn of the nineteenth century, thanks to discoveries made by Friedrich
Lorentz, that the Kashubs rediscovered their far older writing tradition,
which at that time was almost extinct.

The transition from orality to literacy, from a verbal culture to a written
one, obviously creates significant changes in communication patterns and
may well result in a new model of culture transmission and accumulation
of values. Who knows how much of the Kashubs' ancient oral cultural
tradition was preserved by the activities undertaken by *Gryf* and its circle?
If it had not been for these initiatives, though, a considerable share of the
Kashubs' cultural legacy could have disappeared totally. The Young-Kashubs
were aware of this, and in the early days of *Gryf*'s publication Jan Karnowski
wrote: 'First of all one should not forget the unwritten Kashubian literature, such as fables and legends. Publication of a collection of fables (in
the dialect) would be of great use. Such an edition would help to protect
not only unique documents of the culture and its own homebred poetry,
being a mirror of ancient traditions, but would also constitute an outright
and valuable contribution to Polish literature in general. A collection of

Kashubian fables should be found in each of our libraries. Such a collection should help us to restore ancient traditions shining from those tales in obscure contours, to restore ancient beliefs of an ancient mythology' (Karnowski 1909: 121). This task was superbly fulfilled by *Gryf*, as attested by the *Bajarz kaszubski* recently published in the series *Biblioteka Kaszubska* (Wejherowo-Gdańsk 2005).

The transition to literacy does not have to signify a decline of the oral tradition, although the latter definitely undergoes changes. One of the most vital elements of Kashubian culture is its verbal element, the culture of the living word, which is kept alive and nourished within the community. For example, the role of the Chmielno-based recitation contest *Rodna mòwa* ('mother tongue') cannot be overestimated. When launched in 1972, it was a modest, almost local initiative, but it soon became one of the biggest cultural events for Kashubian children and young people, gathering several hundred young participants from all over Kashubia. Another event of great interest from the anthropological point of view is the 'Tournament of Folk Story-Tellers', established in 1978. Many story-tellers have found a permanent place in Kashubian literature through this, and have also gained popularity on a local or even regional level in Kashubia. One of the most talented story-tellers has been Jan Piepka, whose one-of-a-kind initiative *Roztrębacze* ('spreaders, blazers') became a para-theatrical presentation of various forms of Kashubian-language creativity. The tournament, organised in Wiele, has helped to preserve this unique Kashubian genre, with new talents still coming to light.

When describing the Kashubian oral culture, it is also important to acknowledge the place of field work which has been carried out by the theatre community. In the 1990s a new form of 'education through theatre' was created by the Parchowo-based theatre *Dialogus*, who were not solely concerned with Kashubian dramatic literature, but also with Kashubian myths, legends and traditions. As its founder wrote: 'the *Dialogus* theatre has taken the path of discovering Kashubian tradition as source of theatrical inspirations, the conviction of the uniqueness of the place having a major influence upon it. To our astonishment, we have discovered that the belief in interference between the world of the deceased and that of the living still exists here – something we knew only from Czesław Miłosz's *Dolina*

*Issy*, from the Kashubian *Remus* or from ethnographical works – such discoveries have inspired the youth and children to further investigations' (Szroeder 2002: 40). These artists from Parchowo have moved away from performing the Kashubian plays already in existence, exploring other cultural layers and creating their own theatre performances, a good example being the spectacle *Drzwi – Misterium kaszubskie*, inspired by traditional pre-funeral-night obsequies. They have also produced a a new interpretation of the most important classical Kashubian literary work *Życie i przygody Remusa*, in the framework of the *Remusonalia* project, which included an outdoor stage adaptation of the novel (2000) in circumstances close to those experienced by the wandering Remus himself.

The transition from an oral to written culture results in the appearance of 'literate' people. Of course literate people had lived in Kashubia in the sixteenth century, but fate was not generous to them. A new stage in the story began with Ceynowa, who deliberately tried to place himself within this 'ancient' tradition: he was an innovator, but at the same time a continuator. During the period when Ceynowa made his attempts to revitalise Kashubian literature, the Kashubs were no longer a preliterate community. They had lived for a couple of hundred years within a tradition of literacy, predominantly in German, but also Latin and Polish. When Ceynowa started writing, school education was obligatory, and when the writings of the Young-Kashubs were published, there was no illiteracy in Kashubia. The Kashubs, and particularly the emerging Kashubian cultural elite, were educated within a multilingual literary tradition, which must inevitably have influenced the reception and formation of Kashubian literature.

Along with literacy, a new aesthetic sensibility develops, which can bring its own problems. For example, there were strong reactions from the Kashubs to Derdowski's epic *O panu Czorlińsczim*, including suspicions of mockery and derision. Another example is the early reaction to the introduction of Kashubian in the Church liturgy – Kashubian was regarded as a language for the farm, not for the Church.

New aesthetic attitudes lead also to debates on language status. In that respect, the old questions has recurred over and over again: the question of the future of Kashubian, its ability to create its own literature and its relations with literature in Polish. Jan Karnowski, in his first lecture for the Circle of Kashubologists, said that the dream of a separate Kashubian literature 'may be called utopian', and that if it was to appear it should remain on a 'dilettantish' level and play the same part 'as the Low German literature in relation to the High German' (Karnowski 1981: 30–1). In his second report, however, Karnowski expressed the hope that an independent Kashubian literature will develop over time and find its own level 'on Parnassus' (Karnowski 1981: 32). Since then Karnowski has systematically proved that Kashubian literature is a specific phenomenon – entirely autonomous and not classifiable solely as a 'folk literature'. He has also shown that, since Kashubian literature has followed its own track and has not become merely a 'dilettantish variety' of Polish folk literature, it has had to cope with three problems. These problems were the dialectal diversification of Kashubian, the lack of a unified and standardised writing system, and the difference in accentuation patterns from the Polish language. As discussed before, these problems (with the exception of the standardisation of the writing system) may well continue to affect the evolution of Kashubian literature.

This literature has been developing in two distinct directions. On the one hand, there has been a noticeable trend for folk literature, rooted in the world of rural or fishing-community tales. However, from its origins, modern Kashubian literature has also attempted to transcend the forms of folk narration typical of many ethnic literatures. This was in many ways a conscious choice made by Ceynowa, and followed by the Young-Kashubs. The journalistic and polemical texts written in Kashubian by Ceynowa were hugely important, exploring the problems of Kashubian-Polish-German relations and examining the very core of Kashubian cultural identity. The stylistic tools and practices used included satire, derision, criticism, polemic, and even attempts at philosophical reflection. It seems that Ceynowa's oeuvre set very high standards for his followers. Nowadays, however, Kashubian writers face entirely new challenges and opportunities.

The first and probably the most important challenge and chance for Kashubian literature is its presence in education. In 1991, the first Kashubian secondary school opened, in Brusy in southern Kashubia. Since then there has been considerable progress in the teaching of Kashubian. According to recent estimates, some 10,000 children in Kashubia learn the language and the literature. Never before in its history has Kashubian had such a multitude of readers, and its literature has never before been present to such a degree in the school curriculum, in textbooks, lesson programmes and recitation and writing competitions. As a result, the first writers have now appeared who learned Kashubian at school. This is a significant change, as in the past all Kashubian authors were without exception self-taught in the Kashubian language.

Besides education, a new factor in the popularisation and dissemination of Kashubian literature is the internet. It is possible to find both classical works and the works of contemporary Kashubian writers online. For example, Majkowski's novel *Remùs* can not only be read but also listened to, and the author's biography is provided alongside. Many Kashubian texts can be found on the website *Kaszëbskô Czëtnica* ('Kashubian reading room'). This site publishes not only older classics (the works of Ceynowa, Karnowski, Heyke, Budzisz and others) and contemporary writings, but also translations from world literature (for example from Agatha Christie, Terry Pratchett and Charles Dickens). What is more, the entire website is in Kashubian.


## Major works of literature in Kashubian


*Florian Ceynowa*

—— 'Kaszebji do Polochów', *Szkoła Narodowa* 1–11 (Chełmno, 1850).
—— *Kile słov wó Kaszebach e jich zem ...* (Kraków, 1850 and Wejherowo, 1985).
—— *Ksążeczka dlô Kaszëbów* (Gdańsk, 1850).
—— *Rozmòwa Pòlôcha z Kaszëbą. Rozmòwa Kaszëbë z Polôchã*, ed. J.Treder (Gdańsk, 2007).
—— *Rozmowa Pólocha z Kaszebą* (Gdańsk, 1850).
—— *Trze rozprave* (Kraków, 1851).

## Hieronim Jarosz Derdowski

—— 'Jasiek z Kniei i Szymek z Wiela w podróży do Ameryki', *Wiarus* (Winona/ Wisconsin, 1889).

—— *Kaszube pod Widnem* (Toruń, 1883, Wejherowo, 1957 and Gdańsk, 1979).

—— *Kaszubes at Vienna. For the 200th Anniversary of the Liberation of Germans and Christianity from the Turkish Yoke in AD 1683.* (*Kaszëbë pod Widnem*), transl. B. Krbechek and S. Frymark (Gdańsk, 2007).

—— *Nórcyk kaszubsci albo koruszk i jedno maca jędrnyj prowde* (Winona/Wisconsin, 1897).

—— *Ò panu Czôrlińsczim, co do Pùcka pò sécë jachôł*, ed. J. Samp, J. Treder & E. Gołąbek (Gdańsk, 2007).

## Poetry

Stanisław Bartelik, *Chòc mie szëmią jiné drzewa* (Gduńsk, 2000).

Stefan Bieszk, *Sonety kaszubskie*, ed. J. Borzyszkowski (Gdańsk, 1975 and 1986).

Agnieszka Browarczyk, *Zimkowë kwiatë* (Gdańsk, 1979).

Józef Ceynowa, *Z Tatczëzné*, ed. J. Samp (Gdańsk, 1982).

Ida Czajinô [Czaja], *Mòjim mùlkã je kam ...* (Kartuzy, 1994).

Jan Drzeżdżon, *Przëszlë do mnie* (Gdańsk, 1994).

Henryk Hewelt, *Nie òdindã bez pòżegnaniô* (Gdynia, 1996).

Leon Heyke, *Dobrogòst i Miłosława* (Gdańsk, 1999).

—— *Kaszëbsczié spiéwë* (Chojnice, 1927, Gdańsk-Wejherowo, 1972, Gdańsk, 1978 and Gdańsk, 1999).

Stanisław Janke, *Do biôłégo rena* (Gduńsk-Wejrowo, 1994).

—— *Ju nie jem Motélnikiem* (Gdańsk 1983).

—— *Kol kuńca wieku* (Gdańsk, 1990).

Jan Karnowski, *Jo bëm leno chcôł ...*, ed. J. Borzyszkowski (Gdańsk, 1986).

—— *Nowotné spiéwë i wiersze*, ed. L. Roppel (Gdynia, 1958).

—— *Nowotné spiéwe* (Poznań, 1910 and Chojnice, 1999).

—— *Wiersze pierwotne*, ed. J. Borzyszkowski (Gdańsk, 1978).

Aleksander Labuda, *Kaszëbsczim jesmë lëdã* (Gdynia, 1996).

Jaromira Labuda, *Korba cëchote* (Gdańsk, 1986).

—— *Słowa òbséwają zemiã* (Gdańsk, 1995).

Jerzy Łysk, *Mój ogródk: wiérzte* (Puck-Gdańsk, 1988).

—— *Sôł miłosc* (Wejherowo, 1994).

Aleksander Majkowski, *Jak w Koscerzenie koscelnygo obrele, abo Pięc kawalerów a jedno jedyno brutka* (Gdańsk, 1899 and Gduńsk-Kòscérzna, 2008).
——*Pielgrzymka wejherowska* (Gdynia, 1992).
——*Spiewe i frantówci* (Poznań, 1905).
——*Wiersze i frantówci* ed. L. Roppel (Gdynia, 1957).
Krystyna Muza, *Mamota*, ed. B. Fac (Gdańsk, 1981).
Alojzy Nagel, *Astrë: wiersze* (Gdańsk, 1975).
——*Cassubia fidelis: poezje* ed. L. Hoppel (Gdańsk-Wejherowo, 1971).
——*Cëdowny wzérnik* (Gdańsk, 1979).
——*Nie spij pusti nocë* (Gdańsk, 1997).
——*Otemknij dwiérze* (Pelplin, 1992).
——*Procem nocë* (Gdańsk, 1970).
Stanisław Okoń, *Za lasã mòrzé* (Krokowa-Gdańsk, 1998).
Stanisław Pestka, *Południca* (Gdańsk, 1976).
——*Wieczórny widnik* (Gdańsk, 2002).
—— *Wizrë ë duchë* (Gdańsk, 1986).
Jan Piepka, *Kamiszczi* (Gdańsk, 1983).
——*Spiewa i lza* (Gdańsk, 2002).
——*Stojedna chwilka: poezje, satyry i obrazek sceniczny* (Gdynia, 1961).
Eugeniusz Prëczkòwsczi [Pryczkowski], *Na jimiã Bòsczé* (Gdańsk, 2000).
Jan Rompski, *Pòmión zwônów* (Gdańsk-Sztutowo, 1970).
——*Wiérzte*, ed. E. Puzdrowski (Gdańsk, 1980).
Marian Selin, *Niech wiater niese pieśń* (Gdynia, 1996).
Franciszek Sędzicki, *Jestem Kaszubą*, ed. L. Roppel (Warszawa, 1956).
Jerzy Stachurski, *Té pokazëją na mnie*, ed. B. Fac (Gdańsk, 1980).
Bożena Szymańska, *Zdebło na swiat cësnãté* (Gdynia-Wejherowo, 1996).
Jan Trepczyk, *Lecë choranko* (Gdańsk-Wejherowo, 1980).
——*Moja stegna*, ed. W. Kiedrowski (Gdańsk, 1970).
——*Odecknienie* (Gdańsk, 1977).
Jan Walkusz, *Jantarowi pôcerz* (Gdynia, 1991).
——*Kańta nôdzeë* (Gdańsk, 1981).
Robert Żmuda-Trzebiatowski, *Òdłómczi* (Gdynia, 1997).


## Drama

Ida Czajinô [Czaja], *Obrôzczi na binã* (Gdańsk, 2005).
Jan Karnowski, *Utwory sceniczne*, ed. K. Ostrowski (Gdańsk, 1970).
Anna Łajming, *Gdzie jest Balbina?* (Gdańsk, 1974).
——*Szczescé: obrazek sceniczny* (Gdańsk, 1959).

Aleksander Majkowski, *Strachë i zrękovjinë: frantówka w trzech aktach*, ed. D. Majkowska (Gdańsk, 1976).
Jan Rompski, *Jô chcę na swiat: komédia w trzech aktach* (Gdańsk, 1987).
Bernard Sychta, *Dramaty*, vol.1: *Dramaty obyczajowe*, ed. J. Treder and J. Walkusz (Gdańsk, 2008).
——*Gwiôzdka ze Gduńska* (Gdańsk, 1988).
——*Ostatniô gwiôzdka Mestwina* (Gdańsk, 1985).
Paweł Szefka, *Dëgusë* (Gdańsk, 1961).
——*Gwiżdże* (Gdańsk, 1957).
——*Sobótka* (Gdańsk, 1958).
——*Wrëjorze jidą* (Gdańsk, 1981).
——*Wyzwoliny kosiarza* (Gdańsk, 1979).


*Prose*


Józef Bruski, *Gadki Józefa Bruskiego* (Gdańsk, 1975).
——*Gôdczi Józwa Brusczié gò. Gadki Józefa Bruskiego* (Chojnice, 2008).
Alojzy Budzysz [Budzisz], *Zemja kaszëbskô; utwory wybrane*, ed. J. Drzeżdżon (Gdańsk, 1982).
——*Dokôzë* (Gdiniô, 2004).
Józef Ceynowa, *Bursztinowé serce* (Puck, 1981).
——*Urënamle: powiôstci z komudnëch lat* (Gdańsk, 1982).
Henryk Dawidowsczi [Dawidowski], *Z Kaszëbama o Kaszëbach. Opowiadania* (Gdańsk, 2007).
Augustyn Dominik, *Gawędy kaszubskie* (Warszawa, 1986).
——*Pokąd bądą bôtë...* (Krokowa-Puck, 1992).
——*Tóna z pustk* (Puck 1983).
Jan Drzeżdżon, *Dzwónnik* (Gdańsk, 1979).
——*Kôl biélawë* (Gdynia 1991).
——*Na niwach* (Gdańsk, 1990).
——*Sklaniane pôcorë* (Gdańsk, 1974).
——*Twarz Smętka* (Gdańsk, 1993).
——*Wniedzelni wieczór* (Gdańsk, 1974).
Stefan Fikus, *Pojmeńczicë* (Gdańsk, 1981).
Eugeniusz Gołąbek, *Pielgrzimkowanié* (Gdańsk, 1982).
Stanisław Janke, *Łiskawica* (Gdańsk 1988).
——*Psë* (Gdynia, 1991).
Bolesław Jażdżewski, *Jôrmark w Bòrzëszkach*, ed. E. Gołąbek (Gdańsk, 2003).
——*Wspomnienia kaszubskiego gbura* (Gdańsk, 1999).

Jan Karnowski, *Sowizdrzôł u Krëbanów*, ed. J. Borzyszkowski (Gdańsk, 1983).
Aleksander Labuda, *Guczów Mack gôdô: chochołk* (Gdańsk, 1979).
——*Guczów Mack gôdô: kąsk do smjechu* (Gdańsk-Wejherowo, 1971).
——*Guczów Mack gôdô: kuku* (Gdańsk, 1974).
——*Guczów Mack gôdô: zupa z Kuszków* (Gdańsk, 1971).
Anna Łajming, *Bajki* (Gdańsk, 1996).
——*Miód i mleko. Opowiastki kaszubskie* (Gdańsk, 1971).
——*Symbol szczęścia* (Gdańsk, 1973).
Aleksander Majkowski, *Life and Adventures of Remus*, transl. B. Krbechek and K. Gawlik-Luiken (Gdańsk, 2008).
——*Žëcé i przigodë Remusa* (Gdańsk, 1974–1976 & 1995).
——*Życie i przygody Remusa*, transl. L. Bądkowski (Gdańsk, 1964).
Marian Miotk, *Swiętim turę starków: zbiérk leżnoscowëch kôzaniów*, ed. J. and J. Treder (Gdańsk, 1991).
——*Séw Bòżégò Słowa na niwie kaszëbsczich serc*, ed. J. Treder (Gdańsk, 2008).
Jon Natrzecy [Piotr Dziekanowski], *Nalazłé w Bëtowie* (Bëtowò, 2008).
Leon Roppel, *Orzechë do ucechë abo pół tësąca kasëbskich zagôdk* (Gdańsk, 1956).
Franciszek Sędzicki, *Baśnie kaszubskie* (Warszawa, 1957).
Jan Szutenberg, *Tabaka dlô Kaszëbów* (Wejrowò, 2005).

## Anthologies

Józef Borzyszkowski (ed.), *Bajarz kaszubski. Bajki z 'Gryfa' (1908–1912)* (Wejherowo-Gdańsk, 2005).
Roman Drzeżdżon and Grzegorz J. Schramke (eds), *Dzëczé gäsë. Antologiô kaszëbsczi pòezji* (Gdynia, 2004).
Stanisław Janke and Jerzy Treder (eds), *Kaszëbskô nôtëra* (Wejrowò-Gduńsk, 2001).
*Modra struna. Antologia poezji kaszubskiej* (Gdańsk, 1973).
Ferdinand Neureiter, *Kaschubische Anthologie* (München, 1973).
Antón and Aleks Peplińscë [Pepliński], *Antologia lëteracczich dokôzów* (Sierakowice, 2009).
Barbara Pisarek and Jan Lipuski (eds), *Domôcô Bina. Dzewiãc dramów do jigrë* (Wejrowò-Gduńsk, 2006).
Eugeniusz and Elżbieta Prëczkòwscze [Pryczkowski] (eds), *Mësla dzecka. Antologiô wiérztów dlô dzôtków i młodzizn* (Banino, 2001).
Eugeniusz Prëczkòwsczi (ed.), *Dërchôj krôlewiónkò. Antologia dzysdniowi prozë kaszëbsczi* (Gdynia, 1996).

Leon Roppel (ed.), *Ma jesma od morza: poezja i proza kaszubska o morzu* (Gdańsk, 1961).

———*Wybór współczesnej poezji kaszubskiej* (Gdańsk, 1967).

Leon Roppel and Jan Piepka, *Nasze stronë: wybór wierszy i opowiadań kaszubskich* (Warszawa, 1955).

*Rost na kamienie. Antologia prozy kaszubskiej* (Gdańsk-Wejherowo, 2008).

Jerzy Samp (ed.), *Poezja rodnej mowy* (Gdańsk, 1985).

———*Zaklęta stegna: bajki kaszubskie* (Gdańsk, 1985).

Jerzy Treder (ed.), *Kaszëbsczé dzeje ë dzysészé żëcé. Dokôzë kaszëbsczi prozë* (Wejherowo, 2004).

Jan Walkusz and Edmund Puzdrowski (eds), *Swięti dzél dësze: antologia kaszubskiej poezji religijnej* (Pelplin, 1981).

*ZYMK. Znudzeni Młodych Ùtwórców Kaszëbsczëch* 1–7 (2001–8).

## Song Collections

Witosława Frankowska and Eugeniusz Prëczkòwsczi (eds), *Tobie Boże chwała. Kaszubskie pieśni katolickie* (Luzino, 1993).

Władysław Kirstein (ed.), *Kaszëbsczié kolęde ë godowé spiewë* (Gdańsk, 1982).

Władysław Kirstein and Leon Roppel, *Pieśni z Kaszub* (Gdańsk, 1958).

Jan Patock, *Kopa szętopórk* (Gdynia, 1936).

Antoni Peplinski, *Kaszëbë wołają nas: kaszëbsczié piesniczczi* (Gdańsk, 1988).

Eugeniusz Prëczkòwsczi (ed.), *Dlô Was Panie. Kòscelny spiéwnik* (Gdańsk, 2006).

Leon Roppel, *Z piesnią do cebie jidzema mateńko* (Gdańsk, 1988).

Antoni Tomaczkowski, *Wybór pieśni* (Gdańsk, 1981).

TOMASZ WICHERKIEWICZ

# Language Policy and the Sociolinguistics of Kashubian

The current sociolinguistic and socio-political position of Kashubian is the result of both the internal linguistic history of the community and external instruments of administrative language policy. The debate about the linguistic status of Kashubian initiated by the publication of Stefan Ramułt's dictionary in 1983 has irrevocably determined the objective and subjective position of the language, on a regional, national and international scale. Declarations made on this subject by successive organisations of nineteenth- and twentieth-century Kashubian activists have already been presented in detail in earlier chapters.

Obracht-Prondzyński (2007c: 16) has stated that:

> The Kashubian ethos consists of such values as language, religion [...], family, origin (genealogy), territory [...], as well as correlated characteristics of the self-stereotype (piety, diligence, persistence, patriotism, etc). Obviously, that system of values has undergone constant changes deriving from global processes and transformations started after 1989, their effect being a weakening of the dominant cultural canon under the conditions of a 'disclosed multiculturalism' and progressing pluralisation, changes in the state policy towards minorities, social acceptance for such aspirations, widespread tolerance and openness of the society, and particularly its elites, etc. Still, the main question remains that of the Kashubian language: not only its condition and use extent, language attitudes of the Kashubs themselves (quite diverse – from profound affirmation to total rejection), but also its prestige and social status.

The same factors have been cited by Synak (2001: 295): 'The Kashubs belong to the ethnic communities whose cultural axis or core value is constituted by their language. The sociological research indicates that the Kashubian identity depends extremely strongly on the Kashubian language, the latter being an important structural element of the definition of Kashubianness'.

In a manifesto on language policy and culture known as the *Strategy for the Protection and Development of the Kashubian Language and Culture* (2006), the Kashubs themselves have declared that 'the Kashubian language constitutes the foundation of the identity of the Kashubs. Fundamental [...] is the conviction that the language and culture constitute an important contribution to the common cultural heritage and avert alienation and uprooting when confronted with globalisation and commercialisation processes. The *Strategy* is based on the confidence that the essential way of preserving one's own identity is the opening to new trends and not separation'.

The debate on the 'Kashubian issue', focusing on the position of Kashubian as a linguistic and cultural complex, for many years constituted the main axis of dynamic development of and within the Kashubian community. The characteristics of this process, and their impact on various aspects of Kashubian linguistic history since the beginnings of the Kashubian movement, are discussed in detail elsewhere in this book. In this chapter, the pivotal role of recent developments in the sociolinguistic situation and the development of modern language policy will be surveyed.

A totally new episode in the modern debate on the 'Kashubian issue', regarded by many Kashubian activists as a proclamation of linguists' new perspective concerning the status of Kashubian, was an article by Alfred F. Majewicz which appeared in a little-read publication, a Festschrift dedicated to the Polish linguist Adam Heinz. Majewicz wrote: 'Labuda's dictionary (1982) is [...] something very much-desired by Kashubian writers or those identifying themselves with the Kashubian tongue as well as to collectors of Cassubiana and as a manifestation of the praiseworthy and prolific, despite multiplying obstacles, activity of the Kashubian-Pomeranian Society (ZKP), but also as an argument in the aged debate on whether Kashubian is a dialect of Polish or if it deserves the status of a separate language. This lamentable and unproductive debate was revived recently after the appearance of a paper on Kashubian and in Kashubian by a very prominent Kashubian poet, writer, singer and story-teller Jan Trepczyk[1] in which its author spoke in favour of the separateness of Kashubian from Polish'.

1    Trepczyk 1980.

In his monumental 1989 handbook on the languages of the world and their classifications, Majewicz cites the debate on the status of Kashubian amongst Polish linguists as an example of 'quite an unserious and futile discussion [...] lasting for a century and still emotionally involving a great number of parties concerned', despite the fact that a majority of international specialists classified Kashubian as separate language, while 'the specialists in dialectology and Kashubian studies in Poland claim to have proven the dialectal status of Kashubian in relation to the Polish language' (Majewicz 1989: 13–14). The case of Kashubian was skilfully and efficiently used by Majewicz to illustrate the decisive role of extra-linguistic factors when determining the status of two closely related ethnolects, as a necessary completion to such criteria as the concept of language change dynamics or mutual intelligibility. The list of those extra-linguistic factors presented in the 1986 paper and later restated, both in his 1989 book and in various public debates concerning the status of Kashubian, included:

- the national and linguistic self-identification of a community;
- the language policy of state institutions (e.g. forcible and artificial treatment as a language minority, denial of status as a language minority, assistance and encouragement by the state, the pretence that linguistic minorities do not exist despite clear evidence, etc);
- the existence or otherwise of a literary form of an ethnolect;
- the existence or otherwise of some literary tradition;
- the existence or otherwise of an orthographic standard;
- the degree of intelligibility in relation to other ethnolects;
- the degree of applicability of a given ethnolect to the expression of ideas from beyond everyday topics;
- the need for and reasonable probability of compiling bilingual dictionaries, if not already in existence;
- the existence or otherwise of a Bible translation in a given ethnolect
  (Majewicz 1986: 97)

Majewicz's handbook explicitly listed Kashubian as a separate language and placed it, together with (extinct) Slovincian, within the West Slavonic sub-family (Majewicz 1989: 35).

Majewicz's publications and lectures, delivered within various Kashubian fora in the 1980s and 1990s, brought him enormous popularity in

Kashubian circles. In 1990 the ZK-P awarded him a prestigious medal named after Bernard Chrzanowski (*Poruszył Wiatr od Morza* – 'He Who Made the Sea Breeze to Blow').[2]Majewicz's arguments were very favourably received by young activists of the Kashubian movement, such as the members of the Students' Club 'Pomorania', who entered public life in or shortly after 1989. Political and social developments of that period induced the ZK-P to move the public debate on the status of Kashubian to a more advanced level. In 1991, the association, together with the Provincial Centre of Culture, the University of Gdańsk and the journal *Pomerania*, convened a symposium in Gdańsk to acquaint both academics and the general public with recent and projected actions concerning the situation of Kashubian. The invitation to the meeting declared openly:

> The Kashubian community has every reason to believe that the scholarly dispute [on language status] cannot influence practical and social solutions, therefore we provide the following established facts to prove the vitality of Kashubian:

> – the lessons *Gôdomë po kaszëbsku* ['we speak Kashubian'] in the magazine *Rôdno Zemia* ['native land'] broadcast every second Sunday on the second channel of Polish TV;
> – a Kashubian language course planned at the University of Gdańsk;
> – endeavours to create Kashubian schools (the [planned] Kashubian Secondary School)[3] and to introduce lessons of Kashubian in primary schools, as an element of the current regionalisation of education;

2    The winners of this high honour also include: Janusz Pasierb (priest, writer and historian), Ferdinand Neureiter (Austrian compiler of an extensive outline of Kashubian literature), Günter Grass (German writer with Kashubian roots, winner of the Nobel Prize for Literature), Gerard Labuda (professor of mediaeval history, specialist in the history of the Kashubs), Edward Pałłasz (composer), Hans-Georg Siegler (German historian), Hanna Popowska-Taborska (leading dialectologist and co-author of an etymological dictionary of Kashubian), Jerzy Ślaski (journalist and writer), Marian Kubera (filmmaker), Bogdan Wachowiak (historian and writer), Dietmar Albrecht (president of the Ostsee Akademie in Lübeck), Shirley Mask Connolly (translator of Kashubian literature), Nelly-Marianne Wannow (German writer and populariser of Gdańsk and Kashubia), Danuta Stenka (popular actress) and Wiesław Boryś (co-author of an etymological dictionary of Kashubian).

3    To be founded shortly afterwards in Brusy, in southern Kashubia.

- the organisation of a seminar focused on improving Kashubian orthography;
- publishing materials aimed at language standardisation;
- church services in Kashubian;
- a Kashubian version of the Bible;
- competitions of folk storytellers in Wiele;
- recitation competitions for children and youth in Chmielno;
- literary seminars for Kashubian writers.

However, as far as scholarly authorities are concerned, we do not expect to settle hereby the dispute on Kashubian as language or dialect ...
(Majewicz and Wicherkiewicz 2001: 83).

## State language policy and the position of Kashubian

Since the beginning of public discussion on the question of the linguistic status of Kashubian, the debate has been directly influenced by the overall guidelines of state language policy. As the situation of the Kashubs and their language in the German state (before 1918 and during the German occupation 1939–45), as well as in the Polish state between the two world wars, is comprehensively discussed in other chapters of this book, this section focuses on the place occupied by the Kashubs and their ethnolect in the general language policy exercised by the Polish state after the Second World War.

The policy of Poland's Communist authorities in relation to (national) minority languages has been recorded in detail by Majewicz and Wicherkiewicz (1990, 1998). To briefly sum up the issue, it should be stated that the recognition of existing minorities was of a marginal and a selective nature. After the shift of political borders to the west, and a dramatic change in its ethnic composition, Poland was proclaimed a (quasi-) mono-ethnic (and as a result a monolingual) state. Official ethnic and language policy was characterised by intermittent periods of limited concessions granted to state-controlled organisations within some minorities (especially the so-called 'socio-cultural societies' established after the thaw of 1956 for Belarusians,

Czechs and Slovaks, Jews, Lithuanians, Roma, Russians and Ukrainians). For these organisations, some forms of education were provided and press organisations were created. The public presence of the minorities and their languages, however, was limited to aspects of folklore. The very existence of other groups, such as Germans or Rusyn Lemkos (accepted exclusively as a sub-group of Ukrainians), was either ignored or overtly denied. The Tatars, Karaims and Armenians were treated principally as exotic religious minorities (Łodziński 2007: 152–3).

The transformations in the system which began in 1989 brought an immediate change in state policy towards minority issues, followed by prevailingly positive societal support expressed in public debates on various levels and a dramatic increase of interest in problems of ethnicity and minorities. The previously recognised groups (Belarusians, Czechs and Slovaks, Jews, Lithuanians, Roma, Russians and Ukrainians, as well as Tatars, Karaims and Armenians) gradually adapted their structures to the new conditions, and started reformulating their (language) policies, even if initially only to a very limited extent. More difficulty was experienced in the process of official and public recognition of the German and Rusyn Lemko minorities, although the existence and official representative structures of both groups were eventually acknowledged at the beginning of the 1990s. At the same time, a new episode in the debate on the status of the Kashubs and their language emerged.

The newly-elected Parliament (in its new bicameral structure) as early as 1990 established a special Committee for National and Ethnic Minorities, whose primary task was to prepare an act which would normalise the situation of and the policy towards ethnically non-Polish citizens of Poland. The preparations, however, were interrupted and resumed several times. It was to take as long as fifteen years before the new Act entered into force in 2005–6.

However, even if detailed regulations concerning the status and position of regional and minority languages were still at the preparation stage, a vital change in official language policy on the highest level was pronounced in the 1997 Constitution of the Republic of Poland, which contained two articles that pertained directly to minority rights:

Art.27 – Polish shall be the official language of the Republic of Poland. This provision shall not infringe upon national minority rights resulting from ratified international agreements.

Art.35 –

1. The Republic of Poland shall ensure Polish citizens belonging to national or ethnic minorities the freedom to maintain and develop their own language, to maintain customs and traditions, and to develop their own culture.

2. National and ethnic minorities shall have the right to establish educational and cultural institutions and organisations designed to protect their religious identity, as well as to participate in the resolution of matters connected with their cultural identity.

The 1999 Act on the Polish Language provided for the possibility of introducing a minority language as auxiliary in those areas with a 'considerable share of the non-Polish population, where minority languages could be used in bilingual place names, in personal names and in local administration'. That regulation was to be extended and specified by the Act on national and ethnic minorities, then still under preparation.

The 1992 Law on Radio and Television Broadcasting contained a general obligation to meet the needs of national and ethnic minorities in public media.

The Act on the System of Education, passed in 1991, granted pupils the right to maintain their national, ethnic, religious and linguistic identity, and in particular to be given classes in/on their mother tongue, as well as their history and culture. In 1992 it was followed by the 'Decree of the Minister of National Education and Sports on conditions and methods for enabling pupils belonging to national minorities and ethnic groups to maintain their national, ethnic, linguistic or religious identity'. The decree was amended in 2002, although the amended version was perceived by minority organisations as being comparatively regressive. It contained no further provisions for pre-school education of/in minority languages, no longer made the teaching of the mother tongue in schools for minorities compulsory, and included the expression 'country of origin' in many regulations (such as the teaching of history and geography). It was argued that this expression could imply that the minority groups concerned were immigrant communities. Most of the regulations referred explicitly or implicitly to national and ethnic minorities. The concept of 'minority', although used quite extensively in pre-2005 legal regulations, was not defined adequately and remained ambiguous. However, most authorities at any level had quite an inclusive approach, and the regulations were applied to all recognised minorities and minority languages, including Kashubian.

At the same time a discussion ensued – both at the national level and within Kashubian organisations – on how the Kashubs as a community and the Kashubian language should be officially classified and to what extent they should exercise their rights as minority, including their linguistic rights.

Under Communist rule, the Kashubs were referred to as an 'ethnographic group'. The term included regional groupings within the Polish nation, such as Kashubs, Silesians, Gorals (highlanders), Mazurians, Warmians or Kurpie, distinguished by some specific features of their local (folk) culture. It was used more by ethnographers and regional organisations than by the official administration. In terms of official linguistic classification, the 'ethnographic groups' were attributed to dialects (Kashubian, Silesian) or even sub-dialects of Polish (e.g. Podhalean, Spisz or Orawa varieties of the Lesser Polish dialect; Mazurian, Warmian or Kurpian varieties of the Mazovian dialect). After the Second World War, when the so-called 'Recovered Lands'[4] were incorporated into the Polish state, a special term 'autochthons' was coined for the regional groups of allegedly Polish nationality who – as German citizens – had inhabited the areas before the war. This included Kashubs (and Pomeranians), Silesians, Mazurians and Warmians.

As described in other parts of this book, the situation of the Kashubs as a regional, ethnographic or 'autochthonous' group between 1945 and 1989 oscillated between obvious discrimination and increasing recognition for their regional identity (Obracht-Prondzyński 2002a). In terms of language policy, the use of Kashubian was limited to the domains of folklore and folk literature. Any attempts to allow some use of the 'dialect' during Polish language classes were severely contested. Official censorship relentlessly suppressed any public presence of the term 'Kashubian

4    The former German regions of Further Pomerania with Stettin, New March, Silesia, East Prussia and the Free City of Danzig.

language' (*język kaszubski / kaszëbsczi jãzek*); instead, a linguistically awk-ward expression *kaszubska mowa* ('Kashubian speech') was coined and commonly used, together with the more neutral *kaszubszczyzna / kaszë-bizna* ('Kashubianness'). Nevertheless, the discussion on the maintenance and standardisation of Kashubian continued and, even if not pronounced explicitly, constituted one of the main fields of activity within the ZK-P. In the 1970s and 1980s, the foundations for the development of a modern (literary) standard of Kashubian were laid, including a popular outline of Kashubian grammar (Breza and Treder 1975),[5] the principles of Kashubian orthography (Breza and Treder 1981), and a bilingual Kashubian-Polish and Polish-Kashubian dictionary (Labuda 1982). Even if marginalised, and perceived mostly as a matter of folklore, Kashubian did not undergo the processes of linguistic disintegration typical of all other regiolects, dialects and sub-dialects in Poland, with the exceptions of Podhalean and Silesian (Hentschel 2000, 2003).

Together with the political and social transformations of 1989, the con-cept of '(national) minority' entered public discourse in Poland, soon gain-ing a generalised sense of referring to the German minority. The Kashubs and their representatives, however, immediately made a decision not to use or even refer to the term 'minority' in any Kashubian context. Hence, the hitherto strictly specialist concept of an 'ethnic group' (which had only used by Polish ethnologists since the 1980s) found its way into mass media and common usage, as well as into political and legal vocabulary, such as the name of the Parliamentary Committee for National and Ethnic Minorities or the title of the Act on National and Ethnic Minorities. The adjective 'ethnic' was used within the Kashubian movement as eagerly as the popular 'regional', the latter becoming particularly prevalent in the context of planned local government reorganisation, which was implemented in 1999. Under this project of decentralisation and regionalisation the entire ethno-linguistic territory of Kashubia was contained within one territorial unit – the newly established Province of Pomerania (*województwo pomor-skie*). Attempts to name the Province 'Kashubian-Pomerania', explored in the next chapter, have so far proved futile.

5    Re-edited and republished in 1984.

As stated above, the authorities included Kashubian in all new legislation concerning minority languages adopted in the 1990s and 2000s, such as the 'Decree of the Minister of National Education and Sports on conditions and methods for enabling pupils belonging to national minorities and ethnic groups to maintain their national, ethnic, linguistic or religious identity', crucial to the organisation of foundations for teaching Kashubian in the schools of Pomerania, and the 'Framework Convention for the Protection of National Minorities', signed by Poland in 1995 and ratified in 2000. The Convention entered into force in April 2001 and included provisions for the national minorities Belarusians, Czechs, Karaims, Lithuanians, Lemkos, Germans, Armenians, Roma, Russians, Slovaks, Tatars, Ukrainians and Jews, as well as a special reference to the Kashubs as an 'ethnic group in the Province of Pomerania, who cultivate their regional traditions and use a language different from the Polish language; their number being estimated at 350–500,000. The provisions of the Convention are extended towards that group in the area of language rights'. Monitoring reports concerning the implementation of the Convention were published in 2002 and in 2007. The 2007 report cited the figure of 52,665 persons 'using the regional language in their home interactions'. This figure emerged as result of two important events:

- The National Population Census conducted in 2002 (results published in 2003)[6]
- The Act on National and Ethnic Minorities and the Regional Language, passed by the Polish Parliament in January 2005.

The 2002 Census was the first since 1931 to include questions concerning nationality and language. Preparations for the Census, its methodology and its organisation ignited much criticism from minority groups and institutions (Kamusella 2009: 637), but its results were regarded as binding by the authorities, as were the later provisions of the Act on National and Ethnic Minorities and the Regional Language. The Census included two questions:

6    The next population census has just started (2011).

   i. What nationality do you consider yourself?
   ii. What language do you use most often in a home context?

According to the Census, 444,590 Polish citizens belonged to a national minority – a number which differed considerably from estimates made earlier by scholars and minority organisations. It was very difficult to give a clear answer to the question about which ethnic or national group a person belonged to. 770,000 participants did not declare their nationality at all.

   The data obtained through the Census included the following figures:

|  | i. nationality | ii. language |
|---|---|---|
| German | 152,897 | 204,573 |
| Silesian[1] | 173,153 | 56,643 |
| Kashubian | 5,062 | 52,665 |
| Belarusian | 48,737 | 40,650 |
| Ukrainian | 30,957 | 22,698 |
| Roma(ni) | 12,855 | 15,788 |
| Russian | 6,103 | 15,299 |
| Lithuanian | 5,846 | 5,838 |
| Lemko | 5,863 | 5,627 |
| Czech | 831 | 1,482 |
| Slovak | 2,001 | 921 |
| Armenian | 1,082 | 872 |
| Jewish | 1,133 | Hebrew: 225 |
| Tatar | 495 | – |
| Karaim | 45 | – |

Table 1 Results of the 2002 National Population Census
[1] Neither the Silesian nationality nor the separate Silesian language have been recognised by the authorities (Kamusella 2009: 637).

The Census constituted the first ever opportunity – as well as an obligation – for the citizens of Poland to officially declare what they perceived to be their nationality and home language. In the case of the Kashubs, the figure of $c.$ 5,000 persons who declared themselves to be of Kashubian nationality merits further research, especially in comparison with the results of the next National Population Census planned for 2012.

Taking into consideration all the reservations concerning the Census guidelines and methodology, the number of 52,665 persons using Kashubian in a home context is the first official figure obtained since the beginning of research on the Kashubs and their language. Earlier numbers quoted in various sources varied from $c.$ 70,000 Kashubs as quoted by Prussian statistics in the 1900s to the figure of $c.$ 500,000 given by Polish encyclopaedias in the 2000s. A complete register of the Kashubian population figures given by various different sources can be found in Porębska (2006: 56). Possibly the most statistically reliable are the results of various sociological research projects carried out:

– in the 1980s: 332,044 Kashubs and 184,117 half-Kashubs (Latoszek 1990);
– in the 1990s: 250 to 300,000 (Synak 2001);
– in the 2000s: 390,509 Kashubs and 176,228 half-Kashubs (Mordawski 2005).

The figures obtained during the 2002 Census therefore surprised analysts, researchers, and above all minority activists and organisations. A full-scale analysis of the quantitative aspects of language use in Kashubia should probably wait until the next Population Census in 2012, whose methodology will not generate so many doubts among sociologists, politicians, regional activists and the respondents themselves.

The results of the 2002 Census were used as a basis for for some regulations within the Act on National and Ethnic Minorities and the Regional Language, adopted by the two chambers of the Polish Parliament in January 2005. The Act introduced Kashubian to the Polish legal system as an officially recognised regional language – 'The Kashubian language shall be a regional language[7] within the meaning of the Act' (Art.19, para.2). There was also an explanatory introduction in paragraph 1 excerpted from Article 1 of the European Charter for Regional or Minority Languages: 'For the purposes of this Act and in accordance with the European Charter [...] "a regional language" shall mean a language that is: (1) traditionally used within a given territory of a State by nationals of that State who form a group numerically smaller than the rest of the State's population; and (2) different from the official language(s) of that State'. It is immediately noticeable that the authors of the Act did not quote the relevant article of the Charter in their own wording, which uses the term 'regional or minority language(s)' both in the quoted passage, and throughout the rest of the Act, without any distinction between the two types of language.

The 2005 Act also recognised nine national minorities: Belarusians, Czechs, Lithuanians, Germans, Armenians, Russians, Slovaks, Ukrainians and Jews (Art.2, para.2). The Act defined them as:

... groups of Polish citizens who jointly fulfil the following conditions:

1. are numerically smaller than the rest of the population of Poland;
2. significantly differ from the remaining citizens in their language, culture or tradition;
3. strive to preserve their language, culture or tradition;
4. are aware of their own historical, national community, and are oriented towards its expression and protection;
5. their ancestors have been living on the present territory of the Republic of Poland for at least 100 years;
6. identify themselves with a nation organised in their own state.
(Art.2, para.1)

---

7    The absence of an (in)definite article in the Polish language may be of crucial importance here for the other language communities who would apply in the future for the status of a regional language. The official Polish text of Article 19, paragraph 2, reads: 'Językiem regionalnym w rozumieniu ustawy jest język kaszubski'. The English quotation here is taken from the official website of the Ministry of the Interior and Administration, <http://www.mswia.gov.pl/portal.php?serwis=planddzial=353and id=4392andsid=a52d5ee252af087abbddb45b9eecof4a>, accessed on 3 January 2010. The legislative and executive bodies (i.e. the Parliament and the Ministry) definitely intended to limit the use of the term 'regional language' solely to Kashubian, although applications to obtain the same status have been already articulated by the Silesians and Wilamowiceans (Kamusella 2009: 951 and 988).

In addition, four groups were granted the status of ethnic minority: the Karaims, Lemko, Roma and Tatar (Art.2, para.4). Their definition (Art.2, para.3) repeats points 1 to 5 of the previous definition, but with different wording in point 6: 'does not identify themselves with a nation organised in their own state'. This artificial terminological division between 'national' and 'ethnic' minorities – where there is actually no distinction in the civil rights granted by the Act to both groups of minorities – has evoked much debate and criticism in legal circles, and further reservations regarding the concept of 'regional language' itself. Virtually all the regulations provided by the Act (including language rights) refer in the same manner to all three groups: national and ethnic minorities, and 'persons using the regional language'.

Article 20 provides details concerning the latter group:

1. The right of the persons using the language referred to in Art.19, to learn or to be instructed in this language, shall be exercised in accordance with the principles and under the procedure specified in the Act referred to in Art.17.
2. Public authorities shall be obligated to take appropriate measures in order to support the activity aimed at preservation and development of the language referred to in Art.19. The provisions of Art. 18 paras 2, 3 and 5 shall apply accordingly.
3. The measures referred to in para.2 may also include financial means transferred from the budget of a local government unit to organisations or institutions performing tasks conducive to the preservation and development of the language referred to in Art. 19.

Article 19, paragraph 2, states that:

The Art. 7–15 shall apply accordingly, provided that 'a number of municipality residents', as referred to in Art.14, should be understood as a number of persons using the regional language, established as a result of the latest national census.

The aforementioned Article 17 regulates education rights:

The exercise of the right of persons belonging to the minority to learn or to be instructed in the minority language, and also the right of these persons to education in the minority history and culture shall be performed in accordance with the principles and procedures specified in the Act of [...] 1991 on the system of education.

Part of Article 18 concerns the obligation of public authorities to take appropriate financial measures in order to support, through subsidies and grants, activities aimed at protecting, maintaining and developing the cultural identity of minorities, including:

> (3) the publication of books, journals, periodicals and leaflets in minority languages or in the Polish language in printed form or by use of other video and sound recording techniques; (4) support for TV and radio programmes made by the minorities; ... (7) the running of libraries and documentation of minority cultural and artistic life; (8) the education of children and youth, in a variety of forms.

Unquestionably, the most innovative provisions have been reserved for Poland's officially recognised minority languages, with amendments voted by the Senate to grant minorities the right to use their languages as 'auxiliary'/'supporting' in those municipalities (*gminy*), where at least 20 per cent of inhabitants declare affiliation to a minority. This is where the authorities have made a very clear and concrete use of the 2002 National Population Census results, without having warned the responding citizens in advance about the legal consequences of their declarations. The Act contains also a somewhat contradictory provision in relation to this. Article 4, paragraph 2, states that: 'No-one shall be obligated, unless by virtue of law, to reveal information on his/her belonging to a minority, origin, minority language or religion.' And yet, in order for their language(s) to be officially recognised as 'auxiliary', we see that members of minorities do have to declare their ethnic affiliation and/or linguistic behaviours in the population census.

Article 9 states that:

> 1. With the municipal authorities, it shall be possible to use, in addition, the minority language as well as the official one. 2. An additional language might be used only in these municipalities where the number of minority residents, whose language is to be used as a supporting one, is no less than 20 per cent of the total number of the municipality residents, and who have been entered into the Official Register of Municipalities [...], where an auxiliary language is used. 3. The possibility of using an auxiliary language shall mean that persons belonging to a minority [...] shall have the right to: 1) apply to the municipal authorities in the additional language, either in a written or oral form; 2) obtain on his/her distinct request, an answer in the auxiliary language, either in written or oral form.

And Article 14 states decisively that: 'The number of municipality residents belonging to a minority [...] shall be constructed as the number officially stated as a result of the latest census'.

The results of the 2002 Census revealed fifty-one municipalities in which over 20 per cent of inhabitants declared affiliation with a minority nationality (in case of the Kashubs the percentage of persons declaring use of the language is crucial). In twenty-seven municipalities the affiliation was German (in the Provinces of Opole and Silesia); in twelve it was Belarusian and Lithuanian (in the Province of Podlasie); and in ten it was Kashubian – Przodkowo (Przedkòwò, 49 per cent), Sulęczyno (Sëlëczëno, 48.6 per cent), Stężyca (Stãżëca, 43.2 per cent), Sierakowice (Serakòjce, 39.9 per cent), Somonino (Somònino, 30.8 per cent), Chmielno (Chmielno, 34.8 per cent), Linia (Lëniô, 35.5 per cent), Szemud (Szëmôłd, 26.3 per cent), Parchowo (Parchòwò, 22.3 per cent) and Puck (Pùck, 30.9 per cent). In all the appropriate municipalities in Kashubia practical preparations have already been made to introduce Kashubian on an auxiliary base, as provided by law.

Another important change in the Polish linguistic landscape has been made possible by the provisions in Article 12:

> 1. It shall be possible to used additional, traditional place-names alongside: 1) official names of places and physiographical objects; 2) street names – established in the Polish language, pursuant to separate regulations. 2. Additional names [...] shall be used solely on the territories of municipalities entered into the Official Register of Municipalities where names are used in the respective minority language [...]. Entries into the Register shall be made [...] on the request of the municipal council [...] 5. The additional names [...] shall be placed after the respective Polish name, and shall not be used separately; 6. The establishment of an additional name in a given minority language shall take place in accordance with the spelling rules of the language concerned. 7. An additional name of a place or physiographical object in a minority language shall be established provided that: 1) the number of municipality residents belonging to a minority is no less than 20 per cent of the total number of this municipality residents or, in case of an inhabited place, in consultations [...] more than a half of its residents who have taken in the consultations were in favour of the establishment of an additional place-name in the minority language; 2) the municipal council's application gained approval of the Committee on Names of Places and Physiographical Objects [...] 8. The relevant provisions of the Act [...] shall apply to the [...] additional street names in a minority language.

Article 15 defines the financial obligations which apply when implementing Articles 9 and 12:

> 1. The costs involved in the introduction and the use of a supporting language on the territory of the municipality and the costs involved in the introduction of additional names [...] shall be borne by the municipal budget [...] 2. The costs involved in the change of information boards, resulting from the adoption of an additional name of a place or physiographical object in the minority language shall be borne by the State budget.

In spite of financial problems in exercising these provisions, more and more villages in the appropriate municipalities are being identified with bilingual information boards. The first road sign with the official bilingual name of the village was placed in Szymbark/Szimbark in the summer of 2008, although unofficial road signs, place-name boards, advertisements and even plates with street names in both Kashubian and Polish had been visible in Kashubia for many years. Some Kashubian mayors and activists believe that most of the territory of Kashubia could be provided with such bilingual place-names by virtue of the referenda mentioned in Article 12, paragraph 7.

The final stage in adopting the state's new (post-transformational) policy towards regional and minority languages was the ratification of the Council of Europe's European Charter for Regional or Minority Languages. Having signed it in 2003 – and after long discussion and debate – Poland ratified the Charter in 2009, as the twenty-fourth member-state. According to the statement contained in the instrument of ratification deposited in Strasbourg:

> The Republic of Poland declares that it shall apply the Charter in accordance with the Act on national and ethnic minorities and on regional language, dated 6 January 2005. The Republic of Poland declares, in accordance with Article 3, paragraph 1, of the European Charter for Regional or Minority Languages that, within the meaning of the Charter, minority languages in the Republic of Poland are: Belarusian, Czech, Hebrew, Yiddish, Karaim, Kashub, Lithuanian, Lemko, German, Armenian, Romani, Russian, Slovak, Tatar and Ukrainian. The regional language is the Kashub language. The national minority languages are Belarusian, Czech, Hebrew, Yiddish, Lithuanian, German, Armenian, Russian, Slovak and Ukrainian. The ethnic minority languages are Karaim, Lemko, Romani and Tatar. The non-territorial languages are Hebrew, Yiddish, Karaim, Armenian and Romani.

This detailed classification into 'national minority' or 'ethnic minority' languages is unprecedented in previous Charter ratifications. Kashubian again has been officially labelled a 'regional language'.

Another surprise was the choice of provisions selected from the Charter by Poland's Ministry of Interior and Administration, as well as the statement that all of them should be applied for all the languages listed. This stands in obvious contradiction to the spirit of the Charter, according to which diverse obligations should be adopted for strong or weak languages, without any differentiation between Part II of the Convention (general obligations) and Part III (detailed provisions). Thus:

> ... the Republic of Poland declares, in accordance with Article 2, paragraph 2 of the Charter, that the following provisions of Part III of the Charter will be applied for the languages listed above:
> Article 8 (Education) – paragraph 1 a (i), b (i), c (i), d (iii), e (ii), g, h, i and Paragraph 2;
> Article 9 (Judicial authorities) – Paragraph 2 a;
> Article 10 (Administrative authorities and public services) – Paragraph 2 b, g, and Paragraph 5;
> Article 11 (Media) – Paragraph 1 a (ii), (iii), b (ii), c (ii), d, e (i), f (ii), g ; Paragraph 2 and 3;
> Article 12 (Cultural activities and facilities) – Paragraph 1 a, b, c, d, e, f, g ; Paragraph 2 and 3;
> Article 13 (Economic and social life) – Paragraph 1 b, c, d, and Paragraph 2 b;
> Article 14 (Trans-frontier exchanges) – Subparagraphs a, b.

It is noticeable that quite a generous selection of provisions in the field of education and media have been made, which would seem rather unfeasible given existing conditions in these areas, while selections made in other areas, in particular the administrative authorities and social life, as well as the judicial authorities, seem quite modest. For instance, the selection of provisions made in the field of education means that:

> With regard to education, the Parties undertake, within the territory in which such languages are used, according to the situation of each of these languages, and without prejudice to the teaching of the official language(s) of the State:
> – to make available pre-school education in the relevant regional or minority languages; [...]

- to make available primary education in the relevant regional or minority languages; [...]
- to make available secondary education in the relevant regional or minority languages; [...]
- to provide, within technical and vocational education, for the teaching of the relevant regional or minority languages as an integral part of the curriculum; [...]
- to provide facilities for the study of these languages as university and higher education subjects; [...]
- to make arrangements to ensure the teaching of the history and the culture which is reflected by the regional or minority language;
- to provide the basic and further training of the teachers required to implement those of paragraphs a to g accepted by the Party ...

All the above commitments are to be implemented in the case of Kashubian, but they are apparently also to be implemented in the case of such language communities as Karaims or Tatars, for which no speakers are indicated in the 2002 Census.

For Kashubian, the obligations selected by the Polish state, although far more generous than previous national regulations, are correspondingly less applicable in practical terms. The first explanatory report on the implementation of the new Convention was published in 2010.[8]

## The concept of 'regional language'

As described above, the term 'regional language' in reference to Kashubian was used for the first time in the working version of what was to become the 2005 Act on National and Ethnic Minorities and the Regional Language. The first precedent for the consistent use of the term 'regional' in relation to a so-called collateral language was made by German legislators when ratifying the Charter in relation to Germany's minority languages

---

8    See <http://www.coe.int/t/dg4/education/minlang/report/PeriodicalReports/ PolandPR1_en.pdf>, accessed 9 April 2010.

(*Minderheitensprachen*), such as Danish, Sorbian and Frisian, as well as *Niederdeutsch* (Low German) as the *Regionalsprache*. The German precedent was the first to highlight the legal problem within Europe of ethnolects which seek to be officially upgraded from the status of dialect – perceived as inaccurate and ethno-linguistically vague – to that of a separate language, the issue being also of a political, historical and terminological nature.

The languages classified as 'regional' share some common features. They generally fit the criteria of what are called *langues collatérales* in French sociolinguistics (Eloy 2004) or *Ausbausprachen*[9] in Heinz Kloss's typology (Kloss 1967). These features include:

- close genetic relationship to the corresponding majority language of the state – regiolects are often regarded as being 'only' dialects of a majority/state language;
- relatively long history of common development, especially socio-political, of the regional and the corresponding majority language;
- lacking in (or without a fully developed) feeling of national separateness within the group of speakers, but displaying strong regional and/or ethnic identity, with the language constituting the main element of the identity/regional ethnicity;
- high dialectal differentiation within the regiolects, often classified as dialect clusters or L-complexes;
- lacking an adopted uniform literary standard or literary norm, or the standard being *in statu nascendi*;
- rich, often very ancient literary tradition of dialectal/regional literature;
- relatively low social prestige of a regiolect, often lower than in the past;
- underdeveloped status of language planning methods;
- opposition within the group against being perceived and officially treated as national minority group, often with a paradoxical resistance against being seen as minority group at all; and a specific 'embedded' national and/or linguistic identity. (Wicherkiewicz, 2003; Coluzzi 2007: 24–5)[10]

---

9   *Ausbausprache* may be translated literally as 'upgraded language' or 'language by development', and refers to a language variety which is used autonomously with respect to other related languages. This typically means that it has its own standardised form independent of neighbouring standard language(s).

10  Besides Low German and Kashubian, ethnolects or regiolects that are often referred to as regional (or collateral) languages and/or strive for official recognition as such are: Occitan in France, the Oïl languages in France and Belgium, Limburgian in the Netherlands, Scots in Scotland, Aragonese and Asturian in Spain, Lombard

Where Kashubian and Low German are concerned, it is clear that in spite of quite obvious terminological and methodological disputes, new elements in national and international language legislation have definitely contributed to upgrading the language status and social prestige of the respective language communities.

## The sociolinguistics of Kashubian

Recent years have brought an enormous increase in scholarly interest in sociolinguistic research on Kashubian. Following studies by Latoszek (1990) and Synak (2001), new projects have been successfully carried out on the qualitative and quantitative aspects of language use, revitalisation measures and the prospective development of Kashubian. Particularly noteworthy are reports by Porębska (2006, 2007) and Nestor and Hickey (2009); both studies are based on thoroughly prepared, methodologically sound and well-documented fieldwork projects.

Porębska's project consisted of an empirical study conducted between 2000 and 2005 and based on a sample survey of 760 Kashubian informants who were asked to answer a questionnaire covering the vital aspects of language use, language preferences and attitudes. The general results of the survey indicate that almost all respondents (90 per cent) want to preserve their (minority) language and culture. Two-thirds of them, however, intend simultaneously to conform to the majority Polish language and culture (see below). These outcomes strongly confirm the previous widespread perception of the existence of a Kashubian double, embedded identity. The results obtained by Porębska from her representative sample give an unprecedented snapshot of language relations and attitudes within the Kashubian community (Porębska 2007: 180–8). The results obtained for the most important questions were as follows:

---

and Piemontese in Italy, Silesian in Poland and in the Czech Republic, Latgalian in Latvia, Samogitian (Žemaitian) in Lithuania and Võro-Seto in Estonia.

- 'Is it important for the Kashubs to preserve their language and culture?'
  90% 'yes', 10% 'no';
- 'Is it important for the Kashubs to conform to the Polish language and culture?'
  64% 'yes', 36% 'no';
- 'What is your identity?'
  19% 'Kashubian', 6% 'more Kashubian than Polish', 45% 'both Kashubian and Polish', 20% 'more Polish than Kashubian', 10% 'Polish';
- 'Mother tongue'
  10% 'Kashubian', 51% 'both [Kashubian and Polish]', 39% 'Polish';
- 'First language acquired'
  21% 'Kashubian', 18% 'both languages', 60% 'Polish', 1% 'German';
- 'Knowledge of Kashubian – understanding'
  39% 'very good', 33% 'good', 15% 'average', 10% 'poor', 3% 'not at all';
- 'Knowledge of Kashubian – speaking'
  23% 'very good', 27% 'good', 25% 'average', 16% 'poor', 9% 'not at all';
- 'Knowledge of Kashubian – reading'
  4% 'very good', 18% 'good', 24% 'average', 24% 'poor', 30% 'not at all';
- 'Knowledge of Kashubian – writing'
  1% 'very good', 6% 'good', 13% 'average', 27% 'poor', 53% 'not at all';
- 'Knowledge of Kashubian as compared with Polish – understanding'
  8% 'much better', 5% 'better', 56% 'equal', 25% 'worse', 6% 'much worse';
- 'Knowledge of Kashubian as compared with Polish – speaking'
  8% 'much better', 5% 'better', 34% 'equal', 37% 'worse', 15% 'much worse';
- 'What language did you earlier speak more often on an everyday basis?'
  17% 'Kashubian', 4% 'more often Kashubian', 27% 'Kashubian and Polish', 22% 'more often Polish', 10% 'Polish';
- 'What language do you speak more often on an everyday basis nowadays?'
  12% 'Kashubian', 5% 'more often Kashubian', 28% 'Kashubian and Polish', 23% 'more often Polish', 31% 'Polish';
- 'Family language'
  15% 'Kashubian', 10% 'more Kashubian than Polish', 38% 'both Kashubian and Polish', 18% 'more Polish than Kashubian', 20% 'Polish';
- 'How often do you pray in Kashubian?'
  3% 'often', 19% 'seldom', 78% 'never';
- 'How often do you confess in Kashubian?'
  less than 1% 'often', 7% 'seldom', 93% 'never'.

Various other sociolinguistic factors were evaluated by Porębska, also on a gradual scale from 1 to 5, including:

- 'Use of Kashubian by respondent's family members' (from 1 – 'never' to 5 – 'always'):

- grandparents                                    - 4.16
- father                                          - 3.60
- mother                                          - 3.47
- spouse                                          - 3.44
- myself                                          - 2.97
- brothers and sisters                            - 2.73
- children                                        - 2.45
- (great-)grandchildren                           - 2.00;
  - 'Language use with children and spouses' (from 1 – 'Polish' to 5 – 'Kashubian'):
    - with spouse at home                         - 3.38
    - with spouse outside                         - 3.26
    - with children at home                       - 2.71
    - with children outside                       - 2.55;
  - 'Language use in semi-official and official situations' (from 1 – 'Polish' to 5 – 'Kashubian'):
    - with neighbours                             - 2.59
    - with relatives                              - 2.53
    - with friends                                - 2.19
    - at village meetings                         - 2.12
    - at parties                                  - 1.84
    - with colleagues at work/school              - 1.78
    - with superiors at work                      - 1.63
    - with priest                                 - 1.49
    - during classes                             - 1.43
    - with a teacher                              - 1.39.

The results show an obviously inferior position – both subjective and objective – for the prestige of Kashubian in relation to the Polish language. The figures for 'understanding', 'speaking', and particularly for 'reading' and 'writing' conform perfectly to the general model for minority languages with newly developed literary standards.

The results obtained by Porębska generally confirm those presented by Synak (2001: 295–315) on the basis of his 1988–96 research, which was carried out in several municipalities in northern and central Kashubia. Older research results published by Latoszek (1996: 87–92) contained several conclusions on the position of the ethnolect in the region. 40.7 per cent of the total population inhabiting the area could understand Kashubian and spoke it every day or often; 26.3 per cent could understand it, but hardly or never used it; 18 per cent could somehow understand Kashubian; and

15 per cent did not understand it at all. The corresponding numbers are highly differentiated in rural and urban areas, e.g. the figure for active and passive knowledge of the ethnolect reaches 68 per cent in the countryside and barely 25 per cent among inhabitants of the towns.

An extensive sociolinguistic survey concerning the use and situation of Kashubian was also carried out in 2004–5 within the framework of a pan-European project ('Kashubian in Poland', 2004) by a team of experts and scientists. This team also drafted a comparative summary providing a general overview of the situation in the Member States who acceded to the European Union in May 2004 (Cyprus, the Czech Republic, Estonia, Hungary, Latvia, Lithuania, Malta, Poland, Slovakia and Slovenia), including a comparison with the fifteen original Member States. For each of the new member states a full report was produced concerning all regional and minority languages spoken there. Additionally, for each of the states, one language group was selected for an in-depth sociolinguistic study. In the case of Poland, the language chosen for thorough investigation was Kashubian. Unfortunately, for reasons which are not clear, the detailed reports for the representative language groups have never been published.

## Kashubian language planning

The Kashubian Language Board, although still in its infancy, aims to play an important role in all aspects of language planning, i.e. corpus, status, acquisition and technology planning, with a special focus on the first domain. The creation and implementation of the Kashubian Language Board was a direct result of the *Strategy for the Protection and Development of the Kashubian Language and Culture* (Gdańsk 2006), discussed, prepared and adopted by the Kashubian-Pomeranian Association, the first and only document of its kind elaborated by a minority community in Poland. The clearly formulated objective of the document is the protection and development of the language and culture of the Kashubs, 'to enable the existence and the development of Kashubian'. In order to achieve this goal:

... the activities undertaken must focus on four priorities:
1. popularisation of Kashubian education, particularly the teaching of Kashubian;
2. promoting and supporting the use of Kashubian;
3. protecting the linguistic and cultural heritage of Kashubian;
4. strengthening the position of Kashubian at regional, national and international levels.

## The Statutes of the Kashubian Language Board list the following tasks (Breza 2007: 11–13):

The analysis and evaluation of the situation of the Kashubian language as well as announcements concerning the language policy of ZK-P:
1. cooperation with administrative authorities, in particular with the Ministry of Interior and Administration, Ministry of Science, Ministry of National Education, Ministry of Culture and National Heritage in matters of the development of Kashubian and its research;
2. spreading knowledge about Kashubian, its varieties, norms, evaluation criteria, as well as organising related discussions and conferences;
3. the evaluation of and commenting on the standards and needs for publications on the Kashubian language and language culture, as well as publishing activity within the ZK-P;
4. resolving linguistic questions concerning the vocabulary, grammar, pronunciation, orthography and punctuation, as well as stylistics of utterances in Kashubian, as well as solving problems concerning usage of Kashubian in various domains of science and technology, particularly in new ones;
5. expressing opinions concerning use of Kashubian in the public sphere and legal transactions, in particular in advertising, press, radio and television, as well as in administration;
6. expressing opinions on names (and their grammatical and orthographic forms) proposed for new goods and services;
7. caring for the Kashubian language culture in school education, including analysis and evaluation of teaching programmes;
8. (...)
9. setting the rules for the orthography and punctuation of Kashubian;
10. cooperation with high schools and academic institutions that are interested in maintenance and development of the Kashubian language.

The Kashubian Language Board consists of fourteen to seventeen members, mainly linguists, writers and teachers, working either together or within four Committees: Standardisation and Normalisation; Education; Media; and Administration and Language Policy. The Board has organised two seminars and published two bulletins (Breza 2007, 2008) disseminating the results of their work. These have included such issues as: preferred syntactic constructions; ambiguous inflectional and spelling forms; school terminology in literary theory, mathematics, geography, etc.; phraseology of standard literary Kashubian; Kashubian forenames; use of the Kashubian normative dictionary; compiling on-line dictionaries for Kashubian; teaching programmes for Kashubian; teaching of language varieties; media terminology; the use of Kashubian in the public sphere and in legal transactions; the use of Kashubian in radio programmes; Kashubian music in regional education; teaching programmes for graduate courses for teachers of Kashubian; the role and application of the 2005 Act on National and Ethnic Minorities and the Regional Language, and of the European Charter for Regional or Minority Languages.

## Kashubian in education

One of the most important actions undertaken by the Kashubian community with reference to their language has been the introduction of Kashubian into the school system. Such a move has faced resistance from the educational administration, from teachers and very often from parents; it has also faced problems caused by the lack of syllabi, textbooks and qualified teachers. Another problem was the usage of two spelling standards, since until the mid-1990s Kashubian had no uniform spelling and orthography, which made language teaching in schools close to impossible. After many years of discussions and argument, the Protocol of agreement on the spelling rules for the Kashubian language was signed in May 1996, during a meeting of the Kashubian-Pomeranian Association Board of Education. Nevertheless, scholars are under no illusions that literary Kashubian is still *in statu nascendi*.

In 2004 a detailed report on Kashubian in education was prepared by Tomasz Wicherkiewicz and published in the series *Regional Dossiers on Languages in Education* by the Mercator Centre in Leeuwarden/Ljouwert in Friesland/the Netherlands (Wicherkiewicz 2004). This was the first volume devoted to a minority language group from a new European Union member state.

The picture of the Kashubian community in the new conditions after the democratic breakthrough of 1989 would not be complete without a mention of regional education. Introducing regional elements into schools has always been a priority for the ZK-P activists. The idea, however, has evolved considerably, from the desire to regionalise the course content in many school subjects to the conception of ethnic language education, which was connected with the wish to protect the Kashubian language and which was made possible by the new legislation of the 1990s. On the other hand, however, owing to the efforts of the ZK-P, theories about regional education have now spread beyond Kashubia, notably into Kociewie (e.g. conferences for teachers from Kociewie who teach about the region) and also into some cities (e.g. Tricity, Słupsk).

ZK-P activists have always attempted to combine practical work with theoretical scholarly reflection. Thus there have been debates about the meaning of the concepts of regional education, regionalisation of education and ethnic education; the position of a Kashubian child within the school system has also been analysed. These ideas have later been transferred to the level of regional activists, teachers and education officials, through countless conferences, debates and seminars. This phenomenon was particularly visible from the end of the 1980s, when, in the new political situation, the regional debate was permitted to enter an entirely new phase.

The beginnings of Kashubian education after the 1989 democratic transformations mainly focussed around the Kashubian Secondary School, launched in 1991 in Brusy in southern Kashubia, as well as the primary school in Głodnica, near Linia. After the establishment of these schools, the teaching of Kashubian became more popular, finding its way particularly into primary and middle schools. In 2003, Kashubian was being taught to 4,780 pupils in eighty-one schools. At the end of 2005, 5,196 pupils were learning Kashubian in some 100 primary schools, 1,345 in twenty-seven middle schools, and 261 students in three high schools. According to the most recent estimations, almost 10,000 children and adolescents have already been offered some form of school education on Kashubian. This progress is enormous. The subjects are 'Kashubian language', 'Kashubian language with elements of regional culture' and 'regional education with elements of Kashubian language', and are taught for between one and three hours per week.

In 2005, for the first time, students could take their high school final exams in Kashubian (at the high school in Strzepcz). This was made possible due to the 2003 Kashubian Language Syllabus and the 2005 Final Examination Prospectus, prepared and approved by the Ministry of National Education.

The greatest problem, however, has been the shortage of teachers, textbooks and teaching programmes. In order to make up for this deficiency, a Kashubian language course was successfully launched at the University of Gdańsk; there have also been attempts to begin a minor programme in Kashubian studies within the major curriculum in Polish philology. This project was finally launched in the autumn of 2010. In the meantime, the first ever master's thesis written in Kashubian has been publicly defended by Hanna Makurat.

A few courses in Kashubian at the College of Pomeranian Studies, the Graduate School for Regional and Alternative Education and the graduate school for teachers of Kashubian have been established; many courses on Kashubian for teachers have been organised in the region. Between 150 and 200 teachers are estimated to have received qualifications for teaching Kashubian, although obviously not all of them have taught the language subsequently. Preparations have also begun in compiling teacher-authored programmes related to regional education (e.g. 'Regional education programmes: Kashubia, Kociewie, Pomerania', Gdańsk 1998), and textbooks for language teaching. As far as Kashubian teaching materials are concerned, in spite of the continuing scarcity of adequate materials, there are also some examples of fine and popular publications, including a very attractively presented primer and an illustrated school dictionary[11]; handbooks

11    W. Bòbrowsczi and K. Kwiatkòwskô [Bobrowski and Kwiatkowska], *Kaszëbsczé abecadło. Twój pierszi elemeńtôrz* (Gdańsk, 2000) and K. Kwiatkòwskô and

for secondary school and university students[12]; and a growing number of textbooks and course books by Danuta Pioch, including recently published course books for adults and teaching programmes for language teachers.[13] *Najô Ûczba* ('Our learning') has appeared regularly since 2007 as a special supplement to *Pomerania*, with texts and methodological aids for teaching Kashubian. Links have been established with similar ethnic communities abroad, with an eye to drawing inspiration from their experience in teaching an ethnic language.

The Education Group at the Executive Board of the ZK-P coordinates regional education in Kashubia and Pomerania. One of the tasks of the group has been participation in the drafting of relevant legislation pertaining to ethnic education. They have been asked to give their opinion on obligatory elements of the curricula in the teaching of an ethnic language, as well as drawing up teaching programmes and preparing textbooks to be approved for use in schools. Of paramount practical importance was the establishment of a group of experts in Kashubian language assessment, appointed by the Executive Board of the ZK-P in October 2003, and including Edward Breza as the chairman, Renata Mistarz as the secretary, and Marek Cybulski, Małgorzata Klinkosz, Wanda Kiedrowska, Jerzy Samp, Tadeusz Linkner and Anna Ziółkowska as members. The role of the group, as the name implies, was the assessment of the Kashubian language skills of teachers, and the certificate issued by the group entitles a teacher to teach the language. In the first few months forty-four teachers passed the examinations administered by the group.

---

W. Bòbrowsczi [Kwiatkowska and Bobrowski], *Twój pierszi słowôrz. Słowôrz kaszëbskò-pòlsczi* (Gdańsk, 2003). Both publications were sponsored by Donald Tusk, then deputy speaker of the Senate and currently Prime Minister of Poland.

12    R. Wosiak-Śliwa and M. Cybulski, *Kaszubski język literacki. Podręcznik dla* lektoratów (Gdańsk: Graf, 1992); M. Cybulski and R. Wosiak-Śliwa, *Ùczimë sã pò kaszëbskù. Ksiązka pomocnicza dla klas starszych* (Gdańsk, 2001).

13    D. Pioch, *Kaszëbë. Zemia i lëdze* (Gdańsk 2001); *Żëcé codniowé na Kaszëbach. Ùczbòwnik kaszëbsczégò jãzëka* (Gdańsk, 2004); *Najô domôcëzna. Ùczbòwnik kaszëbsczégò jãzëka* (Gdańsk, 2005).

The Education Group also organises or co-organises conferences to promote the sharing of experiences, such as the events organised with the Mercator Centre for the project 'Communicating Tubes', or the conference held in Gdańsk in November 2003 under the title *How Do Others Do It?* Other examples include the seminar on Kashubian orthography held at the University of Gdańsk in March 2002, the workshop *Responsibility for the Regional Heritage* held during an education exhibition at the County Centre for In-service Teacher Training in Kartuzy in April 2002, a conference for kindergarten teachers of the Starogard County held in September 2002, or the seminar *The Legal Status of the Kashubs in the Light of the Current Legislation in Poland and Abroad: Language Policy and Language Planning*, which took place at the Kashubian Folk High School in Starbienino in November 2002. In the past few years there have been several such seminars, workshops and training courses annually. The Kashubian Folk High School plays a pivotal role here, organising training courses for teachers within the framework of the College of Regional Studies. Other initiatives include the online portal 'Regional Education. Kashubia Kociewie Pomerania': <http://www.regedu.kaszubi.pl>.

Education is not limited to schools. Another important undertaking is the project Kashubian for Working Adults, set up by the Academy of Vocational Training in Gdańsk in cooperation with the ZK-P. The project was carried out from 2005 within the framework of the *Integrated Operational Programme* for *Regional Development, Action 2.1: 'Developing the vocational skills of adults connected with labour market needs and* increased lifelong learning opportunities in a region'. 75 per cent of the project was financed by the European Social Fund and 25 per cent by the state budget. In 2005, thirteen groups started their training courses in Kartuzy, Kolbudy, Kościerzyna, Żukowo, Wejherowo, Szemud, Gdańsk, Brusy, Puck and Gdynia. In 2006, twelve more groups were created. The course comprised 200 lessons and included 200 working adults. In subsequent years the market for Kashubian language classes developed so strongly that the Academy organised more courses, but this time there were tuition fees covering the entire cost of the training.

According to the 1991 Act on the System of Education and the 2005 Act on National and Ethnic Minorities and the Regional Language (Art.17), persons belonging to minorities are entitled to learn or to be instructed in their own language and have the right to instruction in the history and culture of the minority. In the case of Kashubian, the school system, for the present, focuses solely on the teaching of the language and some aspects of cultural education. Education in a non-Polish language is considerably underdeveloped if all minority or regional languages in Poland are taken into account, the only commendable exception being the schooling system in/for Lithuanian(s) in the region of Sejny in north-eastern Poland. Germans in Silesia also make great efforts to teach in German in their minority schools. The teaching of Kashubian culture is exercised through the so-called 'regional education path'. The teaching of Kashubian/regional history is a much more problematic issue, although local history teachers have already highlighted for this, referring to Article 8.g. of the European Charter for Regional or Minority Languages, which was selected by Poland in its instrument of ratification.

## Corpus language planning

Modern Kashubian has developed new methods and means of corpus language planning, many of the discussed earlier. The most remarkable achievements have been Gòłąbk's 1997 normative orthography and 2005 dictionary, and Treder's 2005 historical outline of literary Kashubian, 2006 encyclopaedic compendium of the Kashubian language and popular handbook of Kashubian linguistics in Kashubian. These have continued the work published by Breza and Treder in 1981 and 1984, Labuda in 1982, Boryś and Popowska-Taborska between 1994 and 2008, and Breza in 2001, as well as the normative regulations published by Breza in 2007 and 2008. New media is now of crucial importance for current and prospective corpus language planning, with projects such as <http://www.cassubia-dictionary.com>, <http://csb.wiktionary.org>, <http://www.rastko.net> and <http://www.naszekaszuby.pl>, to mention only the most ambitious and promising projects.

## The church and the language

There have been some surprising achievements by Kashubian activists during recent years of political and social reform: apart from developments in education, it is also important to look at the introduction of Kashubian into Catholic religious services. The church and religion have always played a vital role as transmitters of traditional culture and values in Kashubia. Until 1991, however, church services had been provided in Polish only, mainly due to a lack of liturgical texts. The years 1992 and 1993 were marked by an extremely important event in the development of the Kashubian language: two independent translations of the New Testament into Kashubian appeared. The ethnolect was first introduced into Catholic services in between eight and ten churches. These initial trials show that the presence of Kashubian in a religious context experiences the same problems and meets the same social prejudices as do most minority languages. Opponents of Kashubian use at church argue that the 'colloquial' and 'uneducated' nature of the ethnolect is inappropriate for religious use.

The case of two parallel Bible translations illustrates the primary problem faced by language planners in Kashubia: the question of spelling. Issues of orthography have been debated since the creation of modern literary Kashubian over 100 years ago, and have often gained a political dimension. Two major reforms of spelling were undertaken by the Young-Kashubs and *Zrzësz* in the 1930s, and by the ZK-P in 1975. Two Bible translations, and two (or more) spelling and dialectal varieties used in literature and in the press, present a crucial difficulty in developing a language standard, still unknown to most users of Kashubian.

## The Kashubian Institute

The idea of setting up a Kashubian institution, which would constitute a base for cooperation between members of the scholarly community who identified with the Kashubian-Pomeranian movement, was present among regional activists for many years. The initiative was referred to in many manifestos issued by the ZK-P Association, stressing the significant achievements of the regional academic community and the need for such an institution. On the assumption that the founding of a Kashubian Institute was vital for the Kashubian movement, a group of representatives of scholarly circles made an effort to prepare for its establishment at the beginning of 1996. The need to broaden and enhance research about the Kashubs was acknowledged, including the need to research their past and present, and their social, economic and ecological problems. The creation and implementation of such a research programme was to constitute the primary goal of the Institute, which would bring together representatives of various specialties and academic centres. Since its inception, the Institute has aimed to bring together Kashubian-Pomeranian scholars from all over Poland, as well as to assist with the development of international cooperation and to promote regional issues abroad. During the implementation meeting it was established that the new organisation would be founded as an independent association with its seat in Gdańsk, under the name of 'Instytut Kaszubski'. The principal goals of the Institute, according to its statute, are: the organisation of scholarly research with reference to the needs and expectations of the Kashubian community and the tradition of Kashubian studies, as well as the dissemination of the results; the enrichment and development of the regional Kashubian-Pomeranian movement; the integration of the regional scholarly community and its development. The Institute aims to achieve these goals through organising conferences and seminars, formulating and implementing various research projects, editing and publishing books, creating library collections, establishing international contacts and providing assistance to young researchers. The preliminary list of the most urgent research themes, accepted as priorities at the beginning of the Institute's scholarly activity, included the following subjects: editing a multi-volume history of the Kashubs as well as a full scholarly monograph on Kashubian-Pomeranian regionalism in comparison with similar movements in Poland and Europe; editing and publishing a series of biographies of the main founders of Kashubian-Pomeranian regionalism; editing and publishing a Kashubian bibliography; preparing an assessment of the Act on National and Ethnic Minorities and the Regional Language; initiating a discussion on the status of the Kashubs as an ethnic group; participating in discussion on projected reform of the territorial structure of the state; participating in the preparation of strategies of regional development in the provinces; research on the sociological profile of the Kashubs, particularly on the influence of changes in the political system; editing and publishing a series of socio-economic monographs on individual communities; editing a history of Kashubian literature and language; research on the history of Pomeranian families; comparative research on the Kashubs and other European ethnic groups.

The Institute's most visible and most valuable output has been its publications. Two particularly noteworthy projects are:

- *Acta Cassubiana*, a renowned opinion-forming annual scholarly publication, edited with great success since 1999;
- a monumental project entitled *Biblioteka Pisarzy Kaszubskich* ('Library of Kashubian writers') – a critical re-edition of essential works of Kashubian literature, with three volumes published thus far: Ceynowa 2007, Derdowski 2007 and Treder and Walkusz 2008.

Another important publication has been Obracht-Prondzyński's *Bibliografia do studiowania spraw kaszubsko-pomorskich* ('Bibliography of Kashubian-Pomeranian Studies') (2004d).

One of the crucial objectives of the Institute is the animation of scholarly life by means of conferences, seminars and workshops. The Institute has successfully organised a number of events, including international conferences, both in Poland and abroad. Conference proceedings have been published on various occasions. The Institute works in collaboration with numerous scholarly circles, museums, and local government, regional and educational institutions, in the interests of teamwork, mutual aid and the exchange of ideas. The topics of the conferences have included: the cultural heritage of the Mennonites on the Lower Vistula; the history of the Union of Poles in Germany; the history of individual towns and communes; libraries, museums, schools and activists dealing with regional culture and literature; the literary heritage of Majkowski and Derdowski; the scholarly output of Lorentz; the history of the Museum of Kashubian-Pomeranian Literature and Music in Wejherowo; the Springtime of Nations in Pomerania; the history of the Pomeranian regional movement; the everyday life of the Kashubs at the turn of the nineteenth century; the history of the Secret Military Organisation *Gryf Pomorski* and the Resistance in Pomerania; the anniversary of the 1920 Plebiscite and the restoration of Polish statehood in Pomerania; the economic development of Kashubia; Pomeranian teachers' families; regional architecture in the Lakeland region; and the history of Kashubian studies in the twentieth century (Borzyszkowski 2005a: 239–43).

## The international context

The Kashubs have successfully sought official recognition of their language and ethnic status beyond the regional and national stage. There have been many years of cooperation and close contact with other ethno-linguistic minorities throughout Europe, including (but not confined to) the Lusatian Sorbs of Germany, the Frisians of the Netherlands and Germany, the Samogitians/Žemaitians of Lithuania, the Crimean Tatars of the Ukraine, the Catalans and various groups from Georgia. In order to actively mark their presence and role in the international community of minorities, the Kashubian-Pomeranian Association, in cooperation with other regional bodies, has organised several events in Gdańsk, including:

- The 39th Congress of the Federal Union of European Nationalities in 1994.
- The 6th International Conference on Minority Languages in 1996, the first conference in the series convened in East Central Europe (Synak and Wicherkiewicz 1997).
- The European Bureau for Lesser-Used Languages conference, Partnership for Diversity, in 2008.

Another expression of international recognition of the upgraded linguistic status of Kashubian was the international ISO-639 code CSB, granted and used by such bodies as the Library of American Congress, the Summer Institute of Linguistics and its register of world languages *The Ethnologue*.[14]

## Conclusion

To assess what has been achieved by the Kashubs and the Kashubian movement in respect of the official status and sociolinguistic position of their ethnolect, we can revisit the theses formulated by Majewicz (1986: 97), as presented at the beginning of this chapter:

- the Kashubs as a community have developed a recognised ethnic/regional and a specific linguistic self-identification;
- Kashubian has been officially recognised as a regional language by national and international instruments concerned with minorities;
- the literary standard of Kashubian is subject to all aspects of language planning (corpus, status and acquisition planning);
- Kashubian literature has a long tradition of uninterrupted development;

14   Recently ISO-639 codes were registered for other two regional languages in Poland: Silesian (*SZL*) and Wilamowicean (*WYM*).

- an agreed orthographic standard constitutes a firm base for the development of the Kashubian literary language;
- higher social prestige for the language and developments in language policy have created the need for teaching/learning Kashubian both as a native and second language;
- Kashubian has achieved a relatively wide degree of functional polysemy;
- recent years have brought a significant increase in publications necessary for corpus language planning, such as dictionaries, grammars, handbooks and teaching aids;
- the two translations of the Bible in 1990s have undoubtedly increased the intra-linguistic polysemy of literary Kashubian.

CEZARY OBRACHT-PRONDZYŃSKI

# Dilemmas of Modern Kashubian Identity and Culture

From the time that scholars first started to show an interest in matters Kashubian, the central question has been: 'Who are the Kashubs?' – who do they feel themselves to be, who are they considered to be by others, and what is the nature of their self-identification? It might seem that these are not difficult issues, but the complicated history of the Kashubs, and their centuries-long existence in a cultural borderland between larger and stronger ethnic groups (the Germans and the Poles), have caused major difficulties for the Kashubs in determining their identity, as it has changed throughout the course of history. This is particularly obvious in the context of developments in the twentieth century: two world wars, the partition of the Kashubian community among three states in the interwar period, the communist era and the unfriendly policy of the communist authorities, as well as the social and cultural transformations after 1989.

Research carried out since the 1970s by sociologists and ethnologists (Synak 1998b; Latoszek 1995; Obracht-Prondzyński 2004c; Kucharska 1985; Mazurek 2008a; Mazurek 2008b; Galus 1990), supported by historians and linguists, has started to define the specificity of Kashubian identity, and to formulate the dynamics of change.

The research results suggest that the foundation of the Kashubs' identity is their culture, and the Kashubian ethos consists of such values as: language, religion (ecclesiasticism), family, origin (genealogy), and territory in its fourfold meaning: the dwelling place, the historical area possessed by the Kashubs, the native land (most often family households), and the landscape. The basic elements of the Kashubian self-stereotype correlate with these values; in their own opinion Kashubs are characterised by piety, diligence, attachment to the land, persistence (to the point of obstinacy) and patriotism (Obracht-Prondzyński 2002a: 340–73; Borzyszkowski 1999: 275–84).

From a group point of view, other essential elements are historical experiences, a common fate, common customs, and the Kashubian intellectual and artistic heritage (Perszon 2001). The importance of community institutions is also developing systematically; for example, the significance of the largest Kashubian organisation, the Kashubian-Pomeranian Association (ZK-P), in strengthening Kashubian identity can hardly be overestimated (Obracht-Prondzyński 2006b).

Among the above-mentioned values, the language is of central importance, and has been a contentious issue since the mid-nineteenth century (Labuda 1995). However, it is worth pointing out that, historically, language was not always the primary feature of Kashubian distinctness. The idea of the land was at one stage equally important, until the territory was gradually lost to the Germans, and religion was also crucial – the strength of religious ties used to be much greater than that of ethnic or linguistic links, as after all it was relatively easier for Kashubs to marry German Catholics than to marry any kind of Protestants, including Lutheran Kashubs. When interventions took place in defence of the language, be it among the Protestant Kashubs in West Pomerania in the eighteenth century, or among the Catholics of Gdańsk Pomerania in the early twentieth century, they focused on the language to be used in religious instructions, such as preparations for confirmation or first communion, rather than on ethnic or national concerns. The latter elements emerged later, when stronger arguments were needed in the struggle for their own group's interests. This central importance of religion is why, during the entire period of Poland's partition and during the interwar period, the dangers of German Catholicism were emphasised so strongly. If ethnic ties had been clearly stronger than those based on religious beliefs, such a danger would not have existed.

Admittedly, the relationship between ethnicity and religion in the Kashubian borderland was highly complicated, and over time, the language became the first and paramount determinant of the Kashubian communities' distinctness. Until quite recently, the position of the Kashubian language, despite all post-war transformations, was unarguably the most essential element of the Kashubs' group ethos, and this is supported by the results of sociological research conducted in the 1980s and 1990s: 'their ethnic language constitutes an important historical value for the Kashubs, being the common form of communication within native communities' (Synak 1998a: 386), and 'the Kashubian language is a common and definitely the strongest culturally and ethnically distinguishing feature, and its distinctness is commonly perceived by the informants, as 83 per cent indicate that the Kashubs "differ considerably" in that regard' (Synak 1991: 114).

However, while in the past Kashubian was predominantly a home language, in recent years it has become present and visible in the public sphere: in education, religious life, politics. Paradoxically, that process of entering into the public sphere has been accompanied by a weakening of the role Kashubian plays in the private, family sphere (Latoszek 1997; Porębska 2006), and consequently it has depreciated as a marker of Kashubian identity. As recent research shows, Kashubian origin and family ties (genealogical criteria) or being born in Kashubia (territorial criteria) (Mazurek 2005: 25–37; Mazurek 2006: 119–38; Mazurek 2008c: 97–108) are of growing importance as determinants and constitutive indicators for Kashubian identity. Therefore, it is possible nowadays to be a Kashub without speaking Kashubian, which was in principle unthinkable in the past. What is more, it is possible to be a 'Kashub by choice', i.e. to identify oneself with the Kashubian community, in spite of lacking any Kashubian roots; it is sufficient to be born and live in Kashubia. This displays one of the typical features of contemporary identities – they are of a hybrid nature and based on selected values (Baker 2005: 27).

This principle, however, also operates in the opposite direction. Cases of people who know Kashubian and have Kashubian roots but do not admit to being Kashubian, or are even ashamed of it, are not infrequent. They prefer to opt for more prestigious identities, usually Polish.

These complexities have been confirmed by the results of Brunon Synak's recent research, which underlies his classification of identity types among the Kashubian community. The largest group among his respondents consisted of persons whose self-identification was described as complete (more than three-quarters of respondents), with two groups of characteristic factors: genealogical and cultural. The former include the fact of being born to a Kashubian family; the latter include knowledge of Kashubian, and attachment to the Kashubian culture and land. Those factors usually come up coupled, intertwined and mutually reinforced, and their separation has only an analytical sense. They underlie a feeling of localness and homeliness, creating an awareness of cultural (family and group) continuity and a regional deep-rootedness (Synak 1998b: 59): 'the Kashubian identity is of a habitual character, it is more constant, obtained, even attributed and binding' (Synak 1998b: 60).

The second group within the classification is the incomplete identity, 'based on some weaker and less explicit declaration of someone's Kashubianness' (Synak 1998b: 66). In the group investigated by Synak, this type of identity was declared by every fifth person. Moreover, two subgroups could be distinguished here, the first being 'indigenous Kashubs who do not perceive their Kashubianness as unarguable', and even 'see this as an unnecessary ballast and "adversity"' (Synak 1998b: 67). When referring to other investigations, the author also uses the concept of an 'idle identity' among people who do not reject their Kashubianness, but do not take any interest in it, feel no significant links with the rest of their ethnic group, declare no knowledge of Kashubian, etc. Such attitudes are typical of young people, who declare aspirations to a better, 'urban' life. Their world has no place for Kashubianness, and they develop an alternative 'transitional identity' (Synak 1998b: 67).

The second subgroup consists of persons of an incomplete Kashubian genealogy. Following Marek Latoszek's study, the category 'half-Kashub' is used in this case. Although declaring no Kashubian origin, these people are well-rooted in the Kashubian culture, chiefly thanks to community, professional and newly-developed family ties. Such a situation may lead to biculturalism and ambivalence, where two cultures are treated as equivalent, with neither seen as more important than the other in determining one's identity (Synak 1998b: 68). One version of such a situation is the phenomenon called autochthonisation, in which the Kashubian identity has an acquired character and is the result of specific choices, and where Kashubian elements (also Kashubian-Pomeranian or Kashubian-Kociewian elements) may be accompanied by those from the Vilnius region, i.e. brought by the 1945 newcomers from the Eastern territories.

Another type of identity, called 'vestigial', refers to people completely indifferent to their Kashubian heritage or even rejecting it totally ('ethnic escapism', Synak 1998b: 70). This can be the source of Kashubian complexes, usually corresponding with complexes based on rural origin: a respondent might see identification with the Kashubian community and culture as relegating them to an unfavourable status. Sometimes this type of identity is of an occasional or situational character (when circumstances impose such declarations or raise hopes of some possible benefit); it is typical of representatives of the younger generation.

As mentioned earlier, the Kashubs have historically occupied a borderland between the Poles and the Germans. The influence of these neighbours upon the formation of Kashubian identity has obviously been enormous. The proximity of the Germans has created many difficulties for the Kashubs, the mass extermination of Kashubs during the Second World War being the most drastic example of the policy aiming at their Germanisation. Kashubian-German relations were always unequal (Bokszański 2005: 92–7), Germans being by far the more dominant group in regard to politics, economy and culture. At the same time, the German culture was attractive to many Kashubs; right up until 1945 the adoption of a German identity signified wider opportunities for social and material advancement. There were frequent examples of Kashubs' voluntary Germanisation (particularly among the Lutheran Kashubs in the western part of Pomerania). Such a choice meant relinquishing Kashubianness, as the Germans had always perceived the Kashubian culture as inferior and treated it with contempt. People who wanted to 'become' German had to reject their Kashubian heritage, and in principle any reconciliation of a German identity with Kashubianness was impossible (Obracht-Prondzyński 2004a: 167–82; Borzyszkowski 1999: 93–8). The Kashubian movement in the nineteenth century was born out of resistance to Germanisation (Ceynowa 1843: 243–7); for these Kashubian leaders it was obvious that one could not be Kashubian and German at the same time.

Yet recent years have also brought some changes in this respect. Many of the people who founded German minority organisations in Pomerania after the 1989 transitions have Kashubian roots, and they actually emphasise this. Research and observation show that identity constituents can vary, and that a German identity and a Kashubian identity are by no means mutually exclusive. This has an obvious historical context and local economic implications (Borzyszkowski and Obracht-Prondzyński 1994: 34–5; Galus 1994; Matelski 1997: 93–105).

On the other hand, many people whose origins lie in Pomerania and who live in Germany have started to discovering their Kashubian roots, making this an attractive element of their own family history. Certainly, the literary output of Günter Grass (Ciemiński 1999) has been very influential here, but also the political changes after 1989, friendly relations between Poland and Germany, and changes in the social climate within Germany itself, where distinctiveness is no longer necessarily perceived as negative. Many people who emigrated to Germany claiming 'German descent' in the 1970s and 1980s quite eagerly declare that they are Kashubian nowadays.

The nature of Kashubian-Polish relations has been different (Obracht-Prondzyński 2007: 55–66). Unlike the Kashubian and German identities, the Kashubian and Polish identities can in no way be described as mutually exclusive! Brunon Synak, on the basis of his empirical research, claims: 'Strong Kashubian identification does not interfere with an explicit definition of and emphasis put on Polish ethnicity/nationality. "Kashubian identity" and "Polish identity" are identities that overlap on various levels of identification (regional and national), yet within the same universal cultural values. (…) Kashubian and Polish identities are not substitutional, thus one of them, when strengthening, does not weaken or detract from the other' (Synak 1998b: 72–3).

However, this theory has recently been the subject of much discussion, as Kashubs have started asking themselves: Do the Kashubs really have a double identity – Kashubian and Polish? And is this a positive thing? Opponents of the thesis, who constitute only a tiny minority among the Kashubs, claim that in making such an assumption, one condemns the Kashubs to inevitable eventual assimilation (Polonisation), as the Polish culture (especially the Polish language) always occupies a dominant position. In other words, Kashubian-Polish relations are not equivalent and will alwys lead to a weakening of the Kashubian element. They argue that in order to protect and develop the Kashubian identity it is necessary to see the Kashubs as a separate West-Slavonic nation – linked strongly with the Poles, but separate. This view has recently caused heated discussions within the Kashubian community, which have not so far been decisively settled. Yet it is beyond all doubt that an absolute majority of Kashubs become identified with(in) the group and at the same time declare their Polish nationality, this identification not causing internal identity conflicts (Obracht-Prondzyński 2004b: 61–72).

Naturally, the Kashubian identity undergoes constant changes. It can be inherited, or unconsciously adopted in the process of socialisation within families and communities. It can be 'recovered' in the case of people who come from families whose Kashubian origin was concealed or regarded as unimportant. It can also be a consequence of a deliberate, conscious choice, the result of one's own cognitive effort or cultural activity. Researchers claim that, in accordance with global tendencies, there is a gradual transition from a passive, inadvertent adherence to one's homeland, native culture and values, to a more and more active search for and deepening of an individual and group identity, i.e. the so-called 'new ethnicity' (Synak 1987). These phenomena have yet to be adequately identified and described. One can also talk about a 'rediscovered', 'recovered' or even 'chosen' identity in the case of persons without Kashubian roots, but identifying themselves with the Kashubs (Obracht-Prondzyński 2004b: 61–72). This may result the recent fashion for Kashubianness: even people with no Kashubian roots may paste up car stickers with a black griffin on a golden background saying 'Kaszëbë', or use single Kashubian phrases or expressions.

Moreover, the Kashubian identity is locally and socially diversified, depending on historical experiences which have been different in various parts of Kashubia. For example, in the former borderland that was left after 1920 within the borders of Germany (the regions of Bytów/Bütow and Lębork/Lauenberg) or in the Free City of Danzig, German culture and ties with family members who live in Germany are stronger than elsewhere, the result being the foundation of German minority organisations, most of whose members have Kashubian roots.

Kashubian identity differs also according to place of residence, being undoubtedly stronger in rural areas, and relatively shallow-rooted in urban environments, especially among Kashubs in the big cities of Gdańsk and Gdynia (Obracht-Prondzyński 2002a: 287–94; Mordawski 2006: 158–75; Mazurek and Michałowski 2007: 24–7). Another factor is generational changes: this does not mean that young people necessarily have a weaker Kashubian identity – quite often it is actually the other way round. Young people who have just discovered their Kashubian descent often cause radicalisation within the Kashubian movement. Kashubian identity is also affected to a certain extent by professional traditions, e.g. among fishermen (Konkel 2003: 71–88), or by remnants of ancient social divisions, such as elements of 'petit-nobility' traditions in south-western Kashubia, marked by the use of double family names (Kukier 1976; Breza 1986).

Explanations for the changes in Kashubian identity should be sought within the wider context of social processes such as: democratisation resulting from the transformations after 1989; pluralism; the weakening of the cultural centre; changes in the cultural canon; multiculturalism (Synak 1997). It is also worth remembering that the 1989 political transformations brought two kinds of 'subjectivity' (Synak's phrasing) to the Kashubs: civic and ethnic. These are closely related and mutually reinforcing. They clearly influence group identity (Synak 1998b: 158) and are accompanied by important transformations in the sphere of consciousness: 'Undoubtedly, ethnic identity can be fully inherited, it can be either attributed or imposed, it can be either a question of choice or a social "gain" as a result of one's own activity and aspirations, when only certain criteria of ethnicity are fulfilled' (Synak 1998b: 66).

Such transformations in identity have also been influenced by processes occurring within the Kashubian community itself. The weakened role and prestige of the Kashubian intelligentsia, who for a long time were the main generators and advocates of Kashubian revival ideas, is worth discussing. The input of the Kashubian middle class (entrepreneurs, freelancers, fourth-sector workers, i.e. computer specialists, financiers, insurance agents) is undoubtedly of growing significance as they influence the economic conditions of Kashubian society. The Kashubs see themselves as very resourceful and enterprising people. This conviction has been confirmed by research results which indicate a high degree of economic activity in Kashubia. Crucially, rural areas in Kashubia have remained strong during the recent transformation period. Even earlier, during the communist era, they were able to preserve their traditional character and their economic potential (Obracht-Prondzyński 2002a: 255–62).

On the other hand, the growing middle class have committed themselves only to a relatively small extent to protecting and developing Kashubian culture, or supporting social and cultural initiatives. Even when such sponsorship activities are undertaken, they usually do not exceed the local scale and focus on supporting folklore with ludic elements (fetes, folk ensemble concerts, amateur theatre shows, etc). It is unlikely that this social group would be able, in the near future, to yield leaders who could re-define the Kashubian identity.

Here we touch upon a wider issue of the changing social composition of Kashubian elites. This can be best exemplified by the case of the Kashubian-Pomeranian Association (ZK-P). In the mid-1990s the tone in the ZK-P was still set by people active in culture, science and education. Since then, a considerable change has taken place, as politicians and civil servants, who were formerly cultural or educational activists, have taken the lead as decision-makers. Therefore, a new problem arises: how to achieve a balance between the influences (and working styles) of politicians and civil servants and those of cultural activists, teachers, and people involved in the arts and sciences – with the business world hardly represented at all (Obracht-Prondzyński 2006b: 445–9).

Another factor to be considered when discussing Kashubian identity is the events which accompanied the 2002 National Population Census and the 2005 Act on National and Ethnic Minorities and the Regional Language (Łodziński 2005: 170–3). The heated discussions which took place between 2000 and 2005 revealed and publicised divisions within the Kashubian community regarding their self-identity and status.

For the umpteenth time the Kashubs faced the question of who exactly they are. A nation? An ethnic group? An ethno-regional group? An ethnographic group? A minority – national or ethnic? The question was also faced by the Polish state and the Polish academy – how to treat the Kashubs? The answer is crucial, because the principles adopted result in specific legal and financial measures.

It is also worth considering this question: who creates the concepts that define the Kashubian group and who gives them their actual meaning? Thus, who determines who the Kashubs are? Who constructs a specific network of terminology to describe the Kashubs? Why does it vary over time and why are some notions accepted by some circles, and others rejected? Is this just a question of verbal conventions, linguistic sensitivity, and cultural-political taboos? Or maybe it is a question concerning authentic social realities?

It should be stressed explicitly that the actual network of terminology used in debates concerning the Kashubs' identity has been created by the scholarly community and by the Kashubian intellectual elite, these groups in fact coinciding with each other. The terminological model was created in the 1980s and 1990s. It includes such concepts as: double identity (ethnic Kashubian and national Polish); the Kashubian ethnolect (recognising the separate linguistic status of Kashubian, and granting it a central position among community values); ethnic (or ethno-regional) group; the Kashubs as a group of long persistence. The concepts can help to define who the Kashubs are (Kashubian, Polish, a separate language community), but also to identify who they are not: German, a national minority, a nation, an ethnographic group (such as the Kurpie or Kociewie), speakers of a dialect (Obracht-Prondzyński 2002a: 88–120).

What seemed to be a mutually agreed conceptual consensus has been called into question since the beginning of the twenty-first century by an emerging circle of people advocating the so-called Kashubian national option. In this case the question of a separate linguistic status for Kashubian has been accepted axiomatically, while the idea of the Kashubs' double identity and their Polish national affiliation have been rejected, as the Kashubs are not an ethnic group but supposedly a separate Western Slavonic nation (Obracht-Prondzyński 2007: 55–66).

The terminology hitherto used to describe the Kashubian community, which has been used generally since the 1980s as a result of educative and popularising actions by the ZK-P, the media and the Church, has suddenly come into question and been denied. It should be stressed, however, that this conceptual discourse is actually limited to intellectual circles, as confirmed by the latest research carried out in the region of Kartuzy: 'Responses collected reveal that the discourse concerning Kashubian and the status of Kashubs as group, or their legal and political situation is conducted predominantly in a narrow circle of intellectuals from Tricity. At the local level it is not perceived as important, but as a specific elites' game [...] On the other hand the topics taken up in those "intellectual" discussions are considered too dangerous and too difficult for the average local resident – therefore, the elites are expected to take a clear position and indicate a definite stand on individual topics' (Komosa 2006: 170–1).

This evidence of social attitudes should not be surprising, as other recent investigations among the Kashubs reveal a confusion of concepts referring to their own group status and identity. It seems that for many Kashubs matters of identity are quite important, but existing terminology is often unable to describe them adequately and efficiently. According to research results, the respondents find it difficult to describe the essence of being Kashubian: 'Not everybody is able to define "Kashubian identity".

Some "feel", but cannot express it, hence the answer: "I don't know – a Kashub is a Kashub", "I'm Kashub, that's it", "I feel Kashubian", "I simply feel it the same way as being Polish"' (Kurczewski 2007b: 316).

It should come as no surprise that Kashubs are confused, when within the social sciences the concepts of nation, nationality, ethnic group and national minority are hazy at best. If scholars cannot reach a consensus, what can be expected from the average Kashub, or even from an educated Kashub? When they try to define their own identity (something which happens predominantly in crisis situations) they search for possible solutions that are accessible to their mental and linguistic competence and are regarded as sufficiently safe. The 'safety' of using specific terminology to define Kashubian identity is not unimportant, inasmuch as in their history the Kashubs have experienced numerous very real political, legal and economic consequences as a result of defining themselves through specific terminology. It is enough to remember what happened before the First World War (opinions on Ceynowa and the Young-Kashubs), during the interwar period (when Kashubs were considered unreliable), between 1939 1945 (when they were recognised as 'Slavonicised Germans' and as such suitable for Germanisation, which resulted in forcible registration for the *Deutsche Volksliste*), and throughout the entire post-War period (consider the consequences of the *Zrzesz* circle's use of the term 'Kashubian language').

Some might argue that these disputes focusing on identity are not really important. Perhaps it is not important what we call ourselves, but what we do (for the language and culture). But for 150 years the question of Kashubian identity has been closely involved with political discourse, having real political and social consequences and influencing the legal position of the community and access to resources and funds, as well as the attitude of authorities towards the Kashubs (Obracht-Prondzyński 2002a: 135–220).

The debates on Kashubian identity continue, although much more quietly than during the 2002–5 dispute, focused on the Kashubian national option. The activities of people representing the national faction have not so far radically influenced social life and practices in Kashubia, or brought about any outstanding artistic, journalistic, ideological or organisational achievements (such as an organisation of Kashubs who acknowledge the national option, for example).

At present, the vast majority of Kashubs perceive themselves as a 'non-nation', as confirmed in the results of the recent population census, where a considerable majority of Kashubs chose the Polish national declaration. Recent research shows that relations between the 'Polish' and 'Kashubian' identity components can be quite diverse: 'It appears that in spite of the fact that almost all Kashubs (96 per cent) from Puck simultaneously consider themselves as Poles, some one fifth of them (21 per cent) still perceive themselves primarily as Kashubs, and only in the second place as Poles. Worth stressing is the fact that almost 80 per cent of Kashubs declare being Polish in the first instance' (Kurczewski 2007: 316).

Many Kashubs still perceive themselves not within the categories of ethnicity, but those of ethnography and folklore, and treat their distinctiveness as similar to that of the Tatra and Podhale highlanders (the Górals). Again, this should be no surprise, as analogous opinions can be found in the modern scholarly literature. For instance, in a recent synthesis of contemporary Polish society, in the chapter devoted to ethnic questions, we read: 'In the related literature we also find the concept of an ethnographic group, an example being the Kashubs or Polish Górals. Here that issue – important for ethnography – will be passed over ...' (Kapralski and Mucha 2006: 438). This passage was not written by authors lacking in knowledge about Poland's ethnic diversity; on the contrary. It is interesting to note that they use the expression 'Polish Górals', without adding the adjective in the case of Kashubs.

## The regional issue in Poland during the period of transformation and the Kashubs: the question of Kashubian regionalism

The so-called regional issue was one of the more important and interesting problems that accompanied Polish transformation. Aldona Jawłowska, among others, has analysed the cultural changes in progress; as early as 1993 she wrote: 'The revival of the feeling of regional identity is a phenomenon of great cultural as well as social relevance; especially considering that it pertains to large and economically and politically important regions' (Jawłowska 1993: 193). The word 'revival' is used because under communism any manifestation of regional specificity was regarded with great suspicion. It was tolerated only as folklore, folk culture and art being considered the preserve of truly national ideas. No less important was the fact that folk art presented the creative activity of the lower classes, and thus could be opposed to the culture of the elite or the intelligentsia. That is why it is so important that, following the changes of 1989, regional identity came to be seen in its full richness, which alongside the folklore aspect included also economic, political and administrative distinctions.

This understanding of the 'regional issue' was described by Bohdan Jałowiecki at the onset of the democratic changes in Poland:

> The regional issue is the result of making a political issue of regionalism, which is a socio-cultural movement aiming to valorise a given region. The regional issue is characterised by a duality: on the one hand, there is the transition from a tendency towards autonomy to federalism, on the other – from nationalism to separatism. At the foundation of the regional issue there are usually ethnic or cultural differences. (...) However, the regional issue may also appear as a result of economic differences. In the latter case, two scenarios are possible. A region may be economically backward, in which case the community takes action to redistribute the national income more evenly. (...) Alternatively, a region may be economically advanced, but the state's redistribution policy leads to a sizeable portion of the nationally produced wealth being transferred to other parts of the country, which is locally perceived as unjust, thus leading to the community's efforts to change the situation. (Jałowiecki 1992: 43–4)

This statement should be placed in the context of the debate initiated in 1991 concerning the regionalisation of the country (into new administrative divisions), as well as the noticeable revival of regional movements in Silesia and Greater Poland (Wielkopolska). There were also visible regional differences already arising concerning the speed of transformation. In some areas economic reforms were leading to development, whereas in others there were issues such as the rapid decline of the state-owned farms, or the problems with restructuring in Silesia.

It does not seem, however – especially with the benefit of hindsight – that the regional issue should be analysed only in its narrower sense, as phenomena and processes within the spheres of politics, economics and administration. Neither the federation scenario nor the separation scenario have come to pass. Granted, the administrative division reform of 1998 resulted in the emergence of sixteen locally governed provinces, but it still left numerous matters in the hands of the central administration and its local representatives (provincial governors). Thus Poland, despite the reforms, is still a relatively centralised country, although the locally governed provinces make systematic efforts to enhance their positions within the system.

It should also be emphasised that the regional movements which appeared in some parts of Poland (in Silesia, for example, or in Greater Poland), and which made far-reaching demands of territorial autonomy, were not successful. It could even be argued that the reaction of journalists and scholars to the vociferous manifestations of regional differences in the 1990s was the result of paying attention chiefly to political postulates, rather than to the regional cultural activities which had been happening successfully for many years, but which often escaped the notice of commentators. A case in point is the ZK-P, which at the beginning of the 1990s was also actively participating in reforming the Polish administrative system and which postulated the creation of a number of sizeable regions with considerable autonomy, but whose activity was by no means limited to that (Obracht-Prondzyński 2002b). The ZK-P considered it of paramount importance that regionalist activity should be perceived primarily as taking place within the spheres of social and cultural life, and secondarily in the economic and political context.

In order to understand Polish debates over the regional issue, and to place the Kashubian issues in this context, it is necessary to examine the way in which regionalism is depicted in the Polish scholarly literature. Four different approaches can be distinguished.

The first way of explaining the term 'regionalism' implies an individual's point of view: emotional attachment to a homeland, the belief that this land and the community which live there are unique and compare favourably with others. This attachment may be manifested in numerous ways: in literary output, artistic work, scholarly research, or involvement in regional activities (Kwiatkowski 1990: 57).

It would be difficult, however, to analyse an individual's attitude without taking into account more complex issues around identity – and identity is not only shaped by a feeling of identifying with one's region or with its inhabitants (who tend to be idealised). Viewing identity as a dynamic or fluid phenomenon, we must explore the concept of 'social cohesion' as understood by Stanisław Ossowski in his analyses of a regional ideological homeland (Ossowski 1967: 251–70). Describing the process of transition from a private homeland to an ideological homeland, Ossowski wrote:

> Along with the growth of territorial communities there comes a split: the private homeland is no longer synonymous with the ideological homeland, the former becoming part of the latter, while at the same time the private homelands of individual members of the bigger community undergo multiplication and differentiation. In a big modern national community particular regions constitute environments so separate that not only the limits of a private homeland but its very nature and the set of representations connected with it differ greatly from region to region. (Ossowski 1984: 35)

On the basis of these differences, a feeling of identification constituted around difference starts to form. This can be seen clearly in the case of Kashubia (and, more widely, throughout Pomerania). Visitors to the region coming from other parts of Poland used to be struck by how different it was, to the extent of perceiving it as 'un-Polish'.

However, as Ossowski emphasises, the process of separating one's private homeland from one's ideological homeland is not always consistent. For one thing, 'in small communities (...) the private and the ideological homeland could share the same territory; in such a case, the very same area would fulfil both functions for all the patriots of this community' (Ossowski 1984: 35). Furthermore, alongside the conviction that the private homeland constitutes part of a national homeland, there may also exist the conviction that 'it is the land of our regional group if we feel deeper solidarity with that group, with the Kashubs, than with the inhabitants of the Łowicz region, or the inhabitants of Polesie' (Ossowski 1984: 44). Such a situation was particularly prevalent in cultural borderlands.

This feeling of a strong bond with a regional homeland and its values may lead to the emergence of a social movement, which is always accompanied by some ideology. The movement and the ideology may be of a different nature and may have different objectives. In the words of Krzysztof Kwaśniewski, regionalism is:

> ... a social movement whose ideology is preserving and developing critically the heritage of the socio-cultural region in order to participate optimally in pursuing the goals of a larger community (nation, state) without losing one's own identity as an integral and specific part of this larger community, this identity playing in the community a unique though changing role. Thus regionalism in fact equals local patriotism, which can be contained in the all-nation patriotism equally well as the relationship with the 'private homeland' that we know personally can be contained in all of the 'ideological homeland'. (Kwaśniewski 1986: 3)

A similar stance is taken by Andrzej Kwilecki, who differentiates between regionalism as 'a socio-cultural movement, that is, an intellectual, literary, social movement connected with the region and resulting from the work of conscious activists (e.g. the Kashubian regionalism)', and regionalism as an artistic work based on regional motifs and as scholarly research (Kwilecki 1992: 42). All the above can nevertheless be included within the notion of 'movement' and regional 'ideology'.

The above definitions all present regionalism in a non-confrontational manner, as a supplement of sorts to national patriotism. This is very typical of Polish writing, and it may be connected with to the very beginnings of Polish regionalism, which coincided with the particular conditions of a partitioned country and as such had to accommodate Polish national aspirations to reconstruct their own state. Focusing on the cultural uniqueness of a particular place, regionalism in this sense tried to show that regional or local culture is truly Polish; the regional community became a substitute for the national society, and the small homeland a substitute for a big one.

Regionalism was also used as an instrument to make the peasant masses part of the nation. It laid great emphasis on folk culture, which was considered to be just valuable as high culture; indeed, folk culture was perceived as more truly 'national'. As Roman Wapiński has written: 'just like in other European countries, the point of departure was a fuller appreciation of peasants, who at that time began to participate in public life as one of its agents. Fascination with folk literature, art and customs was accompanied, just as in the case of other nations deprived of the freedom to shape their fate, by associating peasants with exceptional national values' (Wapiński 1993: 43–4).

The consequence of such an understanding of regionalism was the acceptance of a regional policy which emphasised the unity of the nation's culture and which displayed a reluctance to accept regional ideas that stressed difference. The best example of such a mixture of approval and dislike is the attitude towards Kashubian regionalism, approved as long as it emphasised Kashubian unity with the Polish culture and criticised for all attempts to stress Kashubian uniqueness (especially in the sphere of language).

A slightly different approach is presented in Hieronim Kubiak's classification of the understanding of regionalism. Alongside social movements and ideology, Kubiak distinguishes another sphere: that of political activity (Kubiak 1994: 29). This is a particularly important aspect, since regionalism is also an intellectual effort towards defining 'the regional interest', and can undertake organised activities towards advancing this interest in a political sense. This is not to say that a regional movement will necessarily become a political one (although regional parties do exist). The range of the possible political activity is very broad, and the possibilities countless – from being a member of the local government, to lobbying and organised protests, to active support for movements and political parties.

Regionalism can be said to consist of ideas (ideologies), people (activists and artists, for example), institutions (scholarly, cultural, economic and political) and organisations (foundations, associations, sometimes also political parties). This distinction between institutions and organisations may seem problematic, but is in fact necessary to help distinguish between regional associations and such things as publishing houses, magazines, museums, community centres, art galleries and websites (which does not mean to say that those very associations may not run those institutions). In this way, regionalism stands a chance of being perceived within a wider context, not just in the context of NGOs.

An analysis of regionalism in Kashubia shows examples of each of the above-mentioned senses of the concept, but the most common is definitely that of a social movement. In the beginning, Kashubian regionalism was 'a movement originating from the protest against political integration and cultural homogenisation enforced by the state' (Kubiak 1994: 29). In this

sense, its objective was (and still is) the protection of its own cultural identity and its position in the region. This was particularly visible under the
Prussian partition, especially at the end of the nineteenth and the beginning
of the twentieth centuries, when Kashubian regionalism started to assume
institutionalised forms (the Young-Kashubs' Association came into existence in 1912). It was then that the Kashubian elite realised that the survival
of the Kashubs would only be possible if they could effectively oppose the
assimilationist policy of the Prussian-German state, which was being pushed
forward by rapid modernisation. At that point, creating an independent
Kashubian nation was out of the question, so the only realistic strategy was
(to simplify things a little) to persuade the Kashubs to opt for Poland.

This is what happened in the end, but the process was neither fast nor
simple nor painless. One of the chief reasons for the vigour of Kashubian
regionalism was a reaction to the assimilationist and levelling tendencies
of the Polish state, which many Kashubian activists considered to be too
strong, both before 1939 (Kutta 2003) and after the Second World War.
One could say that a Kashub's dilemma was how, being so different, to be a
Pole, while at the same time not wanting to lose or deny that very distinctness. A Pole's question, on the other hand, was: being so different – and,
what is more, celebrating the difference – how can a Kashub be a Pole?
Bohdan Jałowiecki aptly describes a similar situation: 'Regionalism is typically based on a feeling of identity. (...) Thus the essence of identity is on
the one hand the feeling of a bond with one's own group, on the other – a
greater or smaller distance from other groups. The distance need not necessarily imply alienation from a bigger unit – a group, retaining its identity,
is simultaneously aware of belonging to a larger community' (Jałowiecki
1993: 44). The question about the distance between the Kashubs and the
Polish national community is today one of the main areas of contention
within the Kashubian-Pomeranian movement.

With time, new types of problems began to confront the regional
movement. Hieronim Kubiak has written:

> In their socio-cultural variety, regional movements are a form of protest against
> standardised, universalised, and thus shallow, mass culture created by contemporary
> cities. The overriding objective for such a movement becomes the local character of

the all-nation culture and its defence, revival and development. Finally, (...) regional movements are a form of the articulation of group interests within the framework of a civic society; they strive not to abolish a nation-state but to modify it by self-government, to decompose the prerogatives of the government and to decentralise the state, to increase the pace of the development by releasing social energy. (Kubiak 1994: 30)

Both of these forms appear in the Kashubian movement. Attempts to preserve the local character – by no means solely identified with folklore – were and still are one of the most important domains of the ZK-P and other local organisations active in Kashubia. An equally important sphere of work for Kashubian activists is the civic activism of the Kashubian community.

However, the Kashubian movement should be expressed not only in regional but also in ethnic terms. This distinction is also made by Grzegorz Babiński, who perceives ethnic and regional movements as two types of social movement, and at the same time polar opposites (with the most extreme version of the ethnic movement being nationalism). In between lies a broad spectrum of transitional forms:

So two basic kinds of territorial movements can be distinguished – regional movements and ethnic movements. A regional movement aims to achieve or maintain local autonomy in matters of culture or economics, but always within the existing political and state structures. Its primary aim is to acquire independence from the excessive dominance of a political and cultural-economic centre, which the region is invariably subordinated to, one way or another. In contrast, ethnic movements are always characterised – to a lesser or greater degree – by irredentism. Even where they do not explicitly postulate political independence, the issue of full sovereignty is always there, be it in their ideology, in their general agenda, or in their plans for the very distant future. (Babiński 1995: 48)

Hence these movements are similar to each other in such respects as territorialism (undertaking activities to integrate the group socially), historicity (referring to a symbolic bond, usually the myth of common ancestry) and, frequently, a dislike for others. However, they also differ in many respects. First, there is the attitude towards the state: whereas regionalism strives for autonomy, an ethnic movement (particularly a nationalist movement) is usually separatist in nature. Secondly, there are differences in ideology (regionalism is based on the idea of a private homeland, while an ethnic movement attempts to create an ideological homeland) and in the degree of openness (regionalism accepts ties above the level of a region or state, often finding in them the confirmation and acceptance of its unique identity, while nationalism is wary of the idea of integration above state level and strives to create a closed community free of strangers). Moreover, regionalism is usually traditionalist whereas nationalism is 'modern' in the sense referred to by Ernest Gellner (1991). Finally, regionalism is defeatist because it concentrates on preserving a separate identity, while nationalism is aggressive, expansive and assimilative towards minorities (and it is xenophobic too) (Babiński 1995: 69–72).

Obviously not all ethnic movements are by definition nationalistic. This depends largely on why they came into existence and under what conditions they have been developing (Siemeńska 1976: 61–76). What seems to characterise the Kashubian movement as an ethnic movement is its proclivity for action intended to change the status of the group. It has been not only a 'reactive' movement, acting as a self-defence mechanism in the face of discrimination and persecution, but has also been geared towards the creation of new values and the amelioration of the social situation of the Kashubs (Babiński 1998: 105). As Andrzej Porębski wrote before the democratic breakthrough: 'among the Kashubs of today, most of the conditions for increased activity for ethnic reasons have been fulfilled: the feeling of having been wronged, growing expectations not satisfied by the centre, as well as a lasting feeling of identity' (Porębski 1991: 147).

In the years to follow, activity arising from this 'ethnic' motivation unquestionably increased. It could be argued that the Kashubian movement for a number of years has manifested a shift of focus to matters of ethnic identity, including the Kashubian language – which is understood as the basis for ethnicity, as well as the main parameter that marks out the Kashubs as a separate group. This focus is apparent as well in public displays of 'belonging' to the Kashubian community, in the development of Kashubian education, in efforts to ensure that Kashubian is introduced into the public sphere and in attempts to adopt relevant regulations to legally protect the Kashubs and their language.

Naturally, distinguishing between regionalism and ethnicity within concrete actions and initiatives is very difficult, practically impossible. However, it is possible to examine variations of focus (for instance in policy statements or in speeches by Kashubian leaders). Recent research indicates that there is considerable awareness among Kashubian-Pomeranian activists about ongoing changes leading to the ethnicisation of the movement. Attitudes to such an evolution of the Kashubian movement are varied: some people think that putting Kashubian interests first is not only desirable but downright necessary if – considering the meagre resources available – the rescue operation is to be successful. Others believe that attempts to preserve and develop Kashubian culture do not require opting for ethnicisation, for several reasons. Such an option might lead to the isolation of the Kashubs within the Pomeranian community, which would result in unnecessary divisions; it could also be counterproductive, alienating those who fear they cannot measure up to strict ethnic criteria (Komosa 2006: 148–207).

## What is the nature of the contemporary Kashubian movement?

Analysing the history of the Kashubian movement in the twentieth century, we can see a fairly tendency towards expansion (with the exception of the Second World War period and the first post-war years). The main organisation of the movement is the ZK-P, which came into existence in 1965 (Obracht-Prondzyński 2006b). This has been active uninterruptedly for more than fifty years, and that its structure has expanded to include as many as ninety-two branches and an estimated 4,000–6,000 members. Its branches can be found not only in the Kashubia region but also in nearby Pomerania (hence the name of the organisation). It is active in West Pomerania (in Szczecin), in Krajna, in Kociewie, in the Tuchola Forest, in the region of Powiśle (Lower Vistula), in Toruń and even in Warsaw.

There also exist within the structures of this organisation, or strongly connected with it, various other groups and organisations. These include students' clubs (the oldest one, 'Pomorania', has been active in Gdańsk since 1962; similar clubs are located in Słupsk and Toruń), scholarly organisations (e.g. the Kashubian Institute), editorial offices (e.g. the monthly publication *Pomerania*), educational institutions (e.g. Kashubian Folk High School in Wieżyca), electronic media, museums, folk groups, amateur theatres, choirs, and associations for professional or amateur artists.

Analysing this dense and diverse network, we can see the increasing pluralisation of the Kashubian-Pomeranian movement and its related groups. The process does not necessarily run smoothly. There are definite tensions, and there have even been instances where the role of the ZK-P as the representative of the Kashubian community has been challenged. A generational conflict is at play here, as well as contesting views on how the ethnic status of the group should be perceived: is it an ethnic group with dual identity – Kashubian and Polish – or is it a separate nation? However, a new organisation has not yet emerged which might equal the ZK-P in potential, size or importance. The conflict is largely domestic and centres on attempts to influence the profile and programme of the ZK-P to become a fully ethnic organisation focused on the interests of the Kashubs (e.g. the protection and promotion of the Kashubian language, etc.). This conflict was very visible in the years 2002–5, but the supporters of this 'Kashubian idea' did not set up their own organisation as an alternative to the ZK-P. On the contrary, these people were active within the ZK-P, and one of the leaders of this group – Artur Jabłoński – even became president of the organisation in 2004.

The period after the national breakthrough in 1989 saw considerable changes in the activities of the ZK-P, with countless initiatives and cultural events. Many of these involved the whole region, though the power of the ZK-P has really become apparent in the numerous projects carried out by local branches: competitions, outings, festivals, *Baśka* games (a traditional Kashubian card game that even has its own league), snuff-taking competitions, meetings promoting Kashubian publications, tournaments, language courses, courses in journalism or embroidery, cookery lessons, and much more. All these attract a lot of participants, who become genuine propagators of the Kashubian way of life on a local level.

The first Kashubian convention was organised on 19 June 1999, when a special train went from the Hel Peninsula to Chojnice to celebrate the fact that for the first time ever all Kashubs found themselves living in one province (a result of the reform of administrative divisions in 1998, which led to the creation of the Pomeranian province). In 2000 the visit was returned: on this occasion a train went from Chojnice to the Hel Peninsula. The conventions have become an annual tradition ever since, held in a different place every year: Wejherowo (2001), Kartuzy (2002), Słupsk (2003), Kościerzyna (2004), Łeba (2005), Gdynia (2006), Brusy (2007), Gdańsk (2008) and Bytów (2009).

Another recent initiative is the Day of Kashubian Unity, which takes place on 19 March and commemorates the first time the title 'Kashubian prince' was used, in 1253, as one of the titles of the Pomeranian duke, Barnim. Since 2005 there have been meetings every year beside the Neptune Fountain to celebrate the anniversary of the first written mention of Kashubia. However, what really attracts attention are the accompanying events in Tuchom, Miastko and Bytów, where an attempt is made each year to break the world record in playing the accordion. The event was initiated by Marek Wantoch-Rekowski. The last meeting took place in 2009 in Bytów, gathering over 250 accordionists not only from Kashubia but also from various parts of Poland.

Another high-profile event is the annual Kashubian Spelling Bee, also known as the Kashubian Dictation. The first event took place on 18 May 2002 at the University of Gdańsk, its coordinator being Wanda Kiedrowska.

Many important new initiatives have been launched locally, and more often than not these attract participants from further afield. With time, many branches have come to specialise in organising particular events. These include the Review of Folk Groups in Wierzchucino (this branch also organises the Review of School Folk Groups, *Burczybas*); the Kashubian Review of Folk Art Created by Children and Youth in Bytów, which since 2001 has included the counties of Bytów, Kościerzyna and Kartuzy; Kashubian Saturdays in Bytów and later in Miastko; the Cod Festival in Łeba; a potato festival, *Bulwowi Bãks*, in Stężyca; the Kashubian Fair in Rumia; the Days of the Herring in Gdynia; Kashubian festivities in Rewa, organised by the branch in Dębogórze; the Festival of Kashubian and

Religious Culture in Gościnino; Kashubian Day in Słupsk (organised in the local university, together with the university authorities and students from the club 'Tatczëzna'); an archaeological festival in Leśno (organised in cooperation with the branch in Brusy); Krajna Feasts, organised by the branches in Miasteczko Krajeńskie and Buczek Wielki; a series of scholarly conferences and meetings for the general public in Tczew, entitled 'In the footsteps of the unknown socio-cultural activists of Kociewie'. The Zblewo branch had an interesting event which ran for a couple of years: the so-called white Saturdays, when consultant physicians from the Medical University of Gdańsk examined inhabitants of the district free of charge. This initiative was certainly important locally.

Obviously, there are also undertakings with a longer tradition, such as the canoeing event entitled 'In the footsteps of Remus', the name of which refers to the wandering of the hero of the greatest work of Kashubian literature, *Żecé i przigodë Remusa*. There are many more similar local initiatives involving recreation, sport and tourism.

The ZK-P hands out numerous awards, including the prestigious Medal of Stolem, given by the club 'Pomorania' to those individuals and institutions who have rendered the greatest service to Kashubia and Pomerania. The name refers to a legend about the mythical creatures known as 'stolems', or giants, who according to legend once inhabited Kashubia. Other awards include the Bernard Chrzanowski medal, 'He Who Made the Sea Breeze to Blow', for those who have contributed to making Kashubia and Pomerania famous, in Poland as well as abroad. There is also the *Skra Ormuzdowa* ('Spark of Ormuzd'), given by *Pomerania* to the activists within local communities; the Stamp of Świętopełk the Great, for services to the ZK-P; and the Antoni Abraham Medal Silver Snuffbox of Abraham, awarded by the Gdynia branch of the ZK-P (its first recipients were the magazine *Pomerania*, Rev. Hilary Jastak and the male choir 'Dzwon Kaszubski'). One final example is the new award established by the ZK-P – the Florian Ceynowa Award, 'The One Who Rouses Kashubia'. The first such award went to the newspaper *Dziennik Bałtycki* in 2005; the second, in 2006, went to Wojciech Kiedrowski, a book publisher, who for many years was editor-in-chief of the magazine *Pomerania*.

A significant part of the activity of the ZK-P is devoted to commemorating people and events. Between 1990 and 2001, more than seventy commemorative plaques, monuments and obelisks were unveiled. These activities were decidedly decentralised, for celebrations connected with commemorating people, institutions and historic events took place in several dozen places, some of them outside Kashubia. In 1993, commemorative plaques were unveiled in Wejherowo in honour of Alojzy Jagalski, Florian Ceynowa and Bishop Paweł Rohde. In 1994, an obelisk in honour of Duke Mściwoj II was unveiled in the cemetery in Rumia (the event was connected with the 40th anniversary of the granting of the town charter and the 700th anniversary of the death of the last duke of Pomerania). During the 18th Meeting in Pelplin (7–8 November 1997), the Board of Directors, the Pelplin branch of the ZK-P and the Pelplin Seminary co-organised a commemorative plaque devoted to Rev. Bernard Sychta, to be placed on the old parish priest's house. At the 24th Meeting in Wdzydze in 1998, Izydor Gulgowski, the creator of the open-air museum there, was commemorated with a plaque on the building which once housed the local primary school. In the same year, a plaque commemorating the painter Kazimierz Jasnoch was unveiled in the village of Jasnochówka, near Borsk. A memorable event took place in Gdynia on 23 June 2001, when a monument to Antoni Abraham was unveiled. On 29 June 2002, in the village of Przytarnia, a commemorative plaque was unveiled devoted to Rev. Bolesław Domański, the leader of the Union of Poles in Germany in the inter-war period. There are many further examples.

The democratic breakthrough also brought with it the opportunity to strengthen ties with foreign countries, and the ZK-P joined the Federal Union of European Nationalities, hosting this organisation's 1994 congress in Gdańsk. A delegation of the ZK-P attends the annual FUEN congresses; moreover, university students from the club 'Pomorania' maintain ties with the association Youth of European Nationalities.

Contact with various minority groups in Europe, maintained through the FUEN, has resulted in several new ideas. This is particularly visible in regional education, which has derived inspiration from the Frisian experience. One example of Kashubian-Frisian cooperation was the important visit of representatives of the Frisian Academy in April 1995. During their

stay, the Frisian guests visited the museum in Wejherowo, met representatives of the ZK-P in the Kashubian House, held talks at the University
of Gdańsk, and met with the provincial authorities. This contact led to a
strengthening of ties between the Kashubs and Frisians, especially among
people involved in education. A delegation of the Council of the Frisian
Movement in Kashubia visited in May 1996, and a project entitled 'Communicating Tubes' took place between 1999 and 2000, providing opportunities for skill-sharing regarding the teaching of an ethnic language. 199
people participated in the project, which ended in an international conference in Gołuń in June 2000, attended by the representatives of the local
government, schools, the Polish Ministry of National Education, education offices and Frisian guests. Links have also been established between
Kashubian and Frisian schools.

Another important initiative was the Conferences of the Pomeranian
Community Abroad, organised in the 1990s, which took place in the
Kashubian Folk High School in Starbienino. They owed their existence
to aid from the Voivode of Gdańsk (later of Pomerania), the head of the
Voivodeship executive board, and Stowarzyszenie 'Wspólnota Polska' (the
'Polish Community' Association). Every year they brought together representatives from various different countries: Germany, Norway, France,
Great Britain, Canada, Sweden, the USA, the Netherlands and Australia.
Participants had a chance to learn about the culture and history of Kashubia
and Pomerania, and also to become acquainted with the current socioeco-
nomic situation within Poland. They visited various districts in Pomerania,
and it was an important opportunity to present the work of the ZK-P and
to establish personal contacts. The importance of this event is apparent
in the visible revival of interest in researching family history among many
emigrants.

Although these conferences are no longer held, ties with the Kashubian-Pomeranian community abroad are still very strong. They led, for
example, to the signing of a partnership agreement between Bytów and
Winona, the US city where Derdowski spent the last years of his life and
was buried. Kashubian Americans, in turn, visit their homeland in ever-
increasing numbers, especially in the south-western part of the region
(the vicinity of Bytów, Lipusz and Brusy). Cooperation with America also

resulted in the publishing of English translations of Kashubian literature by Blanche Krbechek, Katarzyna Gawlik-Luiken and Stanisław Frymark. The first Kashubian museum was actually established in Winona, in 1976. It owes its existence to the efforts of Rev. Paul Breza, a descendant of a Kashub family (Szulist 2005: 81–2).

Similarly lively contacts are maintained with Kashubian Canadians. 2008 saw the commemoration of the 150th anniversary of emigration from partitioned Poland to Canada. The first group to reach Canada in 1858 happened to be Kashubian, so in the jubilee year a sizeable group of Kashubian activists went across the ocean to demonstrate the bonds between Kashubs in Poland and those in Canada. Kashubian traditions are still alive in Canada, as demonstrated by the existence of Heritage Park and the Kashub Heritage Museum in the Canadian village of Wilno, Ontario. They are run by the Society of Kashubian Descendants in Wilno, founded in 1998. Its mission is 'to record and commemorate the rich cultural heritage of all Kashubs, both of those who settled amidst the wild nature of Renfrew County, in the town of Renfrew, on the slopes of Polish hills surrounding Otter Lake, and of those from the Province of Quebec or the faraway Western Canada'. The first undertaking of the society was the opening of Heritage Park – an open-air museum in Wilno, which contains memorabilia connected to the first settlers. It exhibits 'Kashubian folk costumes, embroidery and pottery', displayed in 'several historical buildings' with original decoration. There are also artefacts connected with Kashubs serving in the Polish Armed Forces in the West in the Second World War (Mask Connolly 2004: 595–608).

Partnerships were established over several years between the ZK-P and Ostsee Akademie in Lübeck-Travemünde, with seminars and study trips organised. This was an excellent form of Polish-German cooperation and an opportunity to discuss even the most sensitive issues in Polish-German relations. This partnership resulted in the publication in 2000 of a 800-page bilingual book by Jozef Borzyszkowski and Dietmar Albrecht in 2000. The book came to be used a compendium of information about Kashubia and Pomerania. After 2000, this Polish-German cooperation continued with a new partner, Academia Baltica in Lübeck.

There has also been significant contact with Lusatian Sorbs, such as the
Sorbian presence at the second Kashubian Congress, Kashubian attendance at the eightieth anniversary of *Domowina* in Bautzen in 1992, Sorbian
Day in Gdańsk, publications on Sorbian themes, exchange of publications,
and exhibitions devoted to Sorbian matters in Kashubian museums. Links
have been established with the association *Kulturbund Mecklenburg und
Vorpommern* (resulting in the Days of Kashubian Culture in Schwerin
and numerous seminars both in Poland and in Germany), as well as with
Samogitians (Žemaitians) from Lithuania. A series of Days of Samogitian
Culture was organised in Gdańsk.

The Kashubs have always attached great importance to presenting
Kashubian culture abroad. It would be hard to count how many concerts
per year are given abroad by Kashubian folk groups, how many exhibitions
of Kashubian folk art are staged, how many seminars and meetings take
place. One such meeting should be mentioned: the Kashubian Day which
took place in the Polish consulate in Cologne in May 1993. This included
a photography exhibition by Dariusz Zaręba, paintings by Leon Bieszke,
an exhibition of Kashubian folk art curated by Krystyna Szałaśna of the
National Museum in Gdańsk, a stage appearance by the group Sierakowice,
and the presentation of Kashubian publications. The event was organised
by the ZK-P in cooperation with the Baltic Culture Centre, the Kashubian
Open-Air Ethnographic Park in Wdzydze and the Polish embassy in Germany, the ambassador at the time being Janusz Reiter from Kościerzyna.
Since then there have been several dozen similar presentations in various
European countries (most of them, admittedly, in Germany).

These international contacts – especially those which form part of
the process of Polish-German reconciliation, particularly significant and
difficult in Kashubia and Pomerania – have been noticed and appreciated
among the Kashubs, as evidenced by the fact that the ZK-P became the first
recipient of the Erich Brost Award in Gdańsk, in 1996. Brost was a social
democrat in the Free City of Danzig and an opponent of Hitler's regime.
The award ceremony took place in the Gdańsk Artus' Court.

## Kashubian culture today

Kashubian culture has been perceived and defined by scholars and journalists in very disparate ways. To begin with, it used to be defined as a peasant culture, because most Kashubs have been strongly associated with the peasantry for centuries. Traditional folk culture, created by villagers, is documented primarily by open-air museums, which can be found all over Kashubia. But Kashubian culture is not only a peasant culture. There also recur motifs typical of the culture of the nobility (especially the poorer nobility) and the landed gentry. There are also elements of the culture of the bourgeoisie; the historic role of Gdańsk and – more recently – of Gdynia merits a mention in this context. To top it all, we must remember that there are elements of the fishermen's culture, which is so uniquely Kashubian and so different from traditional ideas about peasant culture.

Kashubian culture certainly cannot be perceived solely in terms of folk culture, even setting aside the fundamental question of whether folk culture still exists at all, since that would imply overlooking those elements that belong to the so-called 'high' or elite culture. The same dilemma can be seen in debates about Kashubian literature.

Neither can Kashubian culture be reduced to a kind of local culture created by a small community for its own needs. Admittedly, that was the case for a very long time. But ever since the revolution in communications in the middle of the nineteenth century, which helped to break the isolation of the villages, and ever since Ceynowa and the beginning of the Kashubian regional movement, an all-Kashubian culture been in existence. It is still all-Kashubian today, even though local differences, once so typical of Kashubia, have not disappeared altogether. Anybody acquainted with Kashubia will instantly perceive the differences among such Kashubian subgroups as Bëloks, Krëbans, Gôchs or Lësôks, and those differences are not limited merely to dialectal differentiation.

Thus it can be said that Kashubian culture used to be a peasant, folk and local culture, but today it is something more. It contains motifs characteristic of the gentry, the bourgeoisie, the intelligentsia and the fishermen, and, furthermore, this culture has been affected by more general changes connected with the flourishing of popular, mass culture. Both the creators of and the audience for Kashubian culture have felt the influence of changes which have considerably altered both Polish and European culture in the past few decades. Phenomena as the counterculture, mass culture, the sharp rise in the importance of electronic media, the influence of television on cultural patterns, and – finally – globalisation were bound to influence the Kashubs.

All of the above have had a great impact on current cultural activity among the Kashubs, and this activity has acquired varied forms, aided by the existence of a dense network of cultural institutions, organisations and informal groups.

Literature is discussed elsewhere in this book, but the ways in which Kashubian literature have been popularised merit a mention here. For example, the competition *Poezja rodnej mowë* ('The Poetry of the Mother Tongue') has been organised in Chmielno ever since 1972. It is the biggest Kashubian literature event aimed at children and young people, attracting several hundred participants from Kashubia each year. Similar competitions are organised locally in many Kashubian districts and counties e.g. the declamation contest *Bë nie zabëc mòwë starków* ('Not to Forget the Language of the Forefathers'), in Puck.

Stage productions in Kashubia are of a different nature. There is no professional theatre group in the region, which does not mean that there is no theatre at all. On the contrary, amateur theatre thrives, drawing on Kashubian literature and looking to Kashubian customs for inspiration. More importantly, theatre initiatives are often found locally in small village communities. Interesting examples include the theatre group *BELECO* in Zapceń, active since the mid-1980s, as well as the theatre group *Bina* in Sierakowice. To this one might add the extremely popular revival of the nativity plays, as well as the activities of caroller groups, some of whose performances are quite complex and theatrical.

An absolutely exceptional phenomenon – the theatre *Dialogus* – was set up in 1992 in Parchowo by Jaromir Szroeder. This group produces experimental performances, drawing on Kashubian culture and literature; examples of their productions include *Drzwi. Misterium kaszubskie* and the stage adaptation of *Żëcé i przigodë Remusa*. For several years from 1994, the theatre also hosted the Theatrical Feast, frequented by ensembles from all over Europe.

Professional performances conncted to Kashubian literature and folklore have also been presented by the City Theatre in Gdynia, by the puppet theatres *Tęcza* in Słupsk and *Miniatura* in Gdańsk, and by the TV Theatre, which (more than twenty years ago) presented a production based on Majkowski's novel *Żëcé i przigodë Remusa*. Finally, it is important to mention the phenomenon of Shakespeare in Kashubian. During Shakespeare's birthday anniversary celebrations in the Baltic Culture Centre in Gdańsk, in April 2007, fragments of *The Taming of the Shrew* were presented in Kashubian.

The functioning of literature – and culture more generally – depends on its availability to a potential audience. In this regard, publishing houses play an important role. Before 1989, books about Kashubian matters and in Kashubian were published chiefly by the ZK-P. By 1990 it had published almost 350 titles. All this was done as a grassroots initiative, without any state subventions (or only with token subsidies), without any allocation of paper (which was the usual practice in communist times), with no guarantee of printing (printing being done only in state print shops), with no safeguarding of copyright, and in the context of unending struggle with the state authorities. This achievement indicates how efficient and determined the regional Kashubian elites could be.

As a result of political changes, the publishing market became more diversified. Kashubian books are still produced by regional associations (including the ZK-P), but also by privately owned publishing houses (e.g. Oficyna Czëc, Wydawnictwo Region from Gdynia, Wydawnictwo ROST, Wydawnictwo BiT, Wydawnictwo Nowator), by foundations, by learned societies (before 1989 the Gdańsk Learned Society rendered considerable service to the Kashubs), by museums, by local government (e.g. monographs about specific towns and villages), by universities (especially the University of Gdańsk and the Pomeranian University in Słupsk), by the local press (e.g. *Kurier Bytowski*, *Gazeta Kartuska*), by schools, parishes and dioceses (e.g. the prominent role of the publishing house *Bernardinum* in Pelplin), and by libraries.

There have also been significant developments in the press. When *Biuletyn Zrzeszenia Kaszubskiego* came into existence in 1963, no-one could have predicted that in the years to come it would become the most important and longest-lived Kashubian magazine, the *Pomerania*. The only interruption in its appearance was between 1982 and 1983, when it was suspended as a result of martial law being introduced in Poland on 13 December 1981.

Nowadays in Kashubia there are plenty of local newspapers, several in each county. Their focus might be just one county, or a district, or several districts. There are newspapers published by local governments and by regional organisations (including the ZK-P), but the majority are private ventures. In many of them, not only are Kashubian matters discussed, but they are discussed in Kashubian. Moreover, the biggest daily in the region, *Dziennik Bałtycki*, has a Kashubian insert called *Norda*. *Głos Pomorza*, published in Słupsk, also included a Kashubian insert, *Głos Kaszëb*, for a couple of years.

The Kashubian language has a strong presence within electronic media. On the Gdańsk television channel, there is a Kashubian magazine programme called *Rôdno zemia*, and two Kashubian programmes are broadcast on the public radio station Radio Gdańsk: an hour-long weekly programme, *Na bòtach ë w borach*, and (since 2004) a morning news programme, *Klëka*.

A private radio station called *Radio Kaszëbë* has been in existence since the end of 2004, run by the Association of the Puck Region. It is dedicated entirely to Kashubian culture and to informing its listeners about the most important events in Kashubia.

The internet enjoys ever-increasing popularity as a source of information about Kashubia, its culture, its institutions and events of importance to the Kashubian community. An internet search using words such as 'Kashubia' and 'Kashubs' (in various languages) yields thousands of websites, many of them created abroad. There is a Kashubian version of Wikipedia, <http://www.csb.wikipedia.org>, and a great deal of Kashubian material can be found at <http://www.naszekaszuby.pl>, not only current affairs but also feature articles, academic texts aimed at the general public, rich illustrative materials, a Kashubian bibliography, a bibliography of the contents of *Pomerania* magazine, and a link to an online bookstore with many Kashubian and Pomeranian books on offer. There is also a discussion forum. Another important Kashubian website is <http://www.kaszubia. com>, edited in Kashubian, Polish and German. It contains a Kashubian bibliography, materials on history, language, ethnography and genealogy, many literary and religious texts, and a concordance of place names. Particularly valuable are programmes for computer users, such as *Cassubdict*, a Kashubian dictionary for Windows, *K-Melon*, a Kashubian version of a browser, a Kashubian keyboard set, and a complete Linux programme in Kashubian (*Linuxcsb.org*). The website <http://www.rastko.net/rastko-ka>, the Kashubian sub-site of one of the largest Slavonic portals, has a different profile: it contains a great deal of historical, literary and linguistic material. We can also find an online Kashubian dictionary, <http://www. cassubia-dictionary.com>, a Kashubian word processor called *KaszEd*, <http://kaszed.ZK-P.pl>, an electronic version of the Majkowski's novel *Żecè i przigodë Remusa*, and the websites of Kashubian organisations such as the ZK-P, <http://www.kaszubi.pl>, the Kashubian Institute, <http:// www.instytutkaszubski.pl>, Kashubian museums, schools, local governments, local newspapers and magazines, libraries, and community centres. The internet enables links to be established with Kashubs dispersed all over the world. Kashubian organisations and communities from the USA, Germany and Canada have created their own websites. The website <http://www.studienstelleog.de/kaschuben/kaschub-inhalt.htm> offers German-language texts devoted to Kashubs. KANA, the Kashubian Association of North America, also has a website, <http://www.ka-na.org>, as does the Kashubian Family Research Centre, <http://www.kashuba. org>. Information about Canadian Kashubs can be found on the websites <http://www.wilno.org> and <http://www.kaszuby.net>. The internet also helps to propagate Kashubian literature, both classic and contemporary. A group of young Kashubian writers called *Zymk* meet occasionally in Wejherowo and publish their own literary almanac under the same title (seven volumes have appeared so far). Information about the group and its publications can be found at <http://www.zymk.net>. The classic novel *Żecé i przigodë Remusa* is available online both as an e-book and an audio book at <http://monika.univ.gda.pl/~literat/remus/remusa.pdf>.

Many literary works can be found on the site *Kaszëbskô Czëtnica*, <http://
www.czetnica.org>, which includes classics by Karnowski, Budzisz, Heyke
and Ceynowa as well as works by contemporary writers, and also displays
translations of world literature (e.g. Agatha Christie, Terry Pratchett and
Charles Dickens). There is also a comic strip, *Inverloch*. All text, including
the site descriptions, is in Kashubian.

No discussion of the institutions which currently foster, protect and
propagate Kashubian culture would be complete without mentioning the
role of museums. Kashubia is one of the regions in Poland with the highest
concentration of museums (Obracht-Prondzyński 2008). The best-known
are the open-air museums in Wdzydze (established in 1906 and the oldest
of the kind in Poland) and in Kluki. There are also smaller museums in
Nadole, Sominy and Silno. Sizeable Kashubian and Pomeranian collections are displayed in the ethnographic museums in Oliwa (a division of
the National Museum in Gdańsk), Bytów, Chojnice and Kartuzy, and
in the ethnographic sections of museums in Słupsk, Puck and Lębork.
There are also specialist museums such as the Museum of the Polish School
in Płotowo (which from 1929 housed the first ever Polish school in the
Bytów region, which at that time belonged to Germany), the Museum of
Kashubian Pottery of the Necel Family in Chmielno, the Museum of Fishery in Hel, and the Museum of the National Anthem in Będomin. Józef
Wybicki, author of the anthem, was born in Będomin into a well-known
noble Kashub family.

Not only did the museums not fall into decay after the change of the
political system in 1989: they have actually developed. Alongside those
already in existence, new ones have been established; some of these have
been created by local governments, in villages such as Sierakowice, Łebno
and Lipusz, and also in small towns. For example, the farmstead in Brusy,
combined with the nearby farmstead belonging to Józef Chełmowski, the
most famous folk artist in Kashubia, has created a kind of a local community centre. Other museums have been established by private individuals
(e.g. the Thatched Cottage Museum in Jastarnia, which displays a collection of fishing paraphernalia), by the Church (e.g. at the parish church in
Żukowo and at the Wejherowo monastery), or by branches of the ZK-P
(e.g. the so-called *chëcz*, a fisherman's hut, in Jastarnia). It is estimated that

there are also several dozen regional exhibition rooms (chiefly in schools), some of which with time have evolved into independent museums. The museum in Kościerzyna, for example, was created in the renovated town hall in the market square.

There is one more museum in which Kashubs take special pride: the Museum of Kashubian-Pomeranian Literature and Music in Wejherowo. This is located in the beautifully renovated Palace of the Przebendowski Family and preserves memorabilia connected with the most famous Kashubian and Pomeranian writers, musicians and composers, eminent cultural figures, scholars, and regional activists; for example, Majkowski, Karnowski, Fenikowski, Rogaczewski, Sędzicki, Suchecki, Trojanowska, Rompski and Rydzkowski. The museum owns a sizeable library (including antique books), and an impressive collection of regional publications and maps. Its activities include exhibitions, publishing, lectures and conferences (among others, it regularly co-organises the scholarly conference 'The Regional Variety of Polish in Pomerania'). It is one of the most important cultural and scholarly centres in Kashubia.

Kashubian museums are important not just for the collecting and documenting of past Kashubian culture, but also supporting the development of Kashubian culture today. From the end of the Second World War, the communist authorities did their best to limit this culture to state-approved folklore activities. Their attempts failed, with Kashubian culture preserving its original character based on its rich heritage. After 1990, there was actually a genuine outburst of cultural activity in the domain of folklore. Despite the difficult economic situation, the old folk groups (e.g. dance groups and choirs) not only survived but increased in size considerably. In contemporary Kashubia, there are several dozen folk groups; travelling all over the world, they are the best ambassadors for Kashubian culture (Obracht-Prondzyński, 2002: 781–3). In the 1990s Kashubian Festivals took place in Słupsk, and International Folk Festivals, organised by the group *Krëbanë* from Brusy, still take place in several locations in Kashubia (Bytów, Sierakowice and Chojnice, to name a few). The oldest review of Kashubian folk groups takes place in Chojnice; its history stretches back over thirty years.

One other event that deserves mention was the stage appearance of an improvised choir of several hundred singers – members of Kashubian folk groups – at the papal Mass in Sopot during John Paul II's pilgrimage to Poland in 1999.

We should remember, however, that Kashubian music is not only folk music (Frankowska 2005). New musical undertakings are sometimes very far-removed from the stereotypes of folk culture. In parallel with dozens of folk groups, in Kashubia also has rock bands (*Chëcz, Wãdzëboczi, Pò drëdżi stranie, C.Z.A.D.*), and groups which sing poetry in Kashubian (e.g. *Kùtin*). Kashubian folklore ensembles have played countless times with well-known jazz musicians such as Leszek Kułakowski and Jarosław Śmietana. Kashubian music is also a source of inspiration for professional choirs, such as *Schola Cantorum Gedanensis*, which has made recordings of Kashubian Christmas carols. Finally, a major event for Kashubian music was the publication of the *Kashubian Songbook*, prepared by Katarzyna Gaertner, in 1996.

Kashubia is home to hundreds of active folk artists who specialise in such traditional crafts as embroidery, basketry, pottery, folk sculpture, making objects out of horn (e.g. snuff horns), and painting on glass. A competition called 'Folk Talents' has been running for more than thirty years, and every year it attracts many young people from Kashubia (Szymański 2006). There is also the important and prestigious competition 'Contemporary Folk Art of Kashubia' (Szkulmowska 1997), as well as plenty of local competitions.

Open-air workshops deserve a mention too, including an exceptional sculpture workshop which preceded the 1999 visit of Pope John Paul II to Sopot. During this event several dozen sculptors, chiefly from Kashubia (but also from Kociewie and Krajna), and led by Marian Kołodziej, prepared an altar consisting of dozens of folk sculptures (Hlebowicz and Arabski 1999). It was probably one of the most original altars in the history of papal pilgrimages. Nowadays figures from this altar serve as roadside or yard shrines in various parts of Kashubia and Pomerania; many are also to be found in the sanctuary of Our Lady in Gdańsk-Matarnia.

Folk art has enjoyed a significant revival in popularity, and is now displayed in all ethnographic museums in Kashubia and Pomerania; it has also become an important source of income for artists, who display their work during festivals and fairs in the tourist season. The most popular event of the kind is probably the Wdzydze Fair, which takes place in the open-air museum in Wdzydze. Art has also found its way into shops specialising in Kashubian souvenirs. Naturally, there emerges the question of the thin line between art and its commercial production.

Apart from museums and regional organisations, there is one further institution whose importance for the propagation and development of Kashubian folk art cannot be overestimated. This is the Kashubian Folk High School in Wieżyca. It was established in 1983 and ever since its foundation its focus has been Kashubian culture, along with ecology, education and civic matters. Even before 1989 the School was a very important centre, preparing independent local government personnel and political leaders. For the new political elites from the provinces of Gdańsk, Bydgoszcz and Słupsk, the School was also seen as in some way trustworthy, because of the involvement of the leaders of the ZK-P in the organisation of training. From 1989 onwards the ZK-P made strenuous efforts to take the institution over, finally succeeded in 1994. A year later the School opened another branch in Starbienino in northern Kashubia (near Choczewo). A Centre for Ecological Education was established here, and the entire complex (a period manor house and an outbuilding) has been fitted with very advanced equipment (including a wind power station, an ecological heating system and solar batteries). The centre was through cooperation between the ZK-P, the Gdańsk University of Technology, the Polish Ecological Club and the Danish SFOF Club. In 1997 the School was named after Józef Wybicki.

The scope of the School is extremely wide. It looks after folk artists – organising open-air workshops, social gatherings, discussions, seminars and workshops presenting traditional crafts, participating in the project 'Vanishing Professions', and collecting folk art and displaying it in its own art gallery. It also organises seminar and conferences on ecological matters and presentations of modern ecological technologies. Other activities include international exchanges for young people and the organisation of youth camps for participants from East and West. The School also specialises in civic education and work for the local government (it was the School that gave rise to the Pomeranian Association of Rural Districts, and it holds courses in the basics of democracy for teachers, young people and local politicians); regional education (mostly seminars and workshops for those who teach about the region); courses in journalism and tourism; courses for ZK-P activists (on how to run social projects, how to raise funds, etc.); the dissemination of knowledge (e.g. organising scholarly conferences); the dissemination of information about the European Union (especially among farmers); and adult and continuing education (e.g. meetings and workshops for specialists in andragogy from Poland and beyond. Between 2001 and 2003, an international project called 'Folk High School – a School for Life' was carried out (Byczkowski, Maliszewski and Przybylska 2003; Byczkowska and Maliszewski 2005). The Kashubian Folk High School is also the venue for many ZK-P events.

The School is one of the best Polish centres for the reinvention of folk high schools, and has taken full advantage of the experience of countries in Western Europe. Unfortunately, the proposed legislation about folk high schools has not been passed; however, the School does its best to implement modern educational and ecological projects.

## Scholarship and science

Kashubian issues are inseparably connected with scholarship; it was scholars who first began to research, describe and discuss the problem of Kashubian identity, ethnic origin and language. These discussions, originally held only among small circles, led as early as the nineteenth century to a heated scholarly debate, which resulted in the popularisation of knowledge about the Kashubs, as well as, rather unexpectedly, strengthening Kashubian identity (Borzyszkowski and Obracht-Prondzyński 2001).

Kashubian studies have been important throughout the entire post-war period, but considerable changes took place after the democratic breakthrough in 1989. First of all, there was a marked increase in research, visible in the number of publications and conferences dedicated to Kashubian issues (there have been more than fifty conferences in the last dozen years). Before 1989 almost every scholarly book about Kashubia was an event, whereas now so many are published that every novice in the field of Kashubian studies has to face an avalanche of literature.

At the same time, there has been a qualitative change in the progress of Kashubian studies. A case in point, within the field of history, is the scholarly output of Zygmunt Szultka, which has transformed our knowledge about the Kashubs of West Pomerania and has provided a wealth of new information on the oldest relics of Kashubian literature (Szultka 1991, 1992, 1994). New historical studies of Kashubian towns and villages are appearing all the time.

A comparable breakthrough in sociology is the work of Marek Latoszek and Brunon Synak. Recent linguistic work within Kashubian studies has also been impressive (Breza 2001; Treder 2005).

Of equal significance are achievements in ethnography such as a three-volume monograph on musical folklore by Ludwik Bielawski and Aurelia Mioduchowska (1997), and monographs by Tadeusz Sadkowski (1997) and Jan Perszon (1999); in musicology such as Witoslawa Frankowska's monograph (2006); in the history of literature; and in biography, particularly the recent scholarly biographies of Majkowski (Borzyszkowski 2002), Karnowski (Obracht-Prondzyński 1999) and Sędzicki (Schodzińska 2003).

The list could be extended, to include for example new publications in pedagogy, political science and geography. A synopsis of the present state of knowledge about the Kashubs across various fields (ranging from geography, through history, sociology and literature to ethnography) is the bilingual monograph by Jozef Borzyszkowski and Dietmar Albrecht published in 2000. A considerable portion of scholarly output up until 2004 is listed in Obracht-Prondzyński (2004d), published by the Kashubian Institute and including nearly 10,000 entries.

The role of the Catholic church in the Kashubian community

In the new situation after the democratic breakthrough, co-operation with church institutions no longer equalled dissent. Before this, Kashubs were frequently accused of clericalism by the communist authorities, which was a really grave accusation.

The supreme achievement of the era of democracy was the publication of fundamental religious texts in Kashubian. This process started with the translations of the New Testament. The first of those, carried out by Franciszek Grucza and including the four Gospels, appeared in Poznań in 1992. The second, by Eugeniusz Gołabek (vel Gołąbk), was published in fragments, through the efforts of the ZK-P, on the occasion of the papal pilgrimage in 1987, and as a complete edition in 1993, in partnership with the diocesan publishing house in Pelplin. The third was a Gospel translation carried out by Adam Ryszard Sikora from Poznań. The heated debate that accompanied Grucza's first translation in no way alters the fact that these publications were of paramount importance for the prestige and status of the Kashubian language.

Collections of sermons, hymnbooks and even a lectionary in Kashubian have also been published. The Kashubian community is still linked to the church by a strong bond and many Kashubs are deeply religious. The presence of Kashubian in the life of the church, even if sometimes controversial, certainly contributed to increasing the prestige of the language and broadened the scope of its application. At present there are a number of churches where the Mass is regularly celebrated either partly or entirely in Kashubian (mostly in towns). The first such Mass was introduced in 1987 in the church of Our Lady of the Rosary in Gdańsk-Przymorze by Rev. Bogusław Głodowski. Rosary prayers in church and May devotions to Our Lady (still popular in Kashubia) are celebrated in Kashubian, as are prayers said during the Stations of the Cross (e.g. in the Wejherowo calvary). Following the death of Pope John Paul II, an all-night vigil was held in Sianowo. The church service, attended by several thousand people, was broadcast by the regional television station TVP Gdańsk.

The education of clerical students is obviously of great importance with regard to the presence of Kashubian in church. In the Pelplin Seminary students can learn Kashubian, and can join Klub Sztudérów Kaszëbów *Jutrzniô*, which issues a periodical entirely in Kashubian, called *Zwónk Kaszëbsczi*.

Several spectacular events of considerable symbolic value have taken place in recent years. The first was the Kashubian pilgrimage to the Holy Land in September 2000. 412 pilgrims, including twelve priests and two bishops, were led by Archbishop Tadeusz Gocłowski and by the president of the ZK-P, Brunon Synak. A commemorative plaque with the Kashubian version of the Lord's Prayer was affixed in the Church of the Pater Noster in Jerusalem, among many similar ones in languages from all over the world. The pilgrimage was a great success and was extensively covered by the media, with numerous press reports and feature articles, five television documentaries and a commemorative album. A similar pilgrimage took place a year later, in May 2001. This was led by an honorary member of the ZK-P, Bishop Andrzej Śliwiński. Seventy-eight people took part, and the focal point, as in 2000, was a meeting at the Pater Noster convent on the Mount of Olives. A third pilgrimage to the Holy Land took place in October 2005 and 173 pilgrims participated. It was intended to commemorate the fifth anniversary of unveiling and blessing of the plaque with the text of the Lord's Prayer.

Another important event was the Kashubs' Pilgrimage to Rome in October 2004, seeking the beatification of Konstanty Dominik. This was not the first attempt by Kashubs to make a pilgrimage to Rome. In 1975, on the occasion of the Holy Year, a Kashubian pilgrimage headed by Rev. Hilary Jastak was to depart for Rome, but they were prevented by the intervention of state authorities and by chaos at the Okęcie airport in Warsaw. Protests and complaints were to no avail. After spending a day waiting at Okęcie, all the pilgrims had to return to Gdynia.

Finally, a pilgrimage to the Tatra Mountains took place in 2006, which served to emphasise the friendship between the Kashubs and the Górals (Highlanders).

Pilgrimages also take place closer to home; during the annual Boat Pilgrimages fishermen from the Hel Peninsula go to the parish church in

Puck on the Day of St Peter and St Paul, at the end of June. This is not only a religious experience but also a tourist attraction. Regional ZK-P branches from north Kashubia have been organising these pilgrimages for many years, while branches from central Kashubia co-organise church fêtes in Sianowo every year.

The Pope's visit to Pomerania in 1999 was also an event of considerable importance. In Sopot, during the ceremonial Mass, a Kashubian choir of several hundred people sang, and the altar was prepared by folk artists, led by Marian Kołodziej. Fishermen also attended the meeting, arriving across the bay on eighty boats carrying 1,400 people in stylised Kashubian costumes. These constituted an important and memorable element of the meeting, particularly at the point where the boats formed the sign of the cross in the middle of the Gulf of Puck.

The picture would be incomplete without a mention of the exceptional involvement of various branches of the ZK-P (especially from the north of Kashubia) in activities intended to bring forward the beatification of Bishop Konstanty Dominik, 'our little Dominik'. In Gdynia, in 1986, a tradition arose of regular Masses dedicated to this aim, and the custom has since spread elsewhere. Bishop Dominik is commemorated in various ways throughout the region, including a stained-glass window in the church of Christ the King in Wejherowo, which was founded by branches of the ZK-P.


# The Kashubs and the Kashubian-Pomeranian Association in politics


Pomerania is unquestionably a specific region, with relatively substantial social capital and 'collective pro-democratic assets', the latter 'consisting not only of local democratic traditions, defined in various ways, but also a moral climate and cultural aura, which determine a public discourse according to principles which grant its participants equal opportunities to express their views' (Kurczewska and Kempy and Bojar 1998: 94). Importantly, there is also a high level of 'civic culture' depending on 'the internalisation of the general values referring to principles ruling the public life: moderation, tolerance, efficiency, participation in public life, knowledge or 'civic involvement' (Kurczewska and Kempy and Bojar 1998: 94). That 'civic culture' in Pomerania has obviously been nurtured by the contribution of the ZK-P, an important institutional actor on the political scene in the region.

During the period of democratic transformations, the ZK-P had several significant advantages (Obracht-Prondzyński 2002b), the most significant being the organisation's substantial experience and deep local roots, in contrast with many of the new political elite. These roots made the organisation an efficient instrument for organising political support. Moreover, local leaders of the organisation were well known and enjoyed high prestige (Jałowiecki 1991: 58). The ZK-P had their own press at their disposal – in particular the opinion-forming monthly *Pomerania*, but also numerous local newspapers and bulletins. They also had a well-developed network of contacts in various circles and a clearly formulated programme, rooted in Bądkowski's political ideas; in addition, there was no clear competition from other regional organisations in Pomerania.

From the very start of the transformation period, the ZK-P was a major actor not only in cultural matters, but also a quasi-political party: 'quasi-' because the Association has never been a regional party in the full sense of the concept. It has never attempted to take over power in the region, which would not have been possible anyway before 1998, as no elective authority structures existed on a regional level (although figures related to the ZK-P did assume power in many municipalities). Moreover, political activity has never been a priority of the ZK-P movement, its key activity being within the fields of culture, education and ecology. According to its statutory regulations and various platforms, the ZK-P has remained a civic organisation (an NGO), and periodic suggestions about transforming it into a political party have been firmly rejected. In 2006, Artur Jabłoński (then the ZK-P president) suggested founding a regional Pomeranian party, in a piece in the Tricity supplement to *Gazeta Wyborcza*, which received considerable news coverage. Although the author made it clear that it was his personal idea, his position meant that it was immediately associated with the entire

Association, causing heated commentary in the media. No great interest has been shown, however, on the part of Pomeranian political circles, or among activists of the ZK-P, and on 3 February 2007, the ZK-P Supreme Council made a resolution firmly dissociating themselves from that initiative and stating that the ZK-P remains a socio-cultural organisation, which refrains from supporting any political party. It seems that in Pomerania a suitable atmosphere does not exist for the creation of a separate political body organised on the model of the regional parties which exist throughout Europe, such as the Convergencia i Unió, Euzko Alderdi Jeltzalea, Partido Nacionalista Vasco EAJ, Coalicion Canaria and Bloque Nacionalista Galego in Spain; the Serbska Ludowa Strona, Wendische Volkspartei-Lausitzer Volkspartei and Schleswig Südschleswigscher Wählerverband in Germany; the Lega Nord and Partito Sardo d'Azione PSd'A in Italy; the Volksunie and the Party of German-Speaking Belgians in Belgium; the Scottish National Party and Plaid Cymru in the United Kingdom; and the Union du Peuple Alsacien and Partitu di a Nazione Corsa in France.

The ZK-P is active in various fields, and it has sometimes proved to be difficult to coordinate all its different activities. The organisation is undoubtedly one of those regional movements which – as emphasised earlier – constitutes an expression of group interests within a civic society. The policy and organisational form of ZK-P was correctly defined by Marek Latoszek as the 'Formula of the three P's: Pragmatism, Professionalism and Politicisation' (Latoszek 1993: 9). However, how can pragmatism be measured – by effectively fighting for power? How does one evaluate professionalism, sometimes confused with bureaucracy? In the case of politicisation, the dispute has focused on such questions as: whether to stand for municipal elections, either alone or in coalition, or to hold back entirely; how to reconcile the diverse political views of ZK-P members with the idea of running independently in elections; how to provide support, and to whom (individual candidates, electoral committees, single parties and their members, or independent members); what should be offered in return for this support (some form of 'gratitude', whatever this means?); how to represent the interests of ZK-P and the Kashubs as a whole in political life; how to protect the organisation from the low standards of political culture; whether referring to Kashubian specificity is politically efficient (e.g. by issuing election leaflets in Kashubian); whether Kashubian interests and expectations should be addressed. Such questions could be multiplied. Various answers have been given in the last two decades, various strategies chosen, and various opinions expressed as regards the organisation itself, its leaders and its members. Developments on a national scale have been crucial, such as the alliances of parties originating from the *Solidarność* movement and their persuasive efforts to put up common candidates for the Senate. This was particularly important 1997, when the ZK-P lent official support to two candidates, Donald Tusk (from *Unia Wolności*) and Edmund Wittbrodt (from *Akcja Wyborcza 'Solidarność'*). Both the candidates successfully won Senate seats.

It is also worth remembering that in 1991 Jozef Borzyszkowski won a seat in the Senate under the auspices of the ZK-P. As a ZK-P candidate he came off second best in Gdańsk province with 30.8 per cent of the vote (155,694 votes), and in twenty-five municipalities (not just in Kashubian territory), he gained over 50 per cent of the vote.

Another element of the ZK-P's strategy has been to assure their representation within the provincial authorities, the most significant examples being the positions of Józef Borzyszkowski as deputy governor of Gdańsk province from 1990 to1996, Kazimierz Kleina as governor of Słupsk province from 1993 to 1997, and Roman Zaborowski as governor of the Pomeranian province since 2007.

Another important question is how to politicise the Kashubian ethnic programme. After the democratic transformations, the Kashubs presented several problems, not only the obvious issue of local administration and territorial structure reform (the latter aimed at including the entire territory of Kashubia within one province, and creating regions such as Vistulan Pomerania). They also made fundamental demands such as:

- the broadcasting of Kashubian programmes in public media
- introduction of regional education in public schools at all grades
- empowering Kashubian representatives to occupy senior posts in government administration (as was already possible through elections on the regional and local level)
- protection of the Kashubian language and culture by legislation
- consideration of Kashubian specificity in planned strategies for regional development.

Many of those demands have already been fulfilled. This does not mean, however, that debate has ceased. The Kashubian movement was never a monolith in the political sense, but under conditions of freedom and democracy, with no fear of the authorities (who formerly used to take advantage of any divisions), there have been numerous tensions and conflicts. The principal object of dispute is how to protect the language: by striving for a minority status for the Kashubs, or a separate national status, as during the National Population Census in 2002? Should the language issue be the focus or should it be perceived as an element of the wider culture? Should the region become bilingual, with Kashubian as the second official language, or should such demands be avoided so as not to encourage anti-Kashub hostility? The political culture in Pomerania does not seem developed enough to accept Kashubian demands without opposition. There was considerable resistance to the adoption of the black griffin against a golden background as the coat of arms of the newly established province of Pomerania, since this is a Kashubian symbol and Pomerania is not only the home of the Kashubs. Ultimately, the coat of arms was adopted, but for the same reasons the proposal to change the name of the province to Kashubia-Pomerania was rejected (although in that case even the ZK-P was divided). The solutions implemented in the province of Friesland in the Netherlands will remain no more than an example for a long time to come.

The political strategy of the ZK-P has not changed significantly since 1989. Their strategy and ideological programme is still rooted in Pomeranian political ideas developed many years previously. The organisation aims to enhance participation in the public life of a civic society, with a focus on the following activity:

- participation in elections: putting up its own candidates or creating coalitions, mainly at the local level, with similar organisations or citizens' groups. Also, engaging the ZK-P structures in electoral activity, such as leading or supporting canvasses, declaring support for individual candidates or programmes, and mobilisation of constituents.
- active membership of ZK-P members in political parties, but without any official alliance between the ZK-P and particular parties. This requirement refers to the organisation as a whole, rather than its local structures, who have frequently formed coalitions with parties

originating from the Solidarność movement or with the Polish People's Party (PSL).
- taking up official positions on the most important political questions affecting the region, especially during apparent political crises.
- organising or supporting various actions aimed at protecting group interests, such as rgw adoption of the coat of arms for the province of Pomerania or proposal to change the province's name, as well as direct support for public protests against closures of rural schools.
- initiating or speaking at public debates concerning crucial questions of regional policy, e.g. development strategy for the province of Pomerania.
- actions supporting legal regulations benefitting the Kashubs, such as the National and Ethnic Minorities and Regional Languages Act, and activity following up on these regulations, such as the introduction of bilingual place names, or the implantation of Kashubian as an auxiliary language in local administration.
- endeavours to gain public subsidies at all levels of government and central administration for various Kashubian initiatives and institutions.
- dissemination of information on the situation of comparable ethnic groups in other European countries and building cooperation with similar organisations, both in Poland and abroad.
- taking various actions relevant to civic education.

It is currently almost possible for a large regional organisation to retain its autonomy and independence, given the rapid mediatisation of politics, the growing party-dependency of democracy (not only on central, but also on regional and local levels), the subjection of community interests to those of party coteries, and the systematic decline of civic activity. The ZK-P is often expected to perform contradictory tasks; on the one hand, it should not engage in political disputes, but on the other, it is expected to take a stand on issues of crucial importance for Pomerania. These issues often require difficult political decisions, so the ZK-P is frequently obliged to take a specific political line. It is expected to avoid this, but at the same time some professional groups (e.g. fishermen) look forward to its support when fighting for their concerns. Various politicians have been attracted to the ZK-P, because it gives them a way to reach potential constituents;

however, they do not always respect its autonomy and independence or the internal diversity of political opinions and views. At the same time, there is a strong conviction within the ZK-P that the strongest politicians in the region should be their allies or (even better) members of the organisation. There is also considerable pride in the achievements of politicians such as Donald Tusk, who went on to become Poland's prime minister.

Relations between the Kashubian community and the world of politics are full of contradictions, a situation which is probably very similar among other ethnic groups within Europe. On the other hand, from the national perspective, Kashubia and the whole of Pomerania have developed a relatively high level of civic culture, which certainly results from the ZK-P's many years of activity and its attempts to promote civic values and attitudes.

# Appendix 1

## Aleksander Majkowski, *Żëcé i przigòdë Remusa*

(passage from Chapter XIV – original version in Kashubian):

(…) W niedzelã pón Józef mie znowù kôzôł przińc. Ten rôz òn òbleczony sedzôł na stółkù przë stole. Bél prawie przë pisaniu. Ale czej jem wszedł, cësnął pióro i rzekł:

– Na cëż to pisanié sã zdô? Za pòzdze dlô mie, bò smierc za dwiérzami. Sadni, chłopkù, bësma pògôdała!

Tej zaczął mie òpòwiadac tak:

– Òd nômłodszich lat szukôł jem taci ksążczi, w chtërny bë zapisóné bëłë dzeje naszégò lëdu kaszëbsczégò. Alem taci ksążczi nie nalôzł w żódny ksãgarni. Czej jem sã tegò doznôł, tej ùwzął jem sã napisac nasze dzeje sóm. Ale dalekò òd òjczëznë, nieùbëtk i wanożenié nie dałë mie leżnoscë k'temù, a terô, czej jem wrócył, lãpka mòjégò żëcô gasnie. Co dzysô piszã, to bôjka, chtërną cë pòwiém.

Żôl mie bëło, ale nie òdrzekł jem nick, bòm wiedzôł, że smierc mù przetnie kòżdą robòtã. A òn zdrzącë długò na mie, rzekł kù reszce:

– Żebës të tak miôł wid i miecz!

W sercu mie zakłóło na te słowa, bòm sobie przëbôcził, co mie ksądz rzekł, jak mie przëjął do wiarë: Dac tobie wid i miecz, a chto wié, czëbës nie zrobił, jak ten pòtcëwi Michôł mówi. A Michôł bél ùdbë, żebëm nieszczescô pò swiece narobił. Przëbôcziwszë sobie ònã rozmòwã, zaczął jem panu Józwòwi wszytko òpòwiadac. Pòwiedzôł jem téż ò grónkù i mieczu, com je nalôzł na zómkòwi górze. A òn pitôł pòlącymi òczama:

– A chdzeżesz pòdzôł złoti miecz?

A jô òdrzekł smùtno:

– Wëzbéł jem miecz! Na kòlana ùklãkłszë dôł jem gò w dôrënkù nôpiã-kniészi z dzéwczãt na swiece, bòm mëslôł, że to królewiónka zaklãtégò zómkù żiwcã na swiat przëszłô.

A òn na to òdwrócył òczë i zapatrził sã w òkno, za chtërnym ju kwiôtczi wëstãpiłë na drzéwiãta w sadze i za całą chwilã tak pòwiedzôł:

– Prôwda! Na cëż cë miecz, czej cë nie delë widu!

Tej znowù sã smùtno ùsmiéchôł do mie i rzekł:

– Wiém wszëtkò ò tobie. Smierc i tobie bëła bliskô. A żôl za ną piãkną panią bezmała cë nie wzął dësze. Czej jes przez taką przeszedł gòrącą kùznią, bãdzesz tëlé cwiardi, żebë jic w żëcu swòją drogą nie bôczącë na cérznie, drodżi i kamienie z rąk lëdzczich.

*Pòtim sztót sedzôł cëchò, le na skarniach zakwitłë mù czerwòné róże a w òczach zażôlëło sã jak òd żëwégò wãgla. Tej zaczął mie tak pòwiadac:*

– Bôczë, chłopkù, coc rzekã dzysô. Bóg wié, czë jesz rôz przë taczi sële z tobą mówic bãdã. Òtwòrzë òkna, żebë wiater niósł wònią kwiatów w mòjã jizbã, bëm zabôcził, żem chòri i że ju na drëdżi rok nie òbôczã kwitnącégò sadu.

Tej pòdniósł ze stołu zwiniãté w długą rurã płótno, a czej je rozwinął, ùzdrzôł jem je pòrësowóné kropkama dużimi i môłimi plachcami różny krôsë i dłudżimi żmijowatimi drogami. Òn wzął, zawiesył płótno na scanie i sã zapitôł:

– A wiész të, co to jesta?

Ale jô so przëbôcził, żem ù ksãdza na nôùce widzôł taczé rësënczi, czej òn mie gwòli mòji skażony gôdczi ùcził òsóbno w swòji jizbie. Tedëm òdrzekł:

– To je gwësno wizerënk jaczégò kraju.

– To je wizerënk naszi òjczëznë! – rzekł pón Józef.

Pòtim kôzôł mie blëżi przëstąpic i jął wëkładac:

– Te dwa krąconé czôrné drodżi, co jidą z półniô kù nocë to dwie wieldżé rzéczi: na wschòdze słuńca Wisła, na zôchòdze Òdra. Tam, chdze Wisła bieżi w mòrze, môsz Gduńsk, tam chdze Òdra, môsz Szczecëno. Zdrzë, jak linijô mòrzô pòdbiégô tãpim klinã do ùscô Òdrë i bôczë, że przeszedłszë rzékã tã na lewi brzég, wiedno jesz stojisz na dôwny zemi kaszëbsczi. Bò òna sã cygnie pò górach bôłtëcczich jaż bezmała tãdë, chdze stoji Berlin, stolëca Niemców i miasto Roztoka, niedalek mòrzô. Òd półniô sznur Wartë i Notecë, jaż do kòlana Wisłë przë Fòrdonie, a òd nocë mòrze: to stôrodôwné granice naszi zemi kaszëbsczi. Na pôłnié zemia sã z nią łączi pòlskô, z chtërną wòlą ksążąt najich i nôrodu jednã twòrzëłasma Rzeczpòspòlitą.

Jô ze zdzëwienim patrzôł i słëchôł, bòm sobie nigdë nie ùwôżôł, żebë krôj Kaszëbów bêł jaż taczi dużi. A òn mówił dali:

– Taczi dużi bêł nasz krôj i wiele w nim żëło lëdu i panów i ksążãta włôsny nimi rządzëlë. A bëlë Kaszëbi bògati na lądze i òkrãtami włôsnymi jezdzëlë pò mòrzu i wòjsk żelôznych wiedlë rejimańtë i mielë wòlã. Bùdowelë wse i miasta. Cëzych przëjimelë gòscynnie a nieprzëjôceli ùmielë pòbic i wënëkac z kraju. – Tak ma wëzdrzała dôwni, szescset lat nazôd. A dzys co mómë?

I przëkrił dwùma rãkama płachc na wizerënkù i rzekł:

– Tëlé nóm òstało z dôwny chwałë.

Mie, chtërnémù nicht jeszcze taczi wiédze nie dôł, żôl sã zrobiło, że naju plemiã jaż tëlé stracëło i jem sã pitôł:

– Jakòż to bëło mòżno?

– Naszedł nieprzëjôcél òd zôchòdu słuńca i ùriwôł jim krôj za krajã, wiedno jidącë na zôchód słuńca. Tak przeszedł Òdrã i mòrził sã nôparce kù Wisle i doparł swégò.

– A czemùż sã naszi nie òbronilë?

A pón Józef długò przemiszlôł i kù reszce pòwiedzôł tak:

– Pitôsz sã, czemù naszi sã nie òbronilë. – Wiãcy niże jedna przëczëna sã zeszłë, bë wëwòłac taczi straszny skùtk. Ale strzôd tich przëczën jedny nie bëło i to ti, żebë jim zbiwało na dzyrżkòscë, dëchù, broni, mòcë. Bëlë bitni i òdwôżny na lądze i mòrzu a mielë spòsób bògati. A jednak stracëlë ... Mòże sã dobierzesz ò przëczënach jich ùpôdkù, czej cë pòwiém co z naszich dzejów. Ùważôj: Czej wińdzesz z tegò pùstkòwiô na swiat, nie zabôczisz zańc do Òliwë, gniôzda dôwnych nôbòżnych cystersów, chtërny tu stąd wiarã swiãtą rozséwelë strzôd naszich przodków. Klôsztor jich zniszcził ten sóm nieprzëjôcél, co nasze kraje zabrôł. Ale wieldżi i pëszny kòscół pò nich jeszcze stoji. Pùdzesz tam jaż przed wôłtôrz wieldżi i klãkniesz przed dużim czôrnym szklącym kamieniã, bò pòd nim głãbòkò w sklepach kòscoła stoją trëmë z kòscami ksążąt kaszëbsczich. Spòmni tam ò nich jak dzeckò nad grobami starszich swòjich i bôczë, że miedzë nimi bëlë taczi, chtërnych dzyrżkòscë i krëwi i prôcë jesz dzysôdnia, pò szesc stach lat, winnismë, że naju nieprzëjôcél nie wëtãpił do nédżi. Nôwiãkszi z nich to Swiãtopôłk. Na smiertelnym jesz łożu kłopòt ò przëchòdné czasë swòjégò lëdu gò nie òpùscył. Kôzôł òn tedë sënów swòjich zawòłac i pòdôł jim pãk zrzeszonych mòcno prãtów, bë gò złómelë. Ale żóden ze sënów ni mógł tegò dokazac. Tak ksãżã Swiãtopôłk wzął i rozrzesził pãk i pòdôł sënóm prãtë kòżdi z òsóbna. A òni je terô letczim spòsobã pòłómelë. – Wezta sobie przikłôd z tich prãtów – rzekł ksãże Swiãtopôłk. – Zrzeszonych waju nicht nie złómie, ale w pòjedinkã waju zniszczą! – Nieszczescé nasze, że wiedno złô rãka rozrzészała pãto, co nas trzimało w gromadze. W tim szukôj, chłopôkù, przëczënë, żesmë sã nie òbronilë.

Bëło mie, jakbë pón Józef òdemknął przede mną dwiérze, co z casny jizbë prowadzëłë na szeroczi krôj. Terô jô miôł na pëtaniô, co mie pòd trzema chòjnami nachòdzëłë głowã, òdpòwiédz gòtowã. Ale pón Józef pòkôzôł rãką na wizerënk naszégò kraju i rzekł:

– Bôczë! Tam dali kù Òdrze nasza mòwa ju wëmarła. Tam bracô naszi pòddelë sã pòrządkòwi i prawóm nieprzëjôcela. A ti, co jesz żëją i mòwã a òbëczôj òjców tu nad Wisłą i mòrzã zachòwelë, ti ju wszëscë ùroslë w niewòli i nie wiedzą, jak bëło dôwni i co jim słëchało. Sąsma, jak serotë na pańsczim chlebie, co nie wiedzą, że jim słëchô panowanié a nié serocy chléb.

Mòcny kaszel jął trząsc panã Józwã i krew pòkôzała sã na jegò wargach. Nie rzekł nic, le rãką dôł znac, żebëm szedł.

Bëła to sobòta, czej przëszedł ksądz z Panã Jezësã. Pòkąd sã pón Józef spòwiôdôł, naszi stojelë na dómie. Bëlë pón i pani i Michôł i Môrcën i knôp òd dobëtkù i Marcyjanna i Marta. Kòbiétë cëchò pôcérz zmówiłë a chłopë stojelë pòkórnie, bò Pón Bóg bêł w gòscënie za dwiérzami. Kù reszce dwiérze sã òdemkłë a wszëscë weszlë do Straszkòwi jizbë i pòklãkelë, bë za ksãdzã pòwtarzac pôcérz.

Pón Józef leżôł bladi na swòjim łóżkù, a jak sã skùńczëło pòjednanié z Bògã, òczë jegò szukałë ze wszëtczich mie. Jak mie ùzdrzôł, ùsmiechnął sã. Ksądz wëszedł. Ùwôżôł jem dobrze, że dim swiéce szedł za nim. Chòri dôł znak rãką, żebë wszëscë wëszlë, ale na mie patrzôł, żebëm òstôł przë nim. Tak jô òstôł i żdôł, co mie pòwié, nim sã wëbierze na to dłudżé pòdróżowanié pòza gwiôzdë.

– Czëjã sã dzys mòcny – rzekł òn. – Tak swiéca jesz rôz sã rozżòli widã, nim zagasnie. Jak ùmrzã, pòwiezeta mie na smãtôrz zabôczoną drogą wedle zómkòwiska, abë jesz dëch mój jidący za trëmą wezdrzôł na môl, chdzem nabrôł mësli i dëcha, co mie bёł wãdrowną palёcą przez całą drogã żёcô. Tobiem bё bёł rôd òstawił napisóné dzeje naszégò lёdu, ale zamiast nich mùszã cё zlecёc bôjkã. Niech cã to nie dzёwi! Żёcé lёdzy i nôrodów wiãcy je bôjką, niże sã zdaje. Mёszlą, że jidą swòją wòlą a to rãka Bòskô jich prowadzy jak gwiôzdё pò drogach le Bògù wiadomich. Tё i jô, i wszёscё na tim pùstkòwiu mają swòje drodżi przepisóné: Trzё kroczi przed sebie widzą, ale môla, dokąd jic mùszą, nie widzą. – Pòwiém cё tã bôjkã ò dzejach kaszёbsczich.

– Biôłi dёch Òrmùzd i czôrny dёch Ariman, a pò naszémù Smãtk, zeszlё sã w zemi kaszёbsczi na górze Rewkòle, co na mòrze patrzi i dzeli tich bracy, co kù Òdrze cygną, òd tich co lgną do Gduńska. I òbrôcôł Òrmùzd widné jak słuńce òczё na niebò i mòrze i ląd i pòwiedzôł tak:

– Ten krôj, to kòlébka i trёma. Ten lud òn ùmarł a żёje. Na biôłi Arkónie stolёmné kamienie, pò chtёrnych wanożi syn dôwnych Weletów z wёstёdzoną dёszą, mòdlący sã Bògù gôdką swich wrogów, sóm wróg krёwi swòji i głёchi na skardżi, co wёchòdzą z mòdżił. Nad ùscami Wisłё i rёbôk i rataj, zgarbiali kù zemi i tcący ikònё przёwãdrów i gòscy a swòje rzucywszё do smiecy. Jô ale jim zbùdzã spòd kamiannych mòdżił ricerzi i wòdzów i rozeżglã płomiéń òd biôłégò Hélu pò Stopienny Kamiéń, bё òżёlё znowù w mòcё i chwale. I òdrzekł Smãtk:

– Smierc jich i zgùba to dobёcé mòje. Pòd Grifòwim znakã bieżelё mòrzami: Piorёnё jich miecze a żôgle jich skrzidła! A wińcã gardów ògrodzёlё ùbёtk wsów swòjich i kòntin. Prёstanie nad mòrzã to zdrzódła jich złota.

– A pùrpùra złoto spiéwałё jich chwałã ze szczitów jich kòntin i biôłich remión jich dzéwcząt i niewiast. – Ale jô do nich spławił z kamiannégò nôrtu zbójników głodnych na mizernych szkùtach. I w granice kraju jô wbił jich jak klinã i pòdparł jich mòcą. Im szedł przed jich wòjskã jak gradowô chmùra. A szpiegami pòszlё i Zôzdrosc i Zwada. Jô mòcné rzãdё jich rodów i plemión rozrzёszôł na snopё, a snopё pòstawił naprocёm sobie, bё zdobiwca z nôrtu mógł żelôznym bótã przeńc pò nich kù słuńcu. Duńszczégò żôłniérza rãkama jô spólił Rujańską Stanicã, a Swiãtowita stolёmny pòsąg

rznął jem na zemiã, a z jegò rzezbą pòkrëtich człónków ùtłukł jem wiorë w
òdżiń pòd grónczi żôłniérsczi strawë. – I ju jich ni ma, pësznych Weletów!
Bò rzãdami leżą w kamiannych grobach òd Matczi Redë do piôsków Hélu.
Le szarô chmara nieswiadomich gbùrów i rëbôków biédnych na smierc
sã spòsobi. Bò kamieni czwioro mechami òbrosłich i sycëna dużô, co we
wietrze rzëzy na pùstim ùgòrze: to grób jich panów.

Ale nie rzekłszë słowa, Òrmùzd wëcygnął rãkã i spòd grobòwégò
kamienia wëdobéł gôrsc prochù bòhaterów i sôł gò jak séwca seje zôrno na
przëchòdné żniwa kù wschòdowi słùńca i zachòdowi, kù nórtu i półniu.
A proch szedł kù zemi jak rój gwiôzd, jak żôlącé skrë. A chdze spadła skra,
tam wëtrisnął òdżiń ze swiãti zemi i łącził sã z ògniã w płom.

A Smãtk sã skrzëwił i lisnął złim òkã i sygnął w durã strëpiałégò wiąza.
Tam sedzôł sãp stôri. A òn gò wzął na dłóń, rozwinął mù skrzidła i pióro
za piórkã wëriwającë pùscył złim wiatrã za skrami. A sãpòwé pióra kù zemi
spôdałë a z kòżdégò lãglë sã sowë i sãpë. I szarim skrzidłã padałë na ògnie
i gasëłë płomiéń.

Ale Òrmùzd biôli nie òprzestôł sôc swiãtich prochów na kaszëbską
zemiã a skrë padałë króm sów i sãpów jak rój gwiôzd.

Takã bôjkã pòwiôdôł pón Józef. Skarnie jemù sã òb ten czas zapôlëłë
jak krew; a z òczu biłë skrë jak te same z Òrmùzdowi rãczi.

– Rozëmiôł të mie? – pitôł pò dłudżi chwilë.

A jô òdrzekł:

– Bãdã skrą Òrmùzdową! (...)

Aleksander Majkowski, *Life and Adventures of Remus*

(passage from Chapter XIV; English translation by B. Krbechek and
K. Gawlik-Luiken, Gdańsk, 2008).

Some time later Pan Józef called for me to come again. This time he was
dressed and was sitting by the table, writing. When I entered, he put down
his pen and said, 'I wonder what purpose will be served by my writing. It

is too late for me, because Death stands on the other side of my door. Sit down, my lad, and let us talk.'

Then he began to tell me, 'Ever since my youngest years, I searched for a book which told the history of our Kaszubian land, but I never was able to find that kind of book in any book store. When I realised that such a book did not exist, I decided to write one myself, but by that time I was far from my Fatherland and with all my wandering and troubles, it was not possible to write. Now that I am back, the light of my life is fading. What I am writing today is a folk tale and I will pass it on to you.'

Sorrow started to fill my heart because I knew Death would cut his work short, but I said nothing. He looked at me for a long time and finally he called, 'Oh, if you only had the light and the sword!'

I felt a tinge in my heart at those words because I remembered what the priest had said when he received me at the altar for my First Holy Communion, 'Let God lead you! If you were to have been given the light and the sword, who knows if you might not do as the honorable Michôł suggests.' Somehow Michôł believed I would bring distress to the world. I remembered that conversation, and I told him everything. I did not even hide the part about the pot and the golden sword that I had found on the castle mountain.

His eyes were aglow with excitement and he asked, 'What have you done with the golden sword?'

I answered regretfully, 'I have lost it. I dropped to my knees and gave it to the most beautiful lady in the world, because I thought she was the young Queen from the sunken castle who had come back to life.'

He turned his eyes away from me and stared out the window and looked at the fruit trees which were already covered with blossoms. After a long while he said, 'It is true! Why would you need the sword if you were not given the light?' Then he smiled sadly and continued, 'I know everything about you. You, too, came face to face with Death. Grief for that beautiful lady almost took your soul away. Since you have been in the forge, you have been hardened enough to go through life on your own without worrying about the wrong ends of thorns, and stones falling off people's hands.'

Again he sat quietly for a while. Red roses bloomed on his cheeks and his eyes sparkled. Then he said, 'Remember, my lad, the things I will tell you today. God only knows whether or not I will be able to talk to you again. Open the window so the breezes can bring the fragrance of the blossoms into my room to help me forget that now I am not well, and will not see the orchard flowering another year.' He picked up a long, rolled parchment from the table. When he unrolled it I could see it was marked with dots, big and small spots of various colours and long curving lines.

He hung the parchment on the wall and asked, 'Do you know what this is?'

I remembered that I had seen such a drawing when I was being schooled by the priest. It hung in the rectory where I was being taught separately, because of my garbled words. So I answered, 'It is probably a picture of some country.'

'This is the picture of our Fatherland,' said Pan Józef. Then he motioned for me to come closer and started to lecture, 'Those two curving black lines which go from south to north are two great rivers, the Wisła (Vistula) to the east and the Odra (Oder) to the west. Where the Wisła River enters the sea you see Gdańsk. Where the Odra River enters you see Szczecin. Look how there is a recess in the coastline which drops to the mouth of the Odra, and remember that after crossing that river to its left bank, one is still in the old Kaszubian land. Long ago, Kaszubia stretched through the fields under the Baltic Sea almost to where the German capital of Berlin now stands, and to the city of Roztoka (Rostock) not far from the sea. To the south you see the curving lines of the Warta and Notec Rivers meeting the Wisła where it bends at Fordon. On the north you see the sea. Those are the old borders of our Kaszubian land. To the south of our land is the Polish land. Together we created one political union with them, by the wishes of our princes and our nation.'

I looked and I listened in utter amazement because it never occurred to me that the Kaszubian land could be so great.

And he continued, 'Our nation was once that large, and many people and lords lived within its boundaries. Our own princes were governing us. The Kaszubes were rich in their land holdings and also rich owners of ships on the sea. They had regiments of iron armies (knights). And, they had freedom. They built villages and cities. They entertained visitors with gracious hospitality. They were able to repel enemies and chase them from their land ... That is how it was six hundred years ago and earlier. And today?'

With both hands he covered only a part of the map and said, 'That is all that is left of our former glory.'

I, who never had such knowledge before, felt saddened that our tribe had lost so much and asked, 'How is that possible?'

'The enemy moved from the west and little by little tore off one piece of our land after another. They crossed the Odra River and pushed relentlessly towards the Wisła River until they accomplished their goal.'

'Why didn't our people defend themselves?'

Pan Józef thought for a long time and finally he said, 'You ask why our people didn't defend ... More than one reason piled up to let that happen, but lack of courage, of spirit, of arms, or of strength were not among them. At that time they were brave and valiant on both the land and the sea and they had enough resources, but still they lost ... Maybe you will be able to discover the reasons why they were overthrown when I tell you a little of our history. Pay careful attention. When you leave this *pustkowie* to go out into the world do not forget to visit Oliwa, the original home of the Cistercian brothers who spread the Holy Faith among our ancestors. The enemy who took our country destroyed their monastery, but their great church is still standing. When you are there, go towards the main altar and kneel in front of the large, shiny black stone, because deep in the undercroft lay sarcophagi with the ashes of the Kaszubian princes. Remember that as you kneel there, you are like the child over the graves of his parents. And remember that among those below you are those for whom we are most grateful, because their bravery, blood and deeds have made it possible for our people to survive the attempts by various enemies to annihilate us, and possible for us to survive up to this very day.

'The greatest among those entombed in the Oliwa church is Prince Swiätopelk. Even on his deathbed he was concerned about the future of his people. He called all his sons together, handed them a bundle of rods, and instructed them to break the bundle. Not one of his sons could break it. Then Prince Swiätopelk untied the bundle and gave each son a separate rod. Now each one was able to break his rod with ease. "Remember the lesson of the rods," said prince Swiãtopelk. "You will be strong when you stand united, and nobody will be able to break you, but if you stand separately you will be weak and be destroyed!" It is our misfortune that some bad hand always untied the knot that had been holding us together. In those thoughts, my lad, look for the main reason of our downfall.'

It seemed as if Pan Józef were opening a door in front of me that led from a confining room into the wide world. Now I had a ready answer to the question that had popped into my head while I was under the three spruce trees. Pan Józef pointed with his hand to the map of our land, 'Look! Farther that way, towards the Odra River and beyond, our language has already vanished. There our brothers surrendered to the order and law of our enemies. Those that today live here closer to the Wisła River and the sea have preserved the tongue and the customs of our fathers. But, they have grown up in captivity and do not know how it was in the far past and what rights they have lost. They are like orphans, raised on the bread of a master, who are not aware that they themselves could produce the bread instead of only eating the crumbs.'

A strong cough shook Pan Józef and blood came to his lips. His words ceased and he only motioned with his hand for me to leave.

It was Saturday when the priest came with the Lord Jesus to give Pan Józef the Last Sacraments. Our people waited in the house while the priest was upstairs hearing the confession. With me were the master and mistress, Michôł, Môrcën, the herding boy, Marcyjanna and Marta. The women prayed quietly and the men stood humbly, because the Lord God was visiting. Finally the door opened and we all walked into the ghost's room to repeat prayers after the priest.

Pan Józef was pale as he lay on his bed. Once he finished his confession, he glanced about the room with his eyes, looking for me. When he caught sight of me, he smiled. The priest left. I noticed that the smoke from the candle followed him. The sick one motioned with his hand for everybody to leave, but he kept looking at me so I would stay with him. I stayed and waited, curious to see what he would tell me before he departed on his long journey beyond the stars.

'I feel strong today,' he said, 'like a candle flame that flares brightly one last time just before it goes out. When I die, you must take me on the forgotten road by the castle mountain. As my spirit walks behind the casket, it will be able to look one last time at the place which shaped my thoughts, and became my spirit's walking cane that supported me throughout my life. I wish I could leave the entire written history of our nation with you, but instead I will just leave you a story. The life of people and nations contains more of a story than we commonly believe. We think people walk according to their own will, but it is God's hand that leads them like stars on a road known only to Him. You and I and all on our *pustkowie* have their way plotted even though they can see only three steps in front of themselves, and cannot see the final destination to which their steps will lead them.

'I will tell you a story from Kaszubian history ... The white god-angel Ormuzd and the black god-angel Aryman, called by us Smętek, met together on our Kaszubian land on the mountain Rowokół which looks down at the sea and separates those brothers who lived towards the Odra from those who lived towards Gdańsk. With eyes as bright as the sun, Ormuzd looked around at the sky, the sea and the land. Then he said, "This country is a cradle and a grave. This nation died, and still it is living. On the white Arkona there are great rocks where the old sons of the *Wieleci* (Veleti tribe) walked with a cold heart. They prayed to a god in the language of their enemy, and were themselves an enemy of their own blood and had turned a deaf ear to the pleas coming from the graves of their ancestors. Where the Wisła enters the sea, fishermen and peasants bowed down to the ground worshipping the icons of the newcomers and flung their own in the rubbish pile. But, I will wake their knights and chiefs from their stony graves and I will light the flame from white Hel to *Stopienny Kamień* (Ger: Stubbenkammer; on Rugia, Ger: Rügen) so they can come back to life in strength and glory".

'And Smętek responded, "Their death and vanquishment is my victory. They sailed throughout the seas under the sign of the *Gryf* (Griffon). Their swords flashed like lightening and their sails were like wings. They protected the peace of their hamlets and temples with fortified villages around the perimeter. Their ports were the source of their gold. Gold and scarlet proclaimed their glory on the poles atop their temples by the sea, and from the white shoulders of their girls and women. But, from the rocky north, I sent hungry warriors on skimpy ships. I pounded the newcomers into the middle of their country like a wedge, and I supported their power. I marched in front of their army like a cloud of doom. Jealousy and Quarreling went among the people. I divided the strong bonds of their families and tribes like grain divided into shocks, and I set those shocks against one another other. Thus, the victor from the north was able to trample them with his iron shoe and continue southward. With the hands of a Danish soldier I burned Rujańska Stanica. I knocked the great statue of Swiãtowid to the ground and carved his ruins into chips which I burned in fires under the soldiers' pots of stew." And so they are gone, the proud Wieleci! They are lying in rows of stony graves stretching from the *Rëde* River (Ger: Recknitz River) to the sands of Hel. Now only a gray mass of simple peasants and poor fishermen still ready themselves for death because four-faced statues became covered with moss and rushes and now only wind howls over fallow ground. Those are the graves of their lords ...

'Without saying a word, Ormuzd reached his hand under the gravestones, and pulled out a handful of the ashes of the heroes. He tossed them towards the east and the west, towards the north and the south, like a farmer sowing grain for a future harvest. The ashes fell to the ground in a storm of blazing sparks. Fires sprouted on the holy ground at each spot where a spark landed. The sparks connected with one another forming one great flame.

'Smętek grimaced and flashed his evil eyes. He reached in a hole of a rotting elm. There sat an old vulture. He took it in his hand, stretched its wings, and pulled out one feather after another from its wings. He sent the feathers to the sparks with an evil wind. They fell to the ground and owls and vultures hatched from each of them. The newly hatched birds used their great wings to suffocate the fires and put out the flames. But white Ormuzd would not stop sowing holy ashes on the Kaszubian soil, and in spite of the vultures and owls, sparks fell like a multitude of stars.'

Such was the story Pan Józef told. Colour came to his cheeks and his eyes were glowing sparks, like those falling from the hand of Ormuzd. 'Did you understand me?' he asked after a long while.

I answered, 'I will be a spark of Ormuzd!'

# Appendix 2: Chronology
(compiled by Cezary Obracht-Prondzyński)

| | |
|---|---|
| Sixth century | Slavonic tribes settle in Pomerania, in the areas between the Vistula and Oder rivers, on the Baltic coast and in the forest belt on the Noteć river, with a centre between Koszalin and Białogard. |
| 966 | Adoption of Christianity in Poland. |
| 997 | Adalbert (Wojciech), Bishop of Prague, baptises Kashubs in Gdańsk during his mission of Christianisation, commended by Prince Bolesław Chrobry 'the Brave'. Adalbert murdered by pagan Prussians and canonised as St Wojciech; his death is the first written mention of Gdańsk, referred to as 'urbs' – an important urban centre on the Baltic. |
| 1000 | Congress of Gniezno: meeting of Emperor Otto III with Bolesław Chrobry 'the Brave'; the first Pomerania diocese founded in Kołobrzeg. |
| 1013 | Pagan unrest within Pomerania; destruction of the first bishopric in Kołobrzeg. |
| 1046 | Pomeranian Duke Siemysł of Szczecin appears at the imperial court in Merseburg on equal terms with the Polish Duke Kazimierz (Casimir) Odnowiciel 'the Restorer', and the Duke of Bohemia, Břetislav (Bretislaus). Beginnings of the dynasty of Griffins (House of Greifen). |
| 1121 | Polish Duke Bolesław Krzywousty 'the Wrymouth' conquers Szczecin; the West-Pomeranian Duke Warcisław (Vartislav) henceforth accounts himself a Polish vassal (he is considered to be the founder of the Greifen state). |
| 1124–1125 and 1128 | Mission of Christianisation in West Pomerania by Bishop Otto of Bamberg. |
| 1138 | Fragmentation of the Polish state following death of Bolesław Krzywousty 'the Wrymouth'; the Dukes of West Pomerania and Gdańsk become indepedent from Polish control. |

| 1140 | Diocese of Wolin established by Pope Innocent II. |
|---|---|
| 1176 | Bishop's residence moved to Kamień Pomorski; establishment of the diocese of Kamień. |
| 1181 | The Duke of Szczecin, Bogusław I, pays homage to Emperor Frederick Barbarossa. |
| 1184–1231 | Danish rule in the Duchy of Pomerania. |
| 1235 | During the reign of Duke Barnim I 'the Good' (1210–78), the capital of the West-Pomeranian Duchy moves from Usedom to Szczecin. |
| 1217/20–1266 | Integration of Duchies in Gdańsk Pomerania during the reign of Świętopełk (Swantopolk) the Great. |
| 1238–1253 | Wars of Świętopełk (Swantopolk) the Great with the Order of the Teutonic Knights. |
| 1282 | Treaty of Kępno between the Duke of Gdańsk, Mestwin II, and the Duke of Wielkopolska (Greater Poland); this is an 'outlive agreement' whereby he who dies first bequeaths his Duchy to the survivor. |
| 1294 | Mestwin II's Duchy taken over by Duke Przemysł II of Wielkopolska after his death. |
| 1295 | Unification of the Duchies of Gdańsk and Wielkopolska (Greater Poland); Przemysł II crowned King of Poland in Gniezno; restoration of Polish Crown and beginning of reconstruction of Polish statehood. |
| 1296–1308 | Struggles for power over Gdańsk Pomerania between the Bohemian Kings Vaclav II and Vaclav III, the King of Poland Władysław Łokietek 'the Elbow-high', and the Brandenburgians. |
| 1308/1309 | Teutonic Knights, called in by Władysław Łokietek 'the Elbow-high' to aid in the war with the Brandenburgians, conquer Gdańsk Pomerania, take it over and incorporate it within their state. |
| 1308–1466 | Teutonic Knights rule in Gdańsk Pomerania. |
| 1410 | Great war with the Order of the Teutonic Knights; victory of Polish-Lithuanian troops in the Battle of Tannenberg/Grunwald. |
| 1440 | Prussian Confederation founded in Kwidzyn/Marienwerde, formed by nobility and townspeople against Teutonic rule. |

| 1454 | Anti-Teutonic uprising; the Prussian Confederation appeal to the King of Poland Kazimierz Jagiellończyk (Casimir Jagiellon) for incorporation of Prussia into the Kingdom of Poland; act of incorporation proclaimed by the King on 6 March 1454; outbreak of war with the Order of the Teutonic Knights. |
|---|---|
| 1454–1466 | Thirteen Years' War between Poland and the Teutonic Knights. |
| 1466 | Second Peace of Toruń and division of the Teutonic Knights' state; Gdańsk Pomerania incorporated into the Polish Crown as the autonomous province of Royal Prussia. |
| 1474 | Power in the Duchy of Szczecin seized by Bogusław X the Great; unification of the Pomeranian state and major reforms. Bogusław X's reign represents the climax of the development of the West-Pomeranian Duchy. |
| 1534 | West-Pomeranian Duchy accepts Protestantism after the Assembly of Trzebiatów. |
| 1569 | Seym of Lublin abolishes the autonomy of Royal Prussia. |
| 1586 | Simon Krofey, a pastor from Bytów, publishes *Duchowne piesnie D. Marcina Luthera y ynszich nabożnich mężów z niemieckiego w Slawięsky ięzyk wilozone ...* in Gdańsk. Probably also publishes *Mały Katechizm*. Both written in a 'Slaviensic' language (i.e. in Old Polish with Kashubian influences), and to be used by Protestant Kashubs in the eastern part of the West-Pomeranian Duchy, they will become the first significant landmark in Kashubian-Polish literature in West Pomerania. |
| 1626–1629 | Truce of Altmark (Stary Targ) ends the Polish-Swedish Wars; Gdańsk Pomerania suffers during the hostilities; the truce causes a slump in Polish trading through Prussian ports, particularly Gdańsk and Królewiec (Königsberg). |
| 1618–1638 | Thirty Years' War; West-Pomeranian Duchy ravaged. |
| 1637 | Duke Bogusław XIV, the last of the dynasty of Griffins (House of Greifen), dies childless. |
| 1637–1657 | Bytów and Lębork (Bütow and Lauenburg) Land, until now a fiefdome in the hands of the Griffins, returns to the Commonwealth of Poland-Lithuania; a process of re-Catholicisation follows, enabling Kashubs to remain there until the twentieth century. |

| 1648 | West-Pomeranian Duchy partitioned as result of the Peace of Westphalia: Szczecin (Stettin) and lands west of the Oder river (known as Vorpommern) taken over by Sweden, lands located to the east (Hinterpommern) incorporated into Brandenburg. |
|---|---|
| 1655–1660 | Swedish invasion of Poland, known as the 'Swedish Deluge'. |
| 1660 | Treaty of Oliva; Brandenburg confirmed a sovereign power in Ducal Prussia and granted feudal sovereignty in Bytów and Lębork Land, as well as the right to transfer troops through the territory of Gdańsk Pomerania; Sweden and Poland-Lithuania maintain their Baltic assets from before the 'Swedish Deluge'; King Jan Kazimierz (John II Casimir) renounces his claim to the Swedish throne; the importance of Poland on the Baltic sea systematically declines. |
| 1683 | Polish troops fight in the Battle of Vienna under the command of King John III Sobieski against the Ottoman army; Kashubian participation is to become a significant factor in the Kashubs' historical consciousness. |
| 1700–1721 | Great Northern War, between the coalition of Sweden and the Ottoman Empire on the one side, and Russia, Denmark, Prussia, Saxony and Poland on the other; most of the warfare takes place in the territory of Poland; Sweden loses most of possessions on the southern Baltic coast; the role of Russia and Prussia increases, mainly at the expense of Poland. |
| 1772 | First Partition of Poland; Gdańsk Pomerania taken over by Prussia, which results in Kashubia being totally incorporated into the Prussian state. |
| 1793 | Second Partition of Poland; Gdańsk and Toruń incorporated into the Prussian state. |
| 1807–1815 | Free City of Danzig (Gdańsk) created during the Napoleonic Wars. |
| 1815 | Congress of Vienna; the whole of Pomerania incorporated into the Prussian state. |
| 1846 | Florian Ceynowa (1817–81) launches an unsuccessful attempt to trigger a Polish uprising; Ceynowa imprisoned and sentenced to death; Ceynowa released from prison after the Berlin revolution of March 1848. |

| 1848 | Springtide of Nations, a wave of revolutionary upheavals throughout Europe. |
|---|---|
| 1826–1827 | Research expeditions to Kashubia by Christoph Coelestin Mrongovius (Krzysztof Celestyn Mrongowiusz), a pastor from Gdańsk (1765–1855); the beginnings of scholarly interest in Kashubia. |
| 1856 | Research expedition to Kashubia by Russian scholar Alexandr Hilferding (1831–72); results published in 1862 in St Petersburg. |
| 1866–1868 | Florian Ceynowa publishes thirteen issues of the first Kashubian periodical, *Skôrb Kaszébskosłovjnskjé Môvé*. |
| 1871–1878 | *Kulturkampf* policy of Germanisation and discriminatory sanctions against the Catholic Church results in strengthening of Polish national identity among Kashubs; Kashubian trust in the Prussian-German state is undermined. |
| 1880 | Hieronim Jarosz Derdowski (1852–1902) publishes his humorous poem *O Panu Czorlińsczim co do Pucka po sece jachoł*. |
| 1893 | Stefan Ramułt publishes *Słownik języka pomorskiego czyli kaszubskiego* in Cracow (Kraków); beginning of heated disputes on the linguistic status of Kashubian. |
| 1906 | Izydor Gulgowski (1874–1925) founds the first Kashubian open-air museum in Wdzydze Kiszewskie. |
| 1908 | Aleksander Majkowski (1876–1938), founder of the Young-Kashubian movement, starts publishing the monthly *Gryf* in Kościerzyna. |
| 1912 | Young-Kashubs' Society founded in Gdańsk. |
| 1913 | Kashubian-Pomeranian Museum founded in Sopot (Zoppot). |
| 1914–1918 | First World War. |
| 1919 | Treaty of Versailles; creation of Free City of Danzig; part of the former West Prussia granted to Poland, together with access to the Baltic Sea. |
| 1920 | Gdańsk Pomerania incorporated into Poland. |
| 1923 | Temporary port opened in Gdynia, which will become the main port of Poland; city rights granted in 1926. |

| 1929 | Regional Association of Kashubs (Zrzeszenie Regionalne Kaszubów) founded in Kartuzy. |
|---|---|
| 1936 | Association of Lovers of Kashubian 'Stanica' (Zrzeszenie Miłośników Kaszubszczyzny) founded in Toruń. |
| 1938 | First edition of the Aleksander Majkowski's novel *Żecë i przigodé Remusa*. |
| 1939 | Outbreak of Second World War; tens of thousands of people murdered during the first months of the 'Bloody Autumn' in Pomerania. |
| 1942 | Introduction of compulsory registration on the German *Volksliste* ('People's List'). |
| 1945 | End of Second World War; 'disastrous liberation' and radical change of Poland's borders. |
| 1946 | First Kashubian Congress convened in January in Wejherowo. |
| 1949–1956 | Stalinist period; suppression of all institutional forms of Kashubian activity, with Kashubian culture allowed to develop only as folklore. |
| 1959 | Foundation of the Kashubian Association as the first mass organisation of the Kashubs (in 1964 its name changes to 'Kashubian-Pomeranian Association'). |
| 1970 | Protests take place in December; Polish army opens fire on protesting workers at the command of the Communist authorities; casualties include Kashubs. |
| 1980–1981 | August strikes in Poland; *Solidarność* Trade Union founded; martial law introduced on 13 December 1981. |
| 1989 | Beginning of democratic transformations in Poland. |
| 1990 | Re-introduction of local self-government. |
| 1998 | Reform of Polish administrative divisions; the whole of Kashubia now located within the new Province of Pomerania ('województwo pomorskie'). |
| 2005, 2009 | Law on National and Ethnic Minorities and the Regional Language passed by Parliament in 2005, with Kashubian officially recognised and protected as a regional language; Council of Europe's European Charter for Regional or Minority Languages ratified in 2009. |

# Appendix 3: Selected Kashubian Institutions

Kashubian-Pomeranian Association, Headquarters
*Zrzeszenie Kaszubsko-Pomorskie, Zarząd Główny*
ul. Straganiarska 20–22
Polish-80–837 Gdańsk
Tel. +48 58301 27 31
Fax +48 58346 26 13
biuro@kaszubi.pl
www.kaszubi.pl

Kashubian Extramural University
*Kaszubski Uniwersytet Ludowy*
Wieżyca 1
Polish-83–315 Szymbark
Tel. +48 58684 38 14
Fax +48 58684 38 01
wiezyca@kfhs.com.pl
www.kfhs.com.pl
Centre in Starbienino
Polish-84–210 Choczewo
Tel. +48 58572 43 43
Fax +48 58572 43 33
ecostarb@kfhs.com.pl

Kashubian Language Board
*Rada Języka Kaszubskiego*
ul. Straganiarska 20–22
Polish-80–837 Gdańsk
Tel. +48 58301 27 31
Fax +48 58346 26 13
edukacja@kaszubi.pl

Centre of Kashubian-Pomeranian Culture in Gdynia
Ośrodek Kultury Kaszubsko-Pomorskiej w Gdyni
Miejska Biblioteka Publiczna w Gdyni (Municipal Library in Gdynia)
al. Piłsudskiego 18
Polish-81–378 Gdynia
Tel. +48 58621 73 25

*Pomerania* editorial office
*Redakcja miesięcznika 'Pomerania'*
ul. Straganiarska 20–22
Polish-80–837 Gdańsk
Tel. +48 58301 90 16, +48 58301 27 31
Fax +48 58346 26 13
red.pomerania@wp.pl

*Academy of Professional Education*
*Akademia Kształcenia Zawodowego*
ul. Straganiarska 20–22
Polish-80–837 Gdańsk
Tel./Fax +48 58346 31 42
gdansk@akademie.com.pl
www.akademie.com.pl

Kashubian Institute
*Instytut Kaszubski*
ul. Straganiarska 20–22
Polish-80–837 Gdańsk
Tel. +48 58346 22 31
Fax +48 58346 23 27
instytutkaszubski@wp.pl
www.instytutkaszubski.pl

Western-Kashubian Museum in Bytów
*Muzeum Zachodnio-Kaszubskie w Bytowie*
ul. Zamkowa 2

Polish-77–100 Bytów
Tel./Fax 59822 26 23
sekretariat@muzeumbytow.pl
www.muzeumbytow.pl

Historical and Ethnographic Museum in Chojnice
*Muzeum Historyczno-Etnograficzne w Chojnicach*
ul. Podmurna 13
Polish-89–600 Chojnice
Tel. 52397 43 92
Fax 52397 43 92
muzeum@chojnicemuzeum.pl
www.chojnicemuzeum.pl

National Museum in Gdańsk
*Muzeum Narodowe w Gdańsku*
ul. Toruńska 1
Polish-80–822 Gdańsk
Tel. +48 58301 68 04
Fax +48 58301 11 25
info@muzeum.narodowe.gda.pl
www.muzeum.narodowe.gda.pl

Ethnographic Museum in Gdańsk
*Muzeum Etnograficzne. Oddział Muzeum Narodowego w Gdańsku*
ul. Cystersów 19
Polish-80–330 Gdańsk
Tel. +48 58552 41 39
etnograf@muzeum.narodowe.gda.pl
www.muzeum.narodowe.gda.pl/mod.php?dz=35

Museum of the Polish National Anthem in Będomin
*Muzeum Hymnu Narodowego w Będominie. Oddział Muzeum Narodowego
w Gdańsku*
Polish-83–422 Nowy Barkoczyn

Tel. +48 58687 71 83
Fax +48 58687 74 24
mhn@muzeum.narodowe.gda.pl
www.muzeum.narodowe.gda.pl/mod.php?dz=39

Municipal Museum in Gdynia
*Muzeum Miasta Gdyni*
ul. Zawiszy Czarnego 1
Polish-81–374 Gdynia
Tel. +48 58662 09 10
Fax +48 58662 09 40
sekretariat@muzeumgdynia.pl
www.muzeumgdynia.pl

Museum of Fishery
*Muzeum Rybołówstwa. Oddział Centralnego Muzeum Morskiego*
Bulwar Nadmorski 2
Polish-84–150 Hel
Tel. +48 58675 05 52
Fax +48 58675 09 05
hel@cmm.pl
www.cmm.pl

Franciszek Treder Kashubian Museum
*Muzeum Kaszubskie im. Franciszka Tredera*
ul. Kościerska 1
Polish-83–300 Kartuzy
Tel. +48 58681 14 42
Tel./Fax +48 58681 03 78
muzeum@muzeum-kaszubskie.gda.pl
www.muzeum-kaszubskie.gda.pl

Museum in Lębork
*Muzeum w Lęborku*
ul. Młynarska 14–15
Polish-84–300 Lębork
Tel./Fax 59862 24 14
biuro@muzeum.lebork.pl
www.muzeum.lebork.pl

Puck Regional Museum
*Muzeum Ziemi Puckiej*
Plac Wolności 28
Polish-84–100 Puck
Tel./Fax +48 58673 22 29; +48 58673 29 96
mzpuck2@poczta.onet.pl
www.muzeumpuck.kaszubia.com

Peasant and Fisherman's Farmstead in Nadole
*Zagroda Gburska i Rybacka. Oddział Muzeum Ziemi Puckiej w Nadolu*
Nadole 16
Polish-84–250 Gniewino
Tel. +48 58676 76 44

Museum of Central Pomerania
*Muzeum Pomorza Środkowego*
ul. Dominikańska 5–9
Polish-76–200 Słupsk
Tel. 59842 40 81
Fax 59842 65 18
muzeum@muzeum.slupsk.pl
www.muzeum.slupsk.pl

Albrecht Farmstead in Swołowo
*Muzealna Zagroda Albrechta w Swołowie. Oddział Muzeum Pomorza Środkowego*
Swołowo 8
Polish-76–206 Słupsk 8
Tel. 59832 48 97
etnografia@muzeum.slupsk.pl
www.muzeum.swolowo.pl

Museum of the Slovincian Village
*Muzeum Wsi Słowińskiej. Oddział Muzeum Pomorza Środkowego*
Kluki
Polish-76–214 Smołdzino
Tel./Fax 59846 30 20
muzeum@muzeumkluki.pl
www.muzeumkluki.pl http://www.muzeum.slupsk.pl/

Museum of Kashubian-Pomeranian Literature and Music in Wejherowo
*Muzeum Piśmiennictwa i Muzyki Kaszubsko-Pomorskiej w Wejherowie*
ul. Zamkowa 2a
Polish-84–200 Wejherowo
Tel. +48 58672 29 56
Fax +48 58672 25 66
sekretariat@muzeum.wejherowo.pl
www.muzeum.wejherowo.pl

Kashubian Open-Air Ethnographic Museum
*Muzeum – Kaszubski Park Etnograficzny*
Wdzydze Kiszewskie
Polish-83–406 Wąglikowice
Tel./Fax +48 58686 11 30; +48 58686 12 88
muzeum@muzeum-wdzydze.gda.pl
www.muzeum-wdzydze.gda.pl

Kashubian Television (CSB TV) and Radio *Kaszëbë*
ul. Pomorska 2
Polish-84–230 Rumia
Tel./Fax +48 58572 57 30
radiokaszebe@radiokaszebe.pl
www.radiokaszebe.pl

Tourist Association *Kaszuby*
*Stowarzyszenie Turystyczne Kaszuby*
ul. Kościuszki 12
PL83–300 Kartuzy
Tel./Fax +48 58685 32 30
stk@kaszuby.com.pl
www.kaszuby.com.pl; www.kaszubylgd.pl

Wilno Heritage Society
Wilno, Ontario, K0J 2N0
Canada
heritage@wilno.org
www.wilno.org

Kashubian Association of North America
P.O. Box 27732
Minneapolis, Minnesota 55427–0732
U.S.A.
kaofna@yahoo.com
www.ka-na.org

# Appendix 4: Selected Kashubian Websites

<http://www.csb.wikipedia.org>
– Kashubian version of Wikipedia

<http://www.csb.wiktionary.org>
– multilingual dictionary in Kashubian

<http://www.naszekaszuby.pl>
– general website about Kashubia

<http://www.kaszubia.com>
– general website about Kashubia in Kashubian, Polish, German and English (with Kashubian bibliography; materials on Kashubian history, language, ethnography and genealogy; literary and religious texts; concordance of placenames; aids and programmes for computer users; CassubDict, Kashubian dictionary programme for Windows; K-Melon, Kashubian internet browser; Kashubian keyboard layout; Linuxcsb.org, Linus operating system in Kashubian)

<http://www.czetnica.org>
– literature in Kashubian

<http://www.zymk.net>
– Kashubian literary group ZYMK

<http://www.dmoz.orgWorld/Kasz%C3%ABbsczi>
– Kashubian *Open Directory Project*

<http://www.monika.univ.gda.pl~literat/remus>
– Aleksander Majkowski's novel *Żecé i przigodë Remusa*

<http://www.rastko.net/rastko-ka>
– Kashubian sub-site of a major web portal on Slavistics, with considerable historical, literary and linguistic materials

<http://www.cassubia-dictionary.com>
– Kashubian online dictionary

<http://www.kaszed.zk-p.pl>
– Kashubian text editor

<http://www.pl.wikibooks.orgwiki/Kaszubski>
– Kashubian language course

<http://www.grzegorj.w.interia.pllingw/kaszub.html>
– information on the Kashubian language in Polish and English

<http://www.szkola.interklasa.plf019/strona/pol/index.html>
– educational material about Kashubia

<http://www.kalwariawejherowska.plplindex.php>
– website of the Calvary of Wejherowo

<http://www.kaszubski.filmjezus.org.pl>
– website about the Kashubian version of the film *Jesus*

<http://www.fif.kaszubia.com>
– website of the Kashubian cabaret group FiF

<http://www.festiwal.brusy.pl>
– website of the International Folklore Festival in Brusy

<http://www.kaszuby.org>
– general information about Kashubia, including tourism

<http://www.kaszuby.info.pl>
– tourist information

<http://www.e-kaszuby.net>
– tourist information

<http://www.kuchnia.wla.com.pl>
– Kashubian cuisine

<http://www.kaszuby.net>
– *Kaszuby* Canada online (in Polish and English)

<http://www.modraglina.republika.plkaszlink.html>
– Kashubian web links in Polish, German and English

<http://www.studiensTelleog.de/kaschuben/kaschub-inhalt.htm>
– German-language texts on the Kashubs

<http://www.kashuba.org>
– Kashubian Family Research Centre

<http://www.glischinski.de/roots/roots.html>
– about the Kashubs and their history, in German

<http://www.pgsa.org/Kashub/kashub.php>
– Kashubian section of the Polish Genealogical Society of America

# Bibliography

E. Achramowicz and T. Żabski, *Towarzystwo Literacko – Słowiańskie we Wrocławiu 1836 – 1886* (Wrocław–Warszawa–Kraków–Gdańsk: Ossolineum, 1973).

M. Andrzejewski, 'Niemieckie zabiegi o uzyskanie wpływu na świadomość polityczną Kaszubów w latach 1924 – 1935. Materiały źródłowe', *Zapiski Historyczne* 2–3 (1990), 37–65.

K.G. Anton, *Erste Linien eines Versuches über der alten Slaven: Ursprung, Sitten, Gebräuche, Meinungen und Kenntnisse*, vol.I–II (Leipzig, 1783, 1789 & Bautzen: Serbski Institut, 1976).

*Atlas językowy kaszubszczyzny i dialektów sąsiednich*, vol.I–VI ed. Z. Stieber, vol. VII–XV ed. H. Popowska-Taborska (Wrocław: Ossolineum, 1964–78).

G. Babiński, 'Nacjonalizmy czy regionalizmy? Ruchy etnoregionalne w Europie', in: G. Babiński and W. Miodunka (ed.) *Europa państw – Europa narodów. Problemy etniczne Europy Środkowo-Wschodniej* (Kraków: NOMOS, 1995), 47–76.

G. Babiński, *Metodologiczne problemy badań etnicznych* (Kraków: NOMOS, 1998).

L. Bądkowski [Bentkowski], *Pomorska myśl polityczna* (Gdynia: Arkun, 1990).

C. Baker, *Studia kulturowe. Teoria i praktyka* (Kraków: Wydawnictwo Uniwersytetu Jagiellońskiego, 2005).

J. Bełkot and M. Wojciechowski, *Powrót. Dokumentacja ustanowienia suwerenności polskiej na Pomorzu w latach 1918 – 1920* (Toruń: Toruńskie Towarzystwo Kultury, 1988).

J. Bernoulli, *Reisen durch Brandenburg, Pommern, Preussen, Curland, Russland und Polen in den Jahren 1777 und 1778*, vol.1 (Leipzig, 1779).

L. Bielawski and A. Mioduchowska, *Kaszuby*, vol.2 *Polska pieśń i muzyka ludowa. Źródła i materiały* (Warszawa: Instytut Sztuki PAN, 1997).

M. Biskup and G. Labuda, *Dzieje zakonu krzyżackiego w Prusach. Gospodarka – Społeczeństwo – Państwo – Ideologia* (Gdańsk: Wydawnictwo Morskie, 1986).

M. Biskup and G. Labuda, *Die Geschichte des Deutschen Ordens in Preußen. Wirtschaft – Gesellschaft – Staat – Ideologie* (Osnabrück: Deutsches Historisches Institut in Warschau, 2000).

M. Boduszyńska-Borowikowa, *Życie jak płomień. O życiu i pracach Józefa Borowika* (Gdańsk: Wydawnictwo Morskie, 1972).

Z. Bokszański, *Tożsamości zbiorowe* (Warszawa: PWN, 2005).

T. Bolduan, *Nie dali się złamać. Spojrzenie na ruch kaszubski 1939 – 1995* (Gdańsk: Zrzeszenie Kaszubsko-Pomorskie, 1996).

W. Boryś and H. Popowska-Taborska, *Słownik etymologiczny kaszubszczyzny*, vol.I–V (Warszawa: Polska Akademia Nauk, Instytut Slawistyki, 1994–2008).

J. Borzyszkowski, *Istota ruchu kaszubskiego i jego przemiany od połowy XIX wieku po współczesność* (Gdańsk: Zrzeszenie Kaszubsko-Pomorskie, 1982 a).

J. Borzyszkowski (ed.), *Trzy pamiętniki pomorskie* (Gdańsk: Zrzeszenie Kaszubsko-Pomorskie, 1982 b).

J. Borzyszkowski, *Inteligencja polska Prus Zachodnich (1848–1920)* (Gdańsk: Wydawnictwo Morskie, 1986 a).

J. Borzyszkowski, *Wielewskie góry. Dzieje Wiela i jego kalwarii* (Gdańsk: Zrzeszenie Kaszubsko-Pomorskie, 1986 b).

J. Borzyszkowski, 'Emigracja polska w Nadrenii – Westfalii a rozwój świadomości narodowej społeczności polskiej Prus Zachodnich przed 1920 rokiem', *Rocznik Gdański* 1 (1993), 5–13.

J. Borzyszkowski, 'Die polnische Emigration nach Nordrhein – Westfalen und die Entwicklung das Nationalbewusstseins der polnischen Bevölkerung Westpreußens vor 1920', *Migration. A European Journal of International Migration and Ethnic Relations* 20 (1993–4), 97–112.

J. Borzyszkowski, 'Od Kongresu Polaków w Niemczech (Berlin 1938) do Kongresu Kaszubów – Polaków – Autochtonów (Szczecin 1946)', in: *Państwo i społeczeństwo na Pomorzu Zachodnim do 1945 r.*, ed. W. Stępiński (Szczecin: Uniwersytet Szczeciński, 1997), 350–60.

J. Borzyszkowski, 'Społeczność kaszubska po 1945 r.', in: M. Giedrojć and J. Mieczkowski (ed.), *Pomerania ethnica. Mniejszości narodowe i etniczne na Pomorzu Zachodnim* (Szczecin: AMP, 1998), 125–44.

J. Borzyszkowski, *Gdańsk i Pomorze w XIX i XX wieku* (Gdańsk: Uniwersytet Gdański, 1999 a).

J. Borzyszkowski: 'Die Kaschuben im 19. und 20. Jahrhundert zwischen Polen und Deutschland', in: H.H. Hahn and P. Kunze (ed.) *Nationale Minderheiten und staatliche Minderheitenpolitik in Deutschland im 19. Jahrhundert* (Berlin 1999 b), 93–8.

J. Borzyszkowski, *Z dziejów Kościoła katolickiego na Kaszubach i Pomorzu w XIX i XX wieku* (Gdańsk-Pelplin: Instytut Kaszubski and Bernardinum, 2000).

J. Borzyszkowski, *Kaszubsko-pomorscy duszpasterze – współtwórcy dziejów regionu* (Gdańsk-Pelplin: Instytut Kaszubski & Bernardinum, 2002).

J. Borzyszkowski, *A. Majkowski (1876–1938). Biografia historyczna* (Gdańsk-Wejherowo. Instytut Kaszubski & Muzeum Piśmiennictwa i Muzyki Kaszubsko-Pomorskiej, 2002).

J. Borzyszkowski (ed.), *Pro memoria Lech Bądkowski (1920–1984)* (Gdańsk: Instytut Kaszubski, 2004).

J. Borzyszkowski (ed.), *Bajarz kaszubski. Bajki z 'Gryfa' (1908–1912)* (Wejherowo-Gdańsk: Muzeum Piśmiennictwa i Muzyki Kaszubsko-Pomorskiej & Instytut Kaszubski, 2005).

J. Borzyszkowski and D. Albrecht (ed.). *Pomorze – mała ojczyzna Kaszubów. (Historia i współczesność). Kaschubisch-pommersche Homeland. (Geschichte und Gegenwart).* (Gdańsk-Lübeck: Ostsee Academie & Zrzeszenie Kaszubsko-Pomorskie & Instytut Kaszubski, 2000).

J. Borzyszkowski and P. Hauser (ed.), *Sejm Rzeczpospolitej o Pomorzu w 1920 roku. Sprawozdanie Komisji Pomorskiej* (Gdańsk: Zrzeszenie Kaszubsko-Pomorskie, 1985).

J. Borzyszkowski, J. Mordawski and J. Treder, *Historia. Geografia. Język i piśmiennictwo Kaszubów. Historia, geògrafia, jãzëk i pismienizna Kaszëbów* (Gdańsk: M.Rożak, 1999).

J. Borzyszkowski and C. Obracht-Prondzyński, 'Mniejszość niemiecka na Pomorzu: Dogadać się można po kaszubsku. (Deutsche Minderheit in Pommern: Man verständigt auf Kaschubisch)', *Dialog* 1–4 (1994), 34–5.

J. Borzyszkowski and C. Obracht-Prondzyński (ed.), *Badania kaszuboznawcze w XX wieku* (Gdańsk: Instytut Kaszubski, 2001).

J. Borzyszkowski and C. Obracht-Prondzyński, 'Serbołużyczanie i Kaszubi a ich pogranicza. Wspólnota dziejów i trwania w XIX i XX wieku', in: M. Buchowski and A. Brencz (ed.), *Polska – Niemcy. Pogranicza kulturowe i etniczne / Poland – Germany. Cultural and ethnic order, Archiwum Etnograficzne / Etnographic Archives* 42 (Wrocław-Poznań: Polskie Towarzystwo Ludoznawcze, 2004), 241–50.

B. Brandt, 'Wypędzeni z domu', *Pomerania* 5 (1996), 38–41.

E. Breza, *Pochodzenie przydomków szlachty pomorskiej* (Gdańsk: Uniwersytet Gdański, 1986).

E. Breza, 'Kształtowanie się kaszubskiego języka literackiego', in: J. Zieniukowa (ed.), *Obraz językowy słowiańskiego Pomorza i Łużyc* (Warszaw: Slawistyczny Ośrodek Wydawniczy, 1997). 247–57.

E. Breza (ed.), *Kaszubszczyzna. Kaszëbizna* (Opole: Uniwersytet Opolski, 2001).

E. Breza and J. Treder, *Zasady pisowni kaszubskiej* (Gdańsk: Zrzeszenie Kaszubsko-Pomorskie, 1975 & 1984).

E. Breza and J. Treder, *Gramatyka kaszubska. Zarys popularny* (Gdańsk: Zrzeszenie Kaszubsko-Pomorskie, 1981).

J. Bugenhagen, *Die pommersche Kirchenordnung von Johannes Bugenhagen 1535. Tex mit Uebersetzung, Erläuterung und Einleitung,* ed. N. Buske (Berlin, 1985).

J. Bugenhagen, *Pomerania*, ed. O. v. Heinemann (Stettin, 1900).

A. Bukowski, *Regionalizm kaszubski. Ruch naukowy, literacki i kulturalny. Zarys monografii historycznej* (Poznań: Instytut Zachodni, 1950).

S. Byczkowska and T. Maliszewski, 'Scandinavian Inspirations: Looking for a True "School for Life"', in: T. Maliszewski, W.J. Wojtowicz and J. Żerko (ed.) *Anthology of Social and Behavioural Sciences* (Linköping: Universitat Linköping, 2005), 135–48.

M. Byczkowski, T. Maliszewski and E. Przybylska (ed.), *Uniwersytet Ludowy – szkoła dla życia* (Wieżyca: Kaszubski Uniwersytet Ludowy, 2003).

F.S. Ceynowa, 'Die Germanisirung der Kaschuben', *Jahrbücher für slawische Literatur, Kunst und Wissenschaften* 4 (1843), 243–7.

F.S. Ceynowa, *Kile słów wō Kaszëbach e jich zemi* (Kraków: Księgarnia Pod Sową, 1850).

F.S. Ceynowa, *Skôrb Kaszébskosłovjnskjè móvé. Pjerszé xęgj pjerszi seszet* (Svjece: J. Hauffe, 1866).

F.S. Ceynowa, *Zarés do Grammatikj Kaśébsko-Słovjnskjè Mòvé. Die Kassubisch-Slovinische Sprache* (Poznań: Wojciech Simon, 1879).

F.S. Ceynowa, *Rozmòwa Pòlôcha z Kaszëbą. Rozmòwa Kaszëbë z Pòlôchã*, ed. J. Treder (Gdańsk: Instytut Kaszubski, 2007).

B. Chrzanowski, A. Gąsiorowski, and K. Steyer, *Polska podziemna na Pomorzu w latach 1939 – 1945* (Gdańsk: Oskar Polnord, 2005).

A. Chołoniewski, *Nad Morzem Polskim* (Warszawa: 1912).

K. Ciechanowski, *Ruch oporu na Pomorzu Gdańskim 1939 – 1945* (Warszawa: Wydawnictwo Ministerstwa Obrony Narodowej, 1972).

K. Ciechanowski, 'Tajna Organizacja Wojskowa "Gryf Pomorski" i inne organizacje konspiracyjne na Pomorzu Gdańskim w latach 1939 – 1945', *Pomerania* 1 (1971), 4–7.

K. Ciechanowski, *TOW 'Gryf Pomorski'* (Gdańsk: Zrzeszenie Kaszubsko-Pomorskie, 1972).

R. Ciemiński, *Kaszubski werblista. Rzecz o Günterze Grassie* (Gdańsk: Oskar-Polnord, 1999).

M. Cybulski, 'Praktyczne aspekty ustawy o mniejszościach narodowych i etnicznych oraz o języku regionalnym', in: J. Treder (ed.) *Kaszubszczyzna w przeszłości i dziś. Kaszëbizna dôwni ë dzys* (Warszawa: Komitet Historii Nauki i Techniki Polskiej Akademii Nauk, 2006), 63–72.

M. Cybulski and R. Wosiak-Śliwa, 'Kaszubskie szkolnictwo i podręczniki', in: E. Wrocławska and J. Zieniukowa (ed.) *Języki mniejszości i języki narodowe* (Warszawa: Slawistyczny Ośrodek Wydawniczy, 2003), 147–58.

P. Czaplewski, *Collegium Marianum. Na stuletnią rocznicę 1836 – 1936* (Pelplin: Collegium Marianum, 1938).

P. Czaplewski, 'Majątki duchowne sekularyzowane po r. 1772 w obrębie województwa pomorskiego i Wolnego Miasta Gdańska', *Rocznik Gdański* 7–8 (1933–4), 385–415.

H. Derdowski, *O Panu Czôrlińsczim co do Pucka po sece jachoł* (Toruń: Buszczyński, 1888 & Gdańsk: Zrzeszenie Kaszubsko-Pomorskie, 1976).

H. Derdowski, *Ò panu Czôrlińsczim co do Pùcka pò sécë jachôł*, ed. J. Samp, J. Treder and E. Gołąbek (Gdańsk: Instytut Kaszubski, 2007).

H. Derdowski, *Jasiek z Knieji* (Toruń, 1885 & Gdańsk: Oficyna Czec, 2001).

A. Dobrowolska, 'O nazwie Kaszuby', *Onomastica* 4 (1958), 333–53.

H. Domańska, *Żarnowiec. Zarys historii wsi i opactwa* (Wejherowo: Muzeum Piśmiennictwa i Muzyki Kaszubsko-Pomorskiej, 1985).

J. Drzeżdżon, *Piętno Smętka. Z problemów kaszubskiej literatury regionalnej lat 1920 – 1939* (Gdańsk: Wydawnictwo Morskie, 1973).

J. Drzeżdżon (ed.), *Modra struna. Antologia poezji kaszubskiej* (Gdańsk: Wydawnictwo Morskie, 1973).

J. Drzeżdżon (ed.), *Współczesna literatura kaszubska 1945–1980* (Warszawa: Ludowa Spółdzielnia Wydawnicza, 1986).

R. Drzeżdżon and G. Schramke, *Dzëcé gäsë. Antologiô kaszëbsczi pòezji* (Gdynia: Region, 2004).

A.D. Duličenko and W. Lehfeldt (ed.), *Kurze Betrachtungen über die kaßubische Sprache, als Entwurf zur Grammatik* (Göttingen: Vandenhoeck and Ruprecht, 1998).

A.D. Dulichenko, *Slavyanskiye literaturnye mikroyazyki. Voprosy formirovaniya i razvitya* (Tallinn: Valgus, 1981).

A.D. Dulichenko, 'Kashubskiy yazyk', in: *Yazyki mira* (Moskva: Academia, 2005), 383–403.

J.-M. Eloy, *Des langues collatérales* (Paris: L'Harmattan, 2004).

J.-L. Fauconnier, 'Les langues d'oïl, des idiomes en voie de reconnaissance': in: Wicherkiewicz and al. (2004), 22–31.

S. Fikus, *Pojmańczicë* (Gdańsk: Zrzeszenie Kaszubsko-Pomorskie, 1981).

A. Fischer, T. Lehr-Spławiński and F. Lorentz, 'Kaszubi. Kultura ludowa i język', *Pamiętnik Instytutu Bałtyckiego* 16, ed. J. Borowik (Toruń: Instytut Bałtycki, 1934).

A. Fischer, T. Lehr-Spławiński and F. Lorentz, *The Cassubian Civilisation* (London: Faber and Faber Ltd, 1935).

W. Frankowska (ed.). *Muzyka Kaszub. Materiały encyklopedyczne* (Gdańsk: Oficyna Czec, 2005).

H. Galus, 'Kaszubi w zbiorowości społecznej Pomorza po 1945 r. – kontynuacja tożsamości', *Przegląd Zachodni* 2 (1990), 1–20.

H. Galus, 'Mniejszość niemiecka na Pomorzu Wschodnim', in: Z. Kurcz and W. Misiak (ed.) *Mniejszość niemiecka w Polsce i Polacy w Niemczech* (Wrocław: Uniwersytet Wrocławski, 1994), 65–80.

A. Gąsiorowski, *Jan Kaszubowski i służby specjalne Gestapo, Smiersz, UB ...* (Gdańsk: Oskar Polnord, 2008).

E. Gellner, *Narody i nacjonalizm* (Warszawa: PIW, 1991).

S. Geppert, 'Język kaszubski uzyskał międzynarodowy kod', *Pomerania* 6 (2003), 48.

T. Główczewski, 'Kronika kaszubskiej rodziny Kossak-Główczewskich', in: *Z południa Kaszub*, ed.. J. Borzyszkowski (Gdańsk: Zrzeszenie Kaszubsko-Pomorskie, 1982), 83–5.

E. Gołąbek, *Kaszëbsczi słowôrz normatiwny* (Gdańsk: Oficyna Czec, 2005).

E. Gołąbk (transl.), *Swięté Pismiona Nowégo Testameńtu* (Gduńsk-Pelplin: Zrzeszenie Kaszubsko-Pomorskie and Bernardinum 1993).

E. Gòłąbk, *Kaszëbsczi słowôrz normatiwny* (Gdańsk: Oficyna Czec, 2005).

H. Gołębiewski, *Obrazki rybackie z półwyspu Helu* (Pelplin: E. Michałowski, 1887 & Gdańsk: Zrzeszenie Kaszubsko-Pomorskie, 1975).

H. Gołębiewski, *Bilder aus dem Fischerleben auf der Halbinsel Hela* (Danzig 1918).

H. Górnowicz, 'Osiągnięcia i postulaty badawcze w zakresie dialektologii i onomastyki na Pomorzu (1945–1965)', *Rocznik Gdański* 24 (1965), 5–34.

G. Grass, *Blechtrommel* (Neuwied/Berlin: Hermann Luchterhand Verlag, 1959). English translation by R. Mannheim, *Tin Drum* (New York: Alfred A Knopf, 1993).

G. Grzelak, 'Lech Bądkowski a Ruch Młodej Polski, 'Solidarność i Lech Wałęsa (1980–1984)', in: *'Solidarność' i opozycja antykomunistyczna w Gdańsku (1980–1989)*, ed. L. Mażewski and W. Turek (Gdańsk: Instytut Konserwatywny im. E. Burke'a, 1995), 29–34.

I. Gulgowski, *Von einem unbekannten Volke im Deutschland. Ein Beitrag zur Volks- und Landeskunde der Kaschubei* (Berlin: Deutsche Landbuchhandlung, 1911).

C.W. Haken, *Bericht über die pommerschen Kaschuben, w: Ausführliche Beschreibung des gegenwärtigen Zustandes des Königl. Preußischen Herzogtums Vor- und Hinterpommern*, vol. 1 (Stettin, 1779).

M. Hejger, *Polityka narodowościowa władz polskich w województwie gdańskim w latach 1945 – 1947* (Słupsk: Pomorska Akademia Pedagogiczna, 1998).

M. Hejger, 'Stosunki polsko-ukraińskie na Pomorzu Zachodnim w latach 1947–1957', in: *Ukraińcy w najnowszych dziejach Polski (1928–1989)*, vol.1, ed. R. Drozd (Słupsk-Warszawa: Pomorska Akademia Pedagogiczna & ZUwP, 2000), 185–96.

A. Hildebrand, *Wiadomości niektóre o dawniejszym archidyakonacie pomorskim, a teraz znacznej części diecezji chełmińskiej* (Pelplin, 1862).

A. Hilferding, *Ostatki Slavyan na yuzhnom beregu Baltiyskogo morya* (Sankt Peterburg: Bezobrazov i Komp., 1856).

A. Hilferding, *Resztki Słowian na południowym wybrzeżu Morza Bałtyckiego*, ed. J. Treder (Gdańsk: Zrzeszenie Kaszubsko-Pomorskie, 1990).

*Historia Pomorza*, vol.I–III, ed. G. Labuda (Poznań: Wydawnictwo Poznańskie & Poznańskie Towarzystwo Przyjaciół Nauk, 1968–2003): vol.IV, 1–2, ed. S. Salmonowicz (Toruń: Towarzystwo Naukowe w Toruniu, 2000–2).

A. Hlebowicz and T. Arabski, *Budujmy ołtarze* (Sopot: Stella Maris, 1999).

B. Jałowiecki, 'Scena polityczna Polski lokalnej', in: B. Jałowiecki and P. Swianiewicz (ed.), *Między nadzieją a rozczarowaniem. Samorząd terytorialny rok po wyborach* (Warszawa: Uniwersytet Warszawski, 1991), 39–74.

B. Jałowiecki, 'Kwestia regionalna', *Studia Socjologiczne* 1 (1992), 43–4.

B. Jałowiecki, 'Kwestia regionalna', in: G. Gorzelak and B. Jałowiecki (ed.) *Czy Polska będzie państwem regionalnym?* (Warszawa: Uniwersytet Warszawski, 1993), 39–74.

W. Jastrzębski, *Polityka narodowościowa w okręgu Rzeszy Gdańsk–Prusy Zachodnie (1939–1945)* (Bydgoszcz: WSP, 1977).

W. Jastrzębski, 'Polityka hitlerowska i straty Pomorza w okresie II wojny światowej', *Studia Pelplińskie* 20 (1989), 11–24.

W. Jastrzębski, *W dalekim obcym kraju. Deportacje Polaków z Pomorza do ZSRR w 1945 r.* (Bydgoszcz: WSP, 1990).

W. Jastrzębski and J. Sziling, *Okupacja hitlerowska na Pomorzu Gdańskim w latach 1939 – 1945* (Gdańsk: Wydawnictwo Morskie, 1979).

A. Jawłowska, 'Kierunki zmiany kulturowej i jej konsekwencje społeczne', in: A. Rychard and M. Fedorowicz (ed.) *Społeczeństwo w transformacji. Ekspertyzy i studia* (Warszawa: IFiS PAN, 1993), 186–200.

E. Kamińska and J. Pałkowska, 'Z historii badań nad gwarami kaszubskimi', *Rocznik Gdański* XV/XVI 1956/57 (1958), 342–92.

S. Kapralski and J. Mucha, 'Kultura polska w oczach mniejszości', in: J. Wasilewski (ed.) *Współczesne społeczeństwo polskie. Dynamika zmian* (Warszawa: Wydawnictwo Scholar, 2007), 429–66.

J. Karnowski, 'O dalszych zadaniach "Gryfa". *Gryf* 4 (1909), 121.

J. Karnowski, *Ludność kaszubska w ubiegłym stuleciu (Szkic społeczno-kulturalny)* (Kościerzyna: Spółka Wydawnicza Gryf, 1911).

J. Karnowski, *Dr F. Ceynowa* (Kościerzyna: Gryf, 1922).

J. Karnowski, *Moja droga kaszubska*, ed. J. Borzyszkowski (Gdańsk: Zrzeszenie Kaszubsko-Pomorskie, 1981).

J. Karnowski, *Dr F. Ceynowa*, ed. J. Treder (Gdańsk: Oficyna Czec, 1997).

W. Kiedrowski (ed.), *Jan Paweł II ze szczególnym słowem do wszystkich nad Bałtykiem* (Gdynia: Arkun, 1990).

J. Kisielewski, *Ziemia gromadzi prochy* (Poznań: Księgarnia św. Wojciecha, 1939).

H. Kloss, '*Abstand* Languages and *Ausbau* Languages', *Anthropological Linguistics* 9 (7) (1967), 29–41.

M. Komosa, 'Kaszëbsczim jesmë ledā. Postawy działaczy ruchu kaszubskiego wobec własnej kultury i tożsamości', in: P. Kalinowski (ed.) *Catering dziedzictwa kulturowego. Kaszubi i Kaszuby w oczach etnologów* (Gdynia: Wydawnictwo Region, 2006), 148–207.

A. Konkel, 'Niektóre elementy tradycji kaszubskich maszoperii żakowych w Jastarni', *Rocznik Helski* 2 (2003), 71–88.

K. Kościński, *Kaszubi giną* (Poznań: Dziennik Poznański, 1908).

S. Krofey, *Duchowne piesnie D. Marcina Luthera ÿ ÿnszich naboznich mężow Zniemieckiego w Slawięsky ięzik wilozone Przes Szymana Krofea, sluge slowa Bozego w Bytowie* (Gdańsk: J. Rhode, 1586).

S. Krofey, *Geistliche Lieder D. Martin Luthers und anderer frommer Männer. Duchowne piesnie D. Marcina Luthera y ynszich naboznich mężów, Danzig 1586*, ed. R. Olesch (Köln-Graz: Böhlau Verlag, 1958).

*Kronika Wielkopolska*, ed. B. Kürbis (Warszawa, 1965).

H. Kubiak, 'Region i regionalizm. Próba analizy typologicznej', *Przegląd Polonijny* 1 (1994), 5–40.

J. Kucharska, 'Kształtowanie się świadomości regionalnej i narodowej ludności kaszubskiej okolic Bytowa', *Acta Universitatis Lodzensis. Folia Ethnologica* 2 (1985), 3–138.

R. Kukier, 'Tradycje kulturowe osadnictwa drobnoszlacheckiego na ziemi człuchowskiej', *Koszalińskie Zeszyty Muzealne* 6 (1976), 139–70.

J. Kurczewska, M. Kempy and H. Bojar, 'Społeczności lokalne jako wspólnoty tradycji – w poszukiwaniu korzeni demokracji', *Studia Socjologiczne* 2 (1998), 3–27.

J. Kurczewski, 'Struktura autoidentyfikacji na Śląsku Opolskim i na Kaszubach: analiza porównawcza', in: C. Obracht-Prondzyński (ed.), *Kim są Kaszubi? Nowe tendencje w badaniach społecznych* (Gdańsk: Instytut Kaszubski, 2007), 305–30.

G. Kustosz, *Święte Góry Wejherowskie* (Gdynia: Arkun, 1991).

J. Kutta, *Regionalizm czy separatyzm? Przyczynek do dziejów integracji społeczeństwa polskiego w latach 1920–1939* (Gdańsk-Bydgoszcz: Zrzeszenie Kaszubsko-Pomorskie, 1989).

J. Kutta, *Druga Rzeczpospolita a Kaszubi 1920–1939* (Bydgoszcz: Wydawnictwo Pozkal, 2003).

K. Kwaśniewski, *Regionalizm* (Poznań: Wydawnictwo Poznańskie, 1986).

P. Kwiatkowski, *Społeczne ramy tradycji. Przemiany obrazu przeszłości Mazowsza Płockiego w publikacjach regionalnych 1918–1988* (Warszawa: Uniwersytet Warszawski, 1990).

A. Kwilecki, 'Region i badania regionalne w perspektywie socjologii', *Ruch Prawniczy, Ekonomiczny i Socjologiczny* 2 (1992), 37–47.

G. Labuda, 'Chrystianizacja Pomorza (X – XIII stulecie)', *Studia Gdańskie* 9 (1993), 45–60.

G. Labuda, *Kaszubi i ich dzieje* (Gdańsk: Oficyna Czec, 1996).

G. Labuda, 'Podłoże polityczne dyskusji nad autonomią języka kaszubskiego na przełomie XIX i XX stulecia', in: H. Horodyska (ed.) *Całe życie pod urokiem mowy kaszubskiej* (Warszawa: Komitet Historii Nauki i Techniki Polskiej Akademii Nauk, 1995), 17–44.

G. Labuda, *Historia Kaszubów w dziejach Pomorza*, vol.I. *Czasy średniowieczne* (Gdańsk: Instytut Kaszubski, 2006).

M. Latoszek (ed.), *Kaszubi. Monografia socjologiczna* (Rzeszów: TNOiK, 1990).

M. Latoszek, 'Regionalizm w procesie przemian – wprowadzenie do zagadnienia', in: M. Latoszek (ed.) *Regionalizm jako folkloryzm, ruch społeczny i formuła ideologiczno-polityczna* (Gdańsk: Gdańskie Towarzystwo Naukowe, 1993), 3–25.

M. Latoszek, 'Grupa etniczna w Polsce – możliwe warianty przemian (ze szczególnym uwzględnieniem Kaszubów)', in: G. Babiński and W. Miodunka (ed.) *Europa państw – Europa narodów. Problemy etniczne Europy Środkowo-Wschodniej* (Kraków: NOMOS, 1995), 141–56.

M. Latoszek, *Pomorze – zagadnienia etniczno-regionalne* (Gdańsk: Gdańskie Towarzystwo Naukowe, 1996).

M. Latoszek, 'Świadomość językowa i kulturowa Kaszubów w kontekście typów orientacji temporalnych i uwarunkowań historyczno-geograficznych, in: J. Zieniukowa (ed.) *Obraz językowy słowiańskiego Pomorza i Łużyc. Pogranicza i kontakty językowe* (Warszawa: Slawistyczny Ośrodek Wydawniczy, 1997), 185–201.

T. Lipski, *Remusowi krôm. Wypisy z literatury kaszubskiej dla nauczycieli języka polskiego* (Gdańsk: Zrzeszenie Kaszubsko-Pomorskie, 1990).

'List pastora Hakena', *Gryf* I, 7 (1908/9), 203–7.

S. Łodziński, *Równość i różnica. Mniejszości narodowe w porządku demokratycznym w Polsce po roku 1989* (Warszawa: Scholar, 2005).

F. Lorentz, *Kaschubische Grammatik* (Danzig: 1919).

F. Lorentz, *Geschichte der Kaschuben* (Berlin: Reimar Hobbing Verlag, 1926).

F. Lorentz, *Gramatyka pomorska* (Poznań 1927–37 and Wrocław: Ossolineum, 1958–62).

F. Lorentz, *Pomoranisches Wörtertuch*, vol.1–5, ed. F. Hinze (Berlin: Akademie-Verlag, 1958–83).

F. Lorentz, A. Fischer and T. Lehr-Spławiński, *Kaszubi. Kultura ludowa i język* (Toruń: Instytut Bałtycki, 1934).

A.F. Majewicz, 'A New Kashubian Dictionary and the Problem of the Linguistic Status of Kashubian', in: *Collectanea Linguistica in Honorem Adam Heinz, Prace Komisji Językoznawczej* 53 (Wrocław: Ossolineum. 1996 a), 95–9.

A.F. Majewicz, 'Kashubian Choices, Kashubian Prospects: a Minority Language Situation in northern Poland', *International Journal of the Sociology of Language* 120, ed. J.A. Fishman, Berlin-New York: Mouton de Gruyter, 1996 b), 39–53.

A.F. Majewicz and T. Wicherkiewicz, 'Polityka językowa na Kaszubach na tle prawodawstwa wobec mniejszości w jednoczącej się Europie (Diagnozy i postulaty)', in: Breza 2001, 81–98.

A.F. Majewicz and T. Wicherkiewicz, 'National Minority Languages in Media and Education in Poland', in: D. Gorter and al. (eds) *Fourth International Conference on Minority Languages*. Vol.II. *Western and Eastern European Papers* (Clevedon-Philadelphia: Multilingual Matters, 1990), 149–74.

A. Majkowski, 'Ruch młodokaszubski', *Gryf* I, 7 (1909), 192–8.

A. Majkowski [J. Starża], 'Nowa wiosna', *Gryf* 1 (1921), 1.

A. Majkowski, *Historia Kaszubów* (Gdynia: Stanica, 1938 and Gdańsk: Zrzeszenie Kaszubsko-Pomorskie, 1991).

A. Majkowski, *Pamiętnik z wojny europejskiej roku 1914*, ed. T. Linkner (Wejherowo-Pelplin: Muzeum Piśmiennictwa i Muzyki Kaszubsko-Pomorskiej, Bernardinum, 2000).

J. Majowa, 'Kaszuby i obszary dialektów sąsiednich jako tereny oddziaływań językowych bieguna zachodnio-i wschodniolechickiego', *Studia z Filologii Polskiej i Słowiańskiej* 17 (1978), 145–82.

F. Manthey, *O historii Kaszubów. Prawda i świadectwo* (Gdańsk: Instytut Kaszubski, 1997).

S. Mask Connolly, 'The Wilno Heritage Society', in: J. Borzyszkowski (ed.), *O Kaszubach w Kanadzie. Kaszubsko-kanadyjskie losy i dziedzictwo kultury* (Gdańsk-Elbląg: Instytut Kaszubski, Elbląska Uczelnia Humanistyczno-Ekonomiczna, 2004), 595–608.

D. Matelski, 'Mniejszość niemiecka na Pomorzu Gdańskim (1920–1996)', *Rocznik Gdański* 1 (1997), 93–105.

M. Mazurek, 'Czynniki wyznaczające tożsamość kaszubską – język, rodzina czy terytorium?' *Acta Cassubiana* 7 (2005), 25–37.

M. Mazurek, 'Język jako wartość u Kaszubów', in: J. Treder (ed.) *Kaszubszczyzna w przeszłości i dziś. Kaszëbizna dôwni ë dzys* (Warszawa: Komitet Historii Nauki i Techniki Polskiej Akademii Nauk, 2006), 119–38.

M. Mazurek, 'Kwestia etnicznej tożsamości nabytej oraz relacji dominacji – podporządkowania – na przykładzie Kaszubów', in: J. Mucha and B. Pactwa (ed.) *'Status mniejszościowy' i ambiwalencja tożsamości w społeczeństwach wielokulturowych* (Tychy: Wyższa Szkoła Zarządzania i Nauk Społecznych, 2008 a), 105–23.

M. Mazurek, 'Tożsamość kaszubska jako tożsamość nabyta- analiza zjawiska', in: A. Sakson (ed.) *Ślązacy, Kaszubi, Mazurzy i Warmiacy – między polskością a niemieckością* (Poznań: Instytut Zachodni, 2008 b), 209–17.

M. Mazurek, 'Tożsamość przestrzenna jako wyznacznik zakorzenienia wśród mieszkańców współczesnych Kaszub': in: M. Kempy, G. Woroniecka and P. Załęcki (ed.) *Tożsamość i przynależność. O współczesnych przemianach identyfikacji kulturowych w Polsce i Europie*, Toruń: Wydawnictwo Naukowe UMK, 2008 c), 97–108.

M. Mazurek and L. Michałowski, 'Kaszubskość Gdyni i Gdańska w oczach ich mieszkańców', *Pomerania* 7–8 (2007), 24–7.

J. Mordawski, *Statystyka ludności kaszubskiej. Kaszubi u progu XXI wieku* (Gdańsk: Instytut Kaszubski, 2005).

J. Mordawski, 'Kaszubi w czasach współczesnych', in: J. Mordawski (ed.) *Gdyńscy Kaszubi*. Gdynia: Zrzeszenie Kaszubsko-Pomorskie, 2006), 158–75.

A. Nadolny, 'Polskie duszpasterstwo w Zagłębiu Ruhry (1871–1894)', *Studia Pelplińskie* 12 (1981), 239–315.

N. Nestor and T. Hickey, 'Out of the Communist frying pan and into the EU fire? Exploring the case of Kashubian', *Language, Culture and Curriculum* 22/2 (2009), 95–119.

F. Neureiter, *Kaschubische Anthologie* (München: Otto Sagner Verlag, 1973).

F. Neureiter, *Geschichte der kaschubischen Literatur Versuch einer zusammenfassenden Darstellung* (München: Otto Sagner Verlag 1978, 1991).

F. Neureiter, *Historia literatury kaszubskiej. Próba zarysu* (Gdańsk: Zrzeszenie Kaszubsko-Pomorskie, 1982).

K. Nitsch, 'Studya kaszubskie: Gwara luzińska', *Materiały i Prace Komisji Językowej AU w Krakowie*, vol.1, 2 (Kraków, 1903), 221–73.

K. Nitsch, 'Historia badań nad dialektami północnej Polski', *Konferencja Pomorska (1954). Prace językoznawcze* (Warszawa: Państwowe Wydawnictwo Naukowe, 1956), 11–20.

C. Obracht-Prondzyński, *Jan Karnowski (1886–1939) – pisarz, polityk i kaszubsko – pomorski działacz regionalny* (Gdańsk: Instytut Kaszubski, 1999 a).

C. Obracht-Prondzyński, 'Wędrówki pomorskich rodzin. Wpływ emigracji na tożsamość regionalną Pomorzan', in: *Rodzina pomorska*, ed. J. Borzyszkowski (Gdańsk: Nadbałtyckie Centrum Kultury, Instytut Kaszubski, 1999 b), 57–72.

C. Obracht-Prondzyński, 'Trudna rzeczywistość – problemy adaptacji Kaszubów do życia w nowych warunkach po 1945 roku', in: *Życie dawnych Pomorzan*, ed. W. Łysiak (Bytów-Poznań: Wydawnictwo Eco, 2001), 247–58.

C. Obracht-Prondzyński, *Kaszubi – między dyskryminacją a regionalną podmiotowością* (Gdańsk: Instytut Kaszubski and Uniwersytet Gdański, 2002 a).

C. Obracht-Prondzyński, *Ku samorządnemu Pomorzu. Szkice o kształtowaniu się ładu demokratycznego* (Gdańsk: Instytut Kaszubski & Uniwersytet Gdański, 2002 b).

C. Obracht-Prondzyński, 'Die Kaschuben – zwischen polnischer Kultur und deutscher Zivilisation', in: R. Schattkowsky and M.G. Müller (ed.) *Identitätenwandel und nationale Mobilisierung in Regionen Diversität. Ein regionaler Vergleich zwischen Westpreussen und Galizien am Ende des 19. und Anfang des 20. Jahrhunderts* (Marburg: Herder-Institut 2004 a), 167–82.

C. Obracht-Prondzyński, 'Kaszubi i ich tożsamość w III Rzeczpospolitej – stare problemy, nowe wyzwania', *Przegląd Polonijny* 3 (2004 b), 61–72.

C. Obracht-Prondzyński, 'Kim są Kaszubi – stare pytania, nowe odpowiedzi?', in: J. Borzyszkowski and C. Obracht-Prondzyński (ed.) *Z dziejów kultury Pomorza XVIII–XX wieku* vol.2. (Gdańsk: Instytut Kaszubski, 2004 c).

C. Obracht-Prondzyński, *Bibliografia do studiowania spraw kaszubsko-pomorskich* (Gdańsk: Instytut Kaszubski, 2004 d).

C. Obracht-Prondzyński, *Dziesięć lat pracy Instytutu Kaszubskiego 1996–2006* (Gdańsk: Instytut Kaszubski, 2006 a).

C. Obracht-Prondzyński, *Zjednoczeni w idei. Pięćdziesiąt lat działalności Zrzeszenia Kaszubsko-Pomorskiego (1956–2006)* (Gdańsk: Zrzeszenie Kaszubsko-Pomorskie, 2006 b).

C. Obracht-Prondzyński, 'Czy tzw. kwestia kaszubska jest nadal kwestią językową?', in: J. Treder (ed.) *Kaszubszczyzna w przeszłości i dziś. Kaszëbizna dôwni ë dzys* (Warszawa: Komitet Historii Nauki i Techniki Polskiej Akademii Nauk, 2006 c), 31–48.

C. Obracht-Prondzyński 'Kaszubi: "inni swoi", czyli o problemie bycia "normalnym Polakiem"', in: M. Głowacka-Grajper and E. Nowicka (ed.) *Jak się dzielimy i co nas łączy. Przemiany wartości i więzi we współczesnym społeczeństwie polskim*, Kraków: NOMOS, 2007), 55–66.

C. Obracht-Prondzyński, *Kaszubskich pamiątek skarbnice. O muzeach na Kaszubach – ich dziejach, twórcach i funkcjach społecznych* (Gdańsk: Instytut Kaszubski, 2008).

W. Odyniec, *Dzieje Prus Królewskich (1454–1772)* (Warszawa: PWN, 1972).

W. Odyniec, 'Kaszubi pod Wiedniem', *Pomerania* 9 (1983), 6–12.

K. Ogier, *Dziennik podróży do Polski 1635–1636* (Gdańsk, 1953).

B. Osmólska-Piskorska, *Pomorskie Towarzystwo Pomocy Naukowej (1848–1898). Pół wieku istnienia i działalności* (Toruń: Towarzystwo Naukowe w Toruniu, 1948).

S. Ossowski, *Z zagadnień psychologii społecznej* (Warszawa: PWN, 1967).

S. Ossowski, *O ojczyźnie i narodzie* (Warszawa: PWN, 1984).

K. Ostrowski, *Pieśniarz z ziemi jezior. O Wincentym Rogali z Wiela* (Gdańsk: Zrzeszenie Kaszubsko-Pomorskie, 1977).

P. Paliński, *Przewodnik po polskim wybrzeżu Bałtyku i po ziemi Kaszubskiej* (Gdynia, 1934).

D. Pandowska, *Kaszuby wśród nazw Pomorza w XII wieku* (Gdańsk: Marpress, 1993).

W. Pepliński, *Prasa pomorska w Drugiej Rzeczypospolitej* (Gdańsk: Wydawnictwo Morskie, 1987).

W. Pepliński, *Czasopiśmiennictwo kaszubskie w latach zaboru pruskiego. Aspekty programmeowe, publicystyczne i wydawnicze* (Gdańsk: Uniwersytet Gdański, 2000).

J. Perszon, 'Kultura ludowa Kaszubów w procesie przemian', in: J. Borzyszkowski and C. Obracht-Prondzyński (ed.) *Badania kaszuboznawcze w XX wieku* (Gdańsk: Instytut Kaszubski, 2001), 56–74.

J. Perszon, *Na brzegu życia i śmierci. Zwyczaje, obrzędy oraz wierzenia pogrzebowe i zaduszkowe na Kaszubach* (Pelplin: Bernardinum, 1999).

G. Pobłocki, 'Doktor Ceynowa', *Gryf* 5 (1909), 128–38.

G. Pobłocki, *Słownik kaszubski z dodatkiem idiotyzmów chełmińskich i kociewskich* (Chełmno: W. Fiałek, 1887).

H. Popowska-Taborska, *Centralne zagadnienie wokalizmu kaszubskiego. Kaszubska zmiana ę ≥ i oraz ĭ, ў, ŭ ≥ ё* (Wrocław: Ossolineum, 1961).

H. Popowska-Taborska, *Kaszubszczyzna. Zarys dziejów* (Warszawa, PWN, 1980).

H. Popowska-Taborska, *Leksyka kaszubska na tle słowiańskim* (Warszawa: Slawistyczny Ośrodek Wydawniczy, 1996).

M. Porębska, *Das Kaschubische: Sprachtod oder Revitalisierung? Empirische Studien zur ethnolinguistischen Vitalität einer Sprachminderheit in Polen* (München: Verlag Otto Sagner, 2006).

A. Porębski, *Europejskie mniejszości etniczne. Geneza i kierunki przemian* (Kraków: Uniwersytet Jagielloński, 1991).

E. Pryczkowski (ed.), *Dërchôj królewiónko. Antologia dzysdniowi prozë kaszëbsczi* (Gdynia: Szos, 1996).

E. and E. Pryczkowski (ed.), *Mësla dzecka. Antologiô kaszëbsczich wiérztów dlô dzôtków i młodzëznë* (Banino: Rost, 2001).

S. Ramułt, *Słownik języka pomorskiego, czyli kaszubskiego* (Kraków: Polska Akademia Umiejętności, 1893).

S. Ramułt, *Statystyka ludności kaszubskiej* (Kraków: Akademia Umiejętności, 1899).

S. Ramułt, *Słownik języka pomorskiego czyli kaszubskiego. Część II*, H. Horodyska (ed.) (Kraków: Polska Akademia Umiejętności, 1993).

S. Ramułt, *Słownik języka pomorskiego czyli kaszubskiego*, ed., integrated and standardised by J. Treder (Gdańsk: Oficyna Czec, 2003).

E. Rogowska-Cybulska, *Poliwalencja kaszubszczyzny a kultura masowa*, in: J. Treder (ed.) *Kaszubszczyzna w przeszłości i dziś. Kaszëbizna dôwni ë dzys* (Warszawa: Komitet Historii Nauki i Techniki Polskiej Akademii Nauk, 2006), 73–98.

A. Romanow, 'Kaszubi i Kaszuby w problematyce pelplińskiego *Pielgrzyma* 1869–1920', *Acta Cassubiana* VI (Gdańsk, 2004), 83–110.

A. Romanow, '*Pielgrzym' pelpliński w latach 1869–1920* (Gdańsk-Pelplin: Instytut Kaszubski, Bernardinum, 2007).

L. Roppel (ed.), *Ma jesma ôd mòrza* (Gdańsk: Zrzeszenie Kaszubskie & Wojewódzki Dom Twórczości Ludowej, 1963).

M. Rudnicki, 'Przyczynki do gramatyki i słownika narzecza słowińskiego', *Materiały i Prace Komisji Językowej AU VI* (Kraków: Polska Akademia Umiejętności, 1913), 1–245.

E. Rymar, *Rodowód książąt pomorskich*, vol.1–2 (Szczecin: Książnica Pomorska im. S. Staszica, 1995).

T. Sadkowski, *Drewniana architektura sakralna na Pomorzu Gdańskim w XVIII–XX wieku* (Gdańsk: Gdańskie Towarzystwo Naukowe, 1997).

J. Samp, 'Literatura bez ludu?', *Pomerania* 8 (1983), 3–4.

J. Samp, 'Literatura kaszubska. Kaschubische Literatur', in: J. Borzyszkowski and D. Albrecht (ed.). *Pomorze – mała ojczyzna Kaszubów. (Historia i współczesność). Kaschubisch-pommersche Homeland. (Geschichte und Gegenwart).* (Gdańsk-Lübeck: Ostsee Academia & Zrzeszenie Kaszubsko-Pomorskie & Instytut Kaszubski, 2000), 653–700.

J. Schodzińska, *Franciszek Sędzicki (1882–1957), działacz narodowy, regionalista i poeta kaszubski* (Gdańsk-Wejherowo: Instytut Kaszubski & Muzeum Piśmiennictwa i Muzyki Kaszubsko-Pomorskiej, 2003).

R. Siemieńska, 'Kategorie analizy przyczyn ruchów etnicznych'. *Studia Socjologiczne*, 2 (1976), 61–76.

B. Śliwiński, *Poczet książąt gdańskich. Dynastia Sobiesławiców XII – XIII wieku* (Gdańsk: Marpress, 1997).

J. Spors, 'Pochodzenie i pierwotny zasięg terytorialny nazwy Kaszuby w znaczeniu politycznym', *Zapiski Historyczne* 3 (1972), 379–400.

J. Spors, 'Przekazy "kaszubskie" w Kronice Wielkopolskiej', *Rocznik Gdański* 1 (1988), 67–82.

J. Spors, 'Geneza i rozwój terytorialny nazwy Kaszuby w znaczeniu etnicznym', *Rocznik Słupski* 5, 1988–9 (1991), 13–44.

Z. Stieber, 'Pierwsza Konferencja Pomorska i jej wpływ na dalsze badania nad dialektami Pomorza', in: *Konferencja Pomorska (1978)* (Warszawa: Ossolineum, 1979), 7–11.

G. Stone, 'Cassubian', in: B. Comrie and G.G. Corbett (ed.), *The Slavonic Languages* (London-New York: Routledge, 1993), 759–94.

*Swięté Pismiona Nowégo Testameńtu*, transl. E. Gołąbek (Gdańsk-Pelplin: Zrzeszenie Kaszubsko-Pomorskie and Bernardinum, 1993).

B. Sychta, *Słownik gwar kaszubskich na tle kultury ludowej*, vol.I–VII (Wrocław: Ossolineum, 1967–1976).

B. Synak, 'Nowa etniczność', *Pomerania* 8 (1987), 2–6.

B. Synak, 'Tożsamość kaszubska – aspekty świadomościowe', *Roczniki Socjologii Morskiej* 6 (1991), 110–23.

B. Synak, 'The Kashubs' Ethnic Identity: Continuity and Change', in: B. Synak (ed.), *The Ethnic Identities of European Minorities* (Gdańsk: Uniwersytet Gdański, 1995), 155–66.

B. Synak, 'Kaszubi w nowych warunkach ustrojowych', in: A. Kapciak, M. Kempy and S. Łodziński (ed.) *U progu wielokulturowości* (Warszawa: Oficyna Naukowa, 1997), 202–15.

B. Synak, 'Ciągłość i zmiana statusu kaszubszczyzny jako etnolektu regionalnej grupy etnicznej' in: *Śląsk – Polska – Europa: zmieniające się społeczeństwo w perspektywie lokalizmu i globalizmu: Xięga X Ogólnopolskiego Zjazdu Socjologicznego* (Katowice: Polskie Towarzystwo Socjologiczne, 1998 a), 384–92.

B. Synak, *Kaszubska tożsamość. Ciągłość i zmiana. Studium socjologiczne* (Gdańsk: Uniwersytet Gdański, 1998 b).

B. Synak and T. Wicherkiewicz (ed.), *Language Minorites and Minority Languages in the Changing Europe. Proceedings of the 6th International Conference on Minority Languages. Gdańsk, 1–5 July, 1996* (Gdańsk: Uniwersytet Gdański, 1997).

W. Szkulmowska (ed.) *Sztuka ludowa Kaszubów. Przeszłość i teraźniejszość* (Bydgoszcz: Kujawsko-Pomorskie Towarzystwo Kulturalne, 1995).

J. and J. Szroeder, 'Teatr edukacyjny jako sposób pobudzania tożsamości i tolerancji kulturowej', *Naji Gòchë* 1 (2002), 40.

W. Szulist, *Kaszubi w Ameryce. Szkice i materiały* (Wejherowo: Muzeum Piśmiennictwa i Muzyki Kaszubsko-Pomorskiej, 2005).

Z. Szultka, *Język polski w Kościele ewangelicko-augsburskim na Pomorzu Zachodnim od XVI do XIX wieku* (Wrocław: Ossolineum, 1991 a).

Z. Szultka, 'Die Reformation und ihre Bedeutung für die pommerschen Kaschuben', in: *Pommern. Geschichte, Kultur, Wissenschaft. 2. Kolloquium zur Pommerschen Geschichte. 13. und 14 September 1991* (Greifswald: Ernst-Moritz-Arndt-Universität Greifswald, 1991 b), 73–83.

Z. Szultka, *Studia nad rodowodem i językiem Kaszubów* (Gdańsk: Zrzeszenie Kaszubsko-Pomorskie, 1992).

Z. Szultka, *Szkoła kadetów w Słupsku (1769–1811)* (Gdańsk: Zrzeszenie Kaszubsko-Pomorskie, 1992).

Z. Szultka 'Kaplica p.w. Najświętszej Marii Panny na Górze Chełmskiej jako miejsce kultowe w średniowieczu', *Studia Gdańskie* 9 (1993), 75–88.

Z. Szultka, 'Rola Kościoła ewangelickiego w procesie germanizacji ludności kaszubskiej wschodniej części Pomorza Zachodniego w XIX wieku', *Studia Gdańskie* 9 (1993), 153–82.

Z. Szultka, *Piśmiennictwo polskie i kaszubskie Pomorza Zachodniego od XVI do XIX wieku* (Poznań: Poznańskie Towarzystwo Przyjaciół Nauk, 1994).

R. Szymański, *Statystyka ludności polskiej w zaborze pruskim* (Poznań, 1874).

T. Szymański, *Ludowe Talenty 1971–2006* (Gdańsk: Oddział Gdański Zrzeszenia Kaszubsko-Pomorskiego and Instytut Kaszubski, 2006).

S. Thugutt, *Autobiografia* (Warszawa: Ludowa Spółdzielnia Wydawnicza, 1984).

Z. Topolińska, *A Historical Phonology of the Kashubian Dialect of Polish* (Hague: Mouton, 1974).

J. Treder, 'Kaszubszczyzna – problemy językoznawców dawniej i dziś', in: J. Borzyszkowski (ed.) *Antropologia Kaszub i Pomorza. Materiały z seminarium* (Gdańsk: Instytut Historii Uniwersytet Gdański and Zrzeszenie Kaszubsko-Pomorskie, 1990), 73–104.

J. Treder, *Polish–Kashubian*, in: P.H. Nelde, Z. Starý, W. Wölck (ed.), *Kontaktlinguistik. Ein internationales Handbuch zeitgenössischer Forschung*, vol. 2 (Berlin–New York: Walter de Gruyter, 1997), 1600–6.

J. Treder, 'Z historii badań kaszubszczyzny. Pierwociny i etapy badań mowy Słowińców i Kabatków', *Studia Bałtyckie* 8. *Polonistyka* vol.I (Koszalin, 1998), 23–44.

J. Treder, 'Z historii badań kaszubszczyzny. Gwara luzińska', *Acta Cassubiana* I (1999), 277–94.

J. Treder, 'Mrongowiusz jako kaszubolog. W dwusetną rocznicę zamieszkania w Gdańsku', *Gdańskie Studia Językoznawcze* VII (2002), 165–236.

J. Treder, 'Piotr I. Prejs i Izmael I. Sriezniewski a Kaszuby', in: *Slavonica Tartuensia* V. *200 let russko-slavyanskoy filologii* (Tartu: Uniersity Press, 2003), 228–44.

J. Treder, *Historia kaszubszczyzny literackiej. Studia* (Gdańsk: Wydawnictwo Uniwersytetu Gdańskiego, 2005).

J. Treder (ed.), *Język kaszubski. Poradnik encyklopedyczny* (Gdańsk: Oficyna Czec, 2002 and Gdańsk: Wydawnictwo Uniwersytetu Gdańskiego, 2006).

J. Treder, 'Tendencje w sferze normalizacji kaszubszczyzny. Rys historyczny', in: J. Sierociuk (ed.), *Gwary dziś 4. Konteksty dialektologii* (Poznań: Wydawnictwo Poznańskiego Towarzystwa Przyjaciół Nauk, 2007), 165–72.

J. Treder, *Dzieje gdańskiej kaszubistyki językoznawczej*, in: J. Borzyszkowski and C. Obracht-Prondzyński (ed.) *Tradycje gdańskiej humanistyki* (Gdańsk: Instytut Kaszubski and Uniwersytet Gdański, 2008 a), 124–36.

J. Treder, 'Język dramatów Bernarda Sychty', in: J. Treder and J. Walkusz (ed.) *Dramaty Bernarda Sychty*, vol..I *Dramaty obyczajowe* (Gdańsk: Instytut Kaszubski, 2008 b), 35–116.

J. Treder, 'Kaszubski w tekstach drukowanych w *Klёce*', in: *Leon Roppel i wejherowska 'Klёka'* Wejherowo: Muzeum Piśmiennictwa i Muzyki Kaszubsko-Pomorskiej, 2008 c), 55–72.

J. Treder, 'Kaszubszczyzna Jana Zbrzycy (S. Pestki)', in: J. Borzyszkowski (ed.), *Z zaborskiego matecznika. O Stanisławie Pestce – Janie Zbrzycy* (Gdańsk: Instytut Kaszubski, 2008 d), 97–124.

J. Treder, *Spòdlowô wiédza ò kaszëbiznie* (Gdynia: Oficyna Czec, 2009).

J. Treder and E. Breza, 'Sytuacja socjolingwistyczna kaszubszczyzny', in: R. Mrózek (ed.), *Kultura – Język – Edukacja* vol.3 (Katowice: Wydawnictwo Uniwersytetu Śląskiego, 2000), 139–66.

J. and J. Treder (ed.), *Domôcé słowo zwęczné. Antologia tekstów kaszubskich dla recytatorów* (Chmielno: ZK-P, 1994 & www.rastkokaszuby.pl).

J. Trepczyk, 'Moje życie', in: Drzeżdżon (1986), 226–46.

B. Wachowiak (ed.), *Źródła do kaszubsko-polskich aspektów dziejów Pomorza Zachodniego do roku 1945*: vol.I *Pomorze Zachodnie pod rządami książąt plemiennych i władców z dynastii Gryfitów (990–1121–1637–1642/1653)*, ed. Z. Szultka: vol. II *Pomorze Zachodnie w państwie brandenbursko-pruskim (1653–1815)*, ed. Z. Szultka: vol.III *Pomorze Zachodnie w XIX i początkach XX stulecia (1815–1918)*, ed. W. Stępiński: vol.IV *Pomorze Zachodnie w okresie od traktatu wersalskiego po klęskę III Rzeszy w 1945 r.*, ed. E. Włodarczyk (Poznań-Gdańsk: Zrzeszenie Kaszubsko-Pomorskie, Wydawnictwo Poznańskie, 2006).

K. Wajda, 'Społeczeństwo polskie i Kościół katolicki na Pomorzu a państwo pruskie w latach 1860–1914', *Studia Pelplińskie* 16 (1985), 99–123.

J. Walkusz (ed.), *Swięti dzél dësze. Antologia kaszubskiej poezji religijnej* (Pelplin: Kuria Biskupia, 1981).

J. Walkusz, *Duchowieństwo katolickie diecezji chełmińskiej 1918–1939* (Pelplin: Bernardinum, 1992).

R. Wapiński, 'Regionalizm – doświadczenia z przeszłości (od schyłku XIX wieku do roku 1939)', in: M. Latoszek (ed.) *Regionalizm jako folkloryzm, ruch społeczny i formuła ideologiczno-polityczna* (Gdańsk: Gdańskie Towarzystwo Naukowe, 1993), 39–64.

M. Wehrmann, *Geschichte von Pommern*, vol. 1–2 (Gotha, 1919–21).

T. Wicherkiewicz, 'Kashubian', in: J. Wirrer (ed.) *Minderheiten- und Regionalsprachen in Europa* (Opladen-Wiesbaden:: Westdeutscher Verlag. 2000 a), 213–21.

T. Wicherkiewicz, 'Lesser Used Languages in Poland', in: *Situation of Minority and Regional Languages in the Countries Applying for Membership in the European Union (Cyprus, Czech Republic, Estonia, Hungary, Poland, Slovenia)* (Strasbourg: European Parliament, 2000 b), 16–23.

T. Wicherkiewicz, 'Becoming a regional leanguage – a method in language status planning?': in: *Actes del 2n Congrés Europeu sobre Planificació Lingüística. Andorra la Vella 14–16 noviembre de 2001* (Barcelona: Generalitat de Catalunya Departament de Cultura, 2003), 473–7.

T. Wicherkiewicz, *The Kashubians in education in Poland* (Ljouwert: Mercator Education, 2004).

T. Wicherkiewicz [Viherkevičs] and al. (ed.), *Regional Languages in the New Europe. Reģionālās valodas mūsdienu Eiropā. Regionaluos volūdys myusdīnu Eiropā – Proceedings of the International Conference 20–23 May 2004* (Rēzekne: Rēzeknes Augstskola, 2004).

M. Wojciechowski, *Powrót Pomorza do Polski 1918–1920* (Warszawa-Poznań-Toruń: Towarzystwo Naukowe w Toruniu, 1981).

H. Wünsche, *Studien auf der Halbinsel Hela* (Leipzig, 1904).

K. Zielińska, *Zjednoczenie Pomorza Gdańskiego z Wielkopolską pod koniec XIII w. Umowa kępińska 1282* (Toruń: Towarzystwo Naukowe w Toruniu, 1968).

K. Zielińska-Melkowska, *Działo się i dan w Kępnie* (Gdańsk: Zrzeszenie Kaszubsko-Pomorskie, 1990).

J. Zieniukowa, 'Stan badań nad dialektami Pomorza Gdańskiego i perspektywy badawcze', in: K. Handke (ed.), *Konferencja Pomorska (1978)* (Wrocław: Prace Slawistyczne, 1979), 149–78.

J. Zieniukowa, 'On the Languages of Small Ethnic Groups – the Case of Sorbian and Kashubian': in: Synak and Wicherkiewicz (1997), 311–16.

J. Zieniukowa, 'Nowe zjawisko w kulturze polskiej – liturgia słowa w języku kaszubskim', in: M. Kamińska and E. Umińska-Tytoń (ed.), *Funkcja słowa w ewangelizacji* (Łódź: Uniwersytet Łódzki, 1998), 111–24.

Z. Zielonka (ed.) *Literatura kaszubska w nauce – edukacji – życiu publicznym* (Gdańsk: Instytut Kaszubski, 2007).

# Index